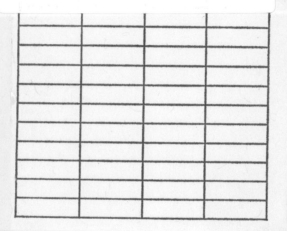

Policing industrial disputes:
1893 to 1985

Policing industrial disputes: 1893 to 1985

Roger Geary

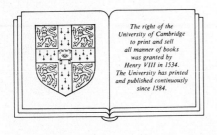

The right of the
University of Cambridge
to print and sell
all manner of books
was granted by
Henry VIII in 1534.
The University has printed
and published continuously
since 1584.

Cambridge University Press

Cambridge
London   New York   New Rochelle
Melbourne   Sydney

Published by the Press Syndicate of the University of Cambridge
The Pitt Building, Trumpington Street, Cambridge CB2 1RP
32 East 57th Street, New York, NY 10022, USA
10 Stamford Road, Oakleigh, Melbourne 3166, Australia

© Cambridge University Press 1985

First published 1985

Printed in Great Britain at the University Press, Cambridge

British Library cataloguing in publication data

Geary, Roger
Policing industrial disputes: 1893 to 1985.
1. Labor disputes – Great Britain – History
2. Police – Great Britain – History
I. Title
331.89′0941   HD5365.A6

Library of Congress cataloguing in publication data

Geary, Roger, 1950–
Policing industrial disputes, 1893 to 1985.
Includes index.
1. Labor disputes – Great Britain – History.
2. Strikes and lockouts – Great Britain – History.
I. Title
HD5365.A6G43   1985   331.89′2941   85-9632

ISBN 0 521 30315 X

BO

Contents

	page
List of illustrations	*vi*
Acknowledgements	*vii*
1 Introduction	1
2 Stoning and shooting	6
3 The pivotal period	25
4 The decline of violent labour protest	48
5 Pushing and shoving	67
6 Victory without violence	116
7 Industrial confrontation after the riots	134
8 Conclusion and implications	146
Notes	152
Index	168

Illustrations

Tables

1 Police forces that co-operated with the research project   *page*   3
2 Numbers and ranks of officers interviewed   4
3 Colliery disturbances reported during March 1912   34
4 Number and sources of statements cited by Churchill in support of the police action during the South Wales coal strike of 1910   43
5 Number of volunteers recruited during the General Strike   57
6 Disturbances, arrests and police injuries during the Roberts–Arundel dispute   70
7 Numbers, injuries and arrests at Saltley   77
8 Numbers, arrests and police injuries during the 1972 Neap House Wharf industrial dispute   83
9 Numbers, arrests and injuries at the Hadfields factory during the 1980 steel strike   91

Figures

1 The changing nature of industrial confrontation   148
2 The escalation of disorder during the 1984–5 miners' strike   150

Acknowledgements

I would very much like to thank the 32 police officers and 69 union officials who assisted me in my research. Their co-operation, hospitality and trust not only made this study possible, but also made the task of data collection a thoroughly enjoyable one. All these people must, of course, remain anonymous.

I am also particularly grateful to Laurie Taylor, Robert Reiner and Peter Jackson who all made valuable suggestions and provided constant encouragement and inspiration.

Finally, my immeasurable indebtedness to Sheila (my wife) cannot be adequately expressed – as always she provided invaluable and indispensable help of many kinds.

1

Introduction

> Police riot squads were used yesterday and several mounted police charges were made. Throughout the day missiles of every size and type were hurled towards police lines . . .
> There were pitched battles inside the coking plant for the first time since picketing began, and the frustration on both sides spilled over into sickening scenes of miners being batoned and of police being attacked with bricks, slivers of glass as well as . . . containers of fuel.[1]

Contemporary events, particularly in an age when most of us receive information secondhand via the media, tend to crystallise into certain dominant images. For many, mention of the miners' strike of 1984 is enough to conjure up pictures of violent confrontations between stone-throwing pickets and baton-wielding police. Such scenes, which seem more reminiscent of the almost forgotten conflicts of social history than modern industrial disputes, inevitably raise issues about the nature of policing and picketing in the 1980s.

One such issue concerns the degree of violence associated with contemporary industrial confrontation. It is readily, perhaps too readily, assumed by commentators of all political views that violent incidents such as that described at the head of this chapter constitute a significant escalation of disorder. Not surprisingly, those at either end of the political spectrum tend to blame each other for the assumed increase in violence. The left point the finger unhesitatingly at the forces of law and order, suggesting that the massive police presence in the coalfields and the use of tactics like the baton-charge have played a major part in bringing about increased levels of violence. At a more sophisticated level this kind of argument develops into the 'strong state' thesis; a theoretical standpoint which identifies the economic crisis of modern capitalism as a motivating force for social polarisation and industrial militancy.[2] This trend, according to the theory, in turn leads to the state maximising repression as the only means of maintaining the *status quo*. The right, a grouping by no means limited to the Conservative Party, equally unhesitatingly attribute picket-line violence to the strikers and vociferously denounce it as an attack on the rule of law and

1

ultimately democracy itself. For them, violent picketing is simply an attempt by the criminally minded to resist the imposition of law and order, a development which requires firm policing.

There are features of both these positions that need to be subject to closer scrutiny so that a clearer understanding of what is going on can emerge. The shared assumption that industrial confrontation is becoming more violent needs to be examined; a detailed historical analysis is necessary to establish precisely how the nature of industrial confrontation has changed and to explain why these changes have occurred.

Such a study would not only plug a gap in the existing literature – somewhat surprisingly there has been comparatively little research on policing in general let alone the policing of industrial disputes – but also enable many of the more controversial aspects of contemporary industrial confrontation to be seen in their historical context. For example, concern generated by the establishment of Police Support Units and the National Recording Centre, about a *de facto* national police force, can be viewed in relation to a changing pattern of formal and informal control of policing policy. Similarly, police riot tactics can be seen not as an isolated development but as a more recent manifestation of a continuing response to industrial disorder.

The main purpose of this book is to question and modify widely held assumptions about the nature of industrial disorder by reaching back beyond the present. The accurate characterisation of historically distinct patterns of confrontation is a prerequisite both for the development of explanatory theory and a better informed public debate.

Methodology

A study of documents such as newspaper reports, parliamentary reports, letters and telegrams sent to and from the Home Office, autobiographies, police and trade union histories was necessary in order to discover how industrial disputes were policed in the past. Fortunately, quite detailed information was discovered. For example, material relating to the South Wales Coal Strike of 1910 includes all the communications between the Home Office and the local Chief Constable, the reports of Home Office officials, senior army officers and the autobiography of the police and army commander.

In order to discover how the major industrial disputes of more recent times – the miners' strikes of 1972, 1974 and 1984–5, the Grunwick dispute of 1976–8 and the steel strike of 1980 – were policed, a number of interviews have been conducted with senior police officers and union officials.

Eleven police forces that have had recent experience of industrial disputes were approached, nine agreed to co-operate with the research project and two refused (see Table 1). The Greater Manchester Police declined to co-

Table 1. *Police forces that co-operated with the research project*

Force	Officers interviewed
Kent County Constabulary	2
Humberside Police	1
Lincolnshire Police	1
Metropolitan Police	3
Nottinghamshire Constabulary	1
South Wales Constabulary	2
South Yorkshire Police	1
West Midlands Police	1
West Yorkshire Police	2
Total	14

operate on the grounds that they were too busy dealing with Home Office researchers following the summer riots of 1981, while Derbyshire Constabulary refused because they had less relevant experience than some other forces.

Those forces that did agree to provide research facilities then nominated a senior officer or officers to be interviewed. As well as these formal interviews informal conversations about the policing of industrial disputes were held with 18 other officers. Altogether 32 policemen were interviewed ranging in rank from Constable to Chief Constable (see Table 2). In addition to these interviews public order training at two police training establishments was observed and the Bramshill Police Staff College was visited on three occasions. The visits to Bramshill were made to interview members of staff, to use the library facilities and to talk to officers attending a course on industrial disputes.

As well as police officers 50 union officials were interviewed during the autumn of 1981. Thirty branch secretaries of the National Union of Mineworkers (NUM) were interviewed together with 20 officials of the Iron and Steel Trades Confederation (ISTC). These respondents were selected at random from lists provided by the Yorkshire and Nottinghamshire area headquarters of the NUM and the Sheffield and Humberside regions of the ISTC. Many of the NUM officials had experience of picketing during the Grunwick dispute and the 1980 steel strike as well as during the miners' strikes of the early 1970s. In addition informal conversations were held with 19 members of the NUM during the 1984 coal strike.

All formal interviews were tape-recorded and lasted from a minimum of forty minutes to a maximum of two hours. The average interview lasted about one hour and fifteen minutes. Of course, the advantages of tape-

Table 2. *Numbers and ranks of officers interviewed (formally and informally)*

Rank	
Chief Constable	1
Assistant Chief Constable	1
Chief Superintendent	3
Superintendent	6
Chief Inspector	4
Inspector	11
Sergeant	4
Constable	2
Total	32

recording are precise reproduction of what is said and discussion uninterrupted by note taking. However, a possible disadvantage is greater inhibition when talking about controversial matters. For this reason all respondents were encouraged to continue the conversation after the tape-recorder had been switched off. Immediately after each interview notes were made from memory of any unrecorded material. In this way it was thought that the best of both the recorded and the unrecorded worlds could be obtained.

The trade unionists enthusiastically co-operated with the research project and openly discussed controversial and sometimes incriminating matters on tape. The police were more cautious and tended to make their most interesting comments after the tape-recorder had been switched off. Most of the union officials automatically assumed that the interviewer was sympathetic towards them and hostile to the police. The police officers tended to make the same assumption. One officer commented 'I'll take my jacket off now because I expect we'll end up scrapping';[3] another accused the interviewer of being a 'political extremist' who had stolen university writing paper in order to gain an interview with him.[4] An Assistant Chief Constable bluntly stated 'You're as biased and as devious as can be.'[5] Overcoming this initial police hostility proved to be easier than one might have supposed. Indeed, there was a certain amount of mock hostility – a deliberate probing of the interviewer to test reactions to allegations of bias and political extremism. After a sometimes hostile start every police respondent settled down to a cordial discussion about the various aspects of policing industrial disputes.

Outline of the book

The next chapter focuses on the use of police and troops to combat industrial disorder during the period from 1893 to 1909, a period which included the infamous 'Featherstone shootings'. In Chapter 3 attention is focused on the increasing use of the police as an order maintaining force during the four years preceding the First World War; the 'Tonypandy riots' of 1910 and the 'Llanelli shootings' are among the incidents examined. The inter-war period is the subject of Chapter 4 which considers the police strikes of 1918 and 1919 and the General Strike of 1926 among others. Chapter 5 addresses itself to the policing of industrial disputes during the period from 1945 to 1980 and includes a discussion of the miners' strikes of the early 1970s, the Grunwick dispute of 1976–8 and the steel strike of 1980.

Some of the factors which have motivated the changes revealed by our investigation are considered in Chapter 6, while the penultimate chapter focuses on industrial confrontation in the 1980s. Our final chapter, as one might expect, states the conclusions and implications of the study.

2

Stoning and shooting

About 9.15 p.m. the magistrate, Mr Hartley, determined that there was no alternative except to fire. A written order was given to Captain Barker to that effect, and Mr Hartley asked him in the first instance to fire with blank cartridge. Captain Barker replied that he had no blank cartridge, and that to use it was against the regulations. Mr Hartley then asked Captain Barker to fire as little as possible. The word was given for a file of two men to fire, the front man kneeling and the rear man standing, and the file was directed to fire at the ground line. The stone throwing still continued while the men were preparing to fire. 'It did not cease for a moment', said Captain Barker. One of the two men firing was struck in the face when he had the rifle at the present. The report of the rifles was followed by silence for a few seconds, but there were then cries from the crowd of 'Go on, it's only blanks', and the stone throwing was resumed. In about five or six minutes Captain Barker, as the shower of stones continued, gave an order for a section of eight men to fire one volley. One soldier, while on the knee and about to fire, had his helmet knocked off by a missile. After the troops had fired the second time, there was a cry from the crowd that two men had been shot.[1]

The first industrial dispute to be described and analysed is also the most violent that will be considered. Two miners were killed and some fourteen others were injured when troops opened fire on strikers in 1893 at Featherstone in West Yorkshire. Although the military were called out on several occasions to deal with disorder associated with industrial disputes during the period between 1893 and 1909, it was only at Featherstone that they actually resorted to shooting. Usually, the implicit threat of shooting that the mere presence of the military conveyed was sufficient to ensure the rapid dispersal of strikers. So the response to disorder revealed by the following account of the Featherstone shootings is both typical and atypical. It is typical in the sense that troops were frequently mobilised and deployed during industrial disputes at this time, but is atypical in that they usually achieved their objectives without abruptly reducing the workforce by discharging their firearms at point blank range.

The aim of our chronology and analysis of the events at Featherstone is to identify specific forms of collective action and order maintenance. Once such a basic pattern of action and reaction has been distilled from the welter of historical facts it becomes possible to chart subsequent modifications of and reversions to the original forms of behaviour. In other words Featherstone provides us with a starting point from which to map the twists and turns in the history of industrial conflict.

The Featherstone shootings 1893: chronology

During the last week of July and the first week of August 1893 miners in many districts either went on strike or were locked-out by their employers. In the West Riding of Yorkshire, where the most violent incidents associated with the strike occurred, over 80,000 men stopped work and 250 pits closed down.[2]

The first disorder occurred on 31 July at the Morley Main Colliery near Dewsbury where between 70 and 100 banksmen had volunteered to continue working during the strike.[3] Naturally, this incensed the strikers who collected at the colliery entrance to jeer and throw stones at the 'blackleg' banksmen. Local police from Dewsbury eventually arrived and succeeded in dispersing the crowd without further violence. However, the following day more serious disorder occurred. According to a report in *The Times* some 4,000 strikers attacked the men who were still working, the 'knobsticks' as they were called, and their police escort before being subjected to repeated baton-charges.[4] But this incident proved to be something of an exception as all remained quiet throughout the West Riding until 30 August when there was another slight disturbance at the Middleton Colliery near Leeds. Once again a small force of police was immediately despatched and order was quickly restored. The strike seemed to be following the pattern of long periods of calm briefly interrupted by isolated incidents of disorder which the police quickly put down. Indeed, Captain Russell, the Chief Constable, was so untroubled by the situation that, in late August, he left the district for a holiday in Scotland. His action reveals a remarkable degree of confidence especially as 259 constables, nearly a quarter of the entire West Riding force, were sent to keep the peace at the Doncaster Races which began on 4 September. Such a drastic reduction in manpower must have seriously affected the capability of the police to deal with outbreaks of disorder. Nevertheless, Captain Russell obviously felt that the situation was sufficiently well in hand to justify his absence.

In the event the Chief Constable's confidence proved to be misplaced for on Monday 4 September minor incidents of disorder occurred at Garforth and the following day witnessed an extension of the disturbances to the Barnsley area. Mr Gill, the Deputy Chief Constable, sent home those Barnsley constables who were on duty at Doncaster and arranged for 188 men from other districts in the West Riding to be drafted into the troubled area. He also sent the following telegram to Captain Russell in Scotland: 'Serious disturbance around Barnsley. Two pits wrecked but all quiet now. Have made all necessary police arrangements. Gill.'[5] Gill, it seems, saw no immediate need for more extreme measures, but this was not a view shared by everyone. At a special meeting of the Barnsley magistrates, held that evening, it was decided that military intervention was required and Gill was instructed to take a requisition to the General commanding the Northern Division at York the next morning. After the meeting the Deputy Chief Constable sent another telegram to his chief which was much less optimistic than its predecessor. 'Serious disturbance expected about Barnsley and Rotherham. I am arranging for military to be in readiness. Doncaster rather crippled me but can manage. Write.'[6] There is a distinct difference in tone between the two communications; a modulation caused, it is suggested, by the influence of the magistrates rather than by any change in the prevailing situation.

In the event Captain Russell received both telegrams within minutes of each other, at approximately 8.10 a.m. on Wednesday the 6th and immediately decided to return to Yorkshire by the next available train. A third telegram from Gill was forwarded on from Scotland in time to be handed to him at York. 'Further riots in Lancashire Division (which means Doncaster Division), and I have obtained order for military just now signed by General Wilkinson. I think you had better return. Urgent. Gill.'[7] Each of Gill's three telegrams is more alarmist than its predecessor. Yet there is no evidence to suggest that the police were unable to restore order or indeed that any significant rioting had taken place.[8] Nevertheless, Captain Russell had been recalled and the military summoned. Such was the general state of affairs in the West Riding up to Thursday 7 September, and it is now necessary to concentrate on the events which transpired at the Ackton Hall Colliery in Featherstone.

Before the strike about 400 men had been employed at the Ackton Hall Colliery as underground workers and about an equal number as surface men who were mainly engaged in building and fitting out new works that were extending the existing buildings. When the strike began in late July all the underground men had been locked out while the surface men continued in employment. Despite this divisive and potentially dangerous situation – the surface workers were bound to be regarded as 'blacklegs' – no disorder of any kind occurred during the first month of the strike at Featherstone. However, this tranquil state of affairs was not to last.

At midday on Tuesday 5 September a crowd of 'men, women and lads' marched into the colliery yard and demanded that the loading of 'smudge' – an operation which the surface men had been carrying out since before the lock-out – be discontinued.[9] The loading of 'smudge' did not involve the getting or working of coal, but it was used to raise steam for the surface engines and surplus amounts were being sold to other collieries. In the event the surface workers, apparently intimidated by the strikers who were armed with sticks and cudgels, decided to discontinue loading.

On the following day, no doubt spurred on by their earlier success, a large number of strikers again visited the colliery and prevented loading. On this occasion, however, they also sent a deputation to see Mr Holiday, the pit manager, with the intention of obtaining an assurance that no more 'smudge' would be extracted and loaded. Holiday went some way towards meeting the strikers' demands by agreeing that henceforth 'smudge' would only be loaded for colliery use and not for sale. With this the deputation appeared satisfied and the crowd dispersed. It is worth emphasising that so far no personal injury or even damage to property had occurred, although there is no doubt that many of the surface workers had been severely frightened. Moreover, once an agreement regarding the loading of 'smudge' had been reached the danger of serious disorder appeared to decline.

However, on Thursday the 7th a crowd of 200 strikers entered the colliery yard and tipped over eight waggon-loads of 'smudge'. Some of the waggons had old tickets on them labelled 'Bradford' and it seems that the crowd was convinced that Holiday was disregarding the previous day's agreement.[10] This misunderstanding leading to a relatively trivial act of lawlessness set in motion a chain of events that culminated twelve hours later in the shooting of sixteen people. The steps in this fatal nexus are clear.

Holiday, no doubt outraged at the vandalism done to his 'smudge' waggons, set off to activate the machinery of social control. As there were only three constables on permanent duty in Featherstone he drove in a dog-cart to Pontefract to request more substantial police protection for the men loading 'smudge'. However, the Pontefract police were unable to help him in this respect as they had received many similar requests and had no men available to assist him. Holiday returned to Featherstone only to find that the strikers had tipped over another seven waggons during his absence. Enough was clearly enough. Holiday caught the midday train to Wakefield with the intention of demanding assistance from the Chief Constable.

At Wakefield police station Holiday was joined by Lord St Oswald, a magistrate and coal owner, who had come on a similar mission. Both men urged the Chief and Deputy Chief Constables to provide protection for their respective pits. When Captain Russell told them that he had no spare manpower available they appealed for military aid. The Chief Constable obediently sent a requisition for soldiers to York only to be told by the military authorities that they too had no available men to send. At this stage Holiday must have despaired of ever obtaining protection for his 'smudge' loaders. However, he need not have worried, for the Deputy Chief Constable contacted the army barracks at Bradford and 50 infantry were immediately despatched for Wakefield by train. It was agreed that if Gill could not arrange for a magistrate to accompany the troops to Featherstone he would telephone Holiday who would then attempt to secure the services of one himself. Satisfied with these arrangements Holiday and Lord St Oswald, who did not need a magistrate since he was one himself, returned to their collieries.

So, after a few false starts the machinery of order maintenance had been finally set in motion. But a misunderstanding was to occur which may have ultimately contributed to the tragic events that followed.

Later that same afternoon the manager of the Sharleston Colliery called on the Chief Constable and, like Holiday and Lord St Oswald, requested police or military assistance. Captain Russell reassured him that troops were on their way and that adequate protection would be provided for the Sharleston Colliery. The manager then secured the services of Mr Clay, a magistrate who had been closeted in the Wakefield Country Club, and accompanied the Chief Constable to the station to meet the soldiers from Bradford. It was at this point that a misunderstanding occurred between Gill and Clay. In his evidence to the committee of inquiry into the subsequent events Gill stated that he asked Clay to meet the soldiers at Sharleston *station* and if all was quiet to accompany them on to Featherstone.[11] According to Clay he was simply asked to meet the troops at Sharleston *Colliery*, no mention being made of going on to Featherstone.[12] In any event Clay and the Sharleston manager returned to the colliery to await the arrival of troops and never went to Sharleston station at all. The effect of this misunderstanding was, as will be made clear, that troops eventually arrived at Featherstone unaccompanied by a magistrate and were therefore reluctant to take any positive action and so totally failed to overawe the crowd.

Meanwhile, Holiday had returned to Featherstone to find that a crowd of about 200 miners, women and pit boys had visited the colliery in his absence and had smashed many of the office windows. However, the crowd had dispersed before his return and he found that all was now quiet.[13]

At about 3.30 p.m. a Captain Barker and 54 men of the South Staffordshire Regiment arrived at Wakefield station. An impromptu council of war was held on the station platform during which Gill urged Captain Barker to divide his men into two groups, one to be sent to Lord St Oswald's colliery at Nostell and the other to Featherstone via Sharleston. At first Captain Barker was somewhat reluctant to divide his relatively small force but eventually agreed to do as Gill suggested. Twenty-five men under a lieutenant left on a branch line for Nostell while the remaining 28 men, commanded by Captain Barker, continued on the main line to Featherstone. Gill informed Captain Barker that a magistrate would meet him at Featherstone station and that on the way he should look out at Sharleston for any sign of disorder. If there were trouble at Sharleston the troops were to stop and deal with it before marching on to Featherstone.[14] Of course, Gill's instructions to Captain Barker were misleading in one very important respect. No arrangements had so far been made for a magistrate to meet the troops at Featherstone station. According to Gill's own version of events (see p. 1) it was at Sharleston that Captain Barker should have been told to look out for not only disorder, but also Clay.

When the soldiers' train arrived at Sharleston, there was no sign of disorder so Captain Barker, unaware that the Deputy Chief Constable was expecting Clay to join him, continued on to Featherstone arriving about 4 o'clock. Meanwhile, Clay was at the Sharleston Colliery office half a mile away patiently awaiting the arrival of troops that never materialised.

On their arrival at Featherstone the troops were met not by the expected magistrate, but by a small group of strikers who jeered them. Captain Barker marched his men from the railway station to the nearby colliery and positioned them out of sight in the engine-house. At this time there was no crowd or any sign of disorder.[15]

At about 6 o'clock a crowd of strikers entered the colliery yard and requested an interview with Holiday. A deputation of four or five men from this crowd came forward and demanded that no more 'smudge' should be loaded. Holiday told the deputation of the informal agreement negotiated the previous day and was then asked to repeat it to the crowd. It was while he was speaking to the crowd that another more menacing group of about 500 men gathered behind him and began to smash the colliery windows. Holiday, now accompanied by two of the local police officers, approached this second more aggressive crowd and asked them what they wanted. It soon became clear that they were not protesting about the loading of 'smudge' but demanding the withdrawal of the military and the police. On being told by Holiday that he had no power to remove either, the strikers crowded around in a menacing manner. A few of the men who had been acting as spokesmen tried to restrain the others but there were several shouts of 'Kill him, kill the — — while you have him',[16] and stones were thrown at both Holiday and the police. In his subsequent report, Inspector Corden, the senior policeman present, explained how he managed to extract Holiday from the middle of the angry crowd by promising to withdraw the police.[17]

The crowd then transferred their attention to the engine-house containing the soldiers. Every window of the building was broken and the doors were smashed in. Captain Barker and his men sought refuge on the third floor but were followed by a deputation of six miners, armed with sticks, who demanded the total withdrawal of the military from the colliery premises. Meanwhile, the crowd below had placed some sacks at the foot of the stairs and one man was trying to set them alight. In the circumstances it is not surprising that Captain Barker offered to withdraw his men on condition that the strikers would disperse and do no further damage. The soldiers, accompanied by a large escort of strikers, evacuated the engine-house and marched back to the railway station.[18]

Once the soldiers had left the premises stacks of pit props, building materials and the joiner's shop itself were set on fire by the strikers who were obviously in no mood to abide by the agreement made with Captain Barker. From their position on the station platform the soldiers could see the flames from the burning colliery buildings, but without a magistrate Captain Barker felt unable to act. Meanwhile, Holiday who had for several hours now been waiting for the promised telephone call from Gill, decided to send one of the local constables to Pontefract to enlist the services of a magistrate. Eventually this officer returned with Mr Bernard Hartley JP who promptly joined the troops at Featherstone station.[19]

A detailed account of what transpired has already been provided (see p. 61). All that is necessary here is to outline the main sequence of events. The troops, this time accompanied by the magistrate, marched for a third time across the land separating the station and the burning colliery. Hartley made several informal calls for the strikers to disperse before finally reading the Riot Act. The soldiers attempted to disperse the crowd by advancing with fixed bayonets and when this did not work by firing a warning volley into the ground. Ultimately the soldiers, who had been stoned by the crowd for some time, were given the order to fire directly and at point blank range into the mass confronting them. As has already been noted this action resulted in two miners being killed outright and some fourteen others being injured.[20]

Following the shootings the stone throwing practically ceased and the troops were left in comparative peace until they were relieved by a stronger force at 11.15 p.m. However, the disturbances were not over; about an hour after the shootings a nearby wooden railway bridge was set on fire and totally destroyed. Waggons were set ablaze early the next morning and a crowd attempted to pull down the brickwork supporting a chimney, but according to *The Times* soldiers and police quickly restored order without further loss of life or injury.[21]

In the aftermath of the shootings a contingent of Metropolitan police were sent to the disturbed area, but the worst disturbances were now over and, aside from a few minor incidents, no further clashes occurred. Eventually, the Metropolitans returned to London and peace prevailed in the Yorkshire coalfield.[22]

The Featherstone shootings 1893: analysis

The strikers

In relation to the behaviour of the strikers two points are worth emphasising: the presence of 'marching gangs' and the almost complete lack of organisational control. It seems clear that a gang, or gangs, of strikers marched to Ackton Hall Colliery to demand that the loading of 'smudge' be discontinued. When these men suspected that their demands were not being met they attempted, as we have already noted, to destroy property. This kind of behaviour was not restricted to Featherstone. Indeed, there are numerous reports of 'marching gangs' in virtually every area affected by the dispute.[23] Of course, this early form of flying picket was nothing new but, as George Rudé points out, part of a long tradition of collective bargaining by riot.[24]

At first sight the persistence of 'marching gangs' into the late nineteenth century is somewhat surprising. After all much political water had flowed under the bridge; two reform acts, the repeal of the Combination Laws, the formation of the Independent Labour Party and the growth of the trade union movement. However, the harsh material conditions of those on strike had hardly changed since the eighteenth century. The only realistic choice facing strikers, particularly in the later stages of a strike when savings had been exhausted, was often sabotage or starvation. During the first month of the strike only very few relatively minor incidents of disorder occurred; it was only when starvation became a distinct possibility in late August and early September that violent incidents began to be regularly reported.[25]

Despite the plight and undoubted frustration of the miners it seems clear that violence was mainly directed at property rather than persons. For example, of the twelve colliery disturbances in the West Riding, only three involved personal violence prior to the arrival of police or troops.[26] However, once the forces of law and order had arrived on the scene the strikers not only attempted to damage property but also to inflict personal injury, usually by stoning. Indeed, if 'stoning' is defined rather broadly to include not only the throwing of missiles at police or troops but also any attempt to destroy property, then it is clear that this was the typical mode of confrontation adopted by the marching gangs.[27]

It is clear that the disorderly behaviour of the miners was accompanied by an almost total lack of organisational control. Both the day-to-day running of the strike and the handling of disorderly incidents were managed, if at all, by situational leaders in a very uncoordinated and ineffective manner. Of course, lack of organisation did not mean that disorder was inevitable. As at Featherstone the 'marching gangs' sought to establish agreements with the pit managers and in those reported cases where an agreement was made and honoured no disorder occurred.[28] However, when the strikers suspected that an agreement was not being adhered to, lack of organisation and control made the occurrence of violence extremely likely. There is evidence that some miners' leaders urged restraint at mass meetings. For example, the *Derbyshire Times* reported that at a large gathering at Alfreton a resolution was passed that 'all miners remain peaceable and orderly'.[29] Similarly, *The*

Times noted a resolution passed by Welsh miners to 'restore peace and good understanding'.[30]

Despite this kind of resolution situational leaders at pit-head confrontations were unable to control those present. Holiday, the manager of Ackton Hall Colliery, revealed in his evidence to the Committee of Inquiry into the 'Featherstone shootings' both the ineffectual attempts of the miners' spokesmen to prevent violence and his apprehension of personal danger:

> I told them I had no power to remove either the military or the police . . . They got very menacing. They closed round me. A few of those who were spokesmen I think, did their best to keep the others back, but the others closed round, and yelled and shouted, and said they would kill me now they had got me . . . – I considered it a miracle that I escaped unhurt.[31]

The military

The focus of our attention now shifts from the action of the strikers to the intervention of the army in the strike of 1893. However, in order to place this military involvement in perspective it is necessary to note briefly the changing historical response of the state to the problem of dealing with civil unrest.

The military tradition of public order maintenance starts with the Anglo-Saxon fyrd or general levy which, until the establishment of a regular army in the seventeenth century, was the only force available to support sheriffs and magistrates in their attempts to put down riots. Even after the formation of the regular army the general levy or militia, as it came to be known, remained the primary anti-riot force of the day. As well as being the ultimate in cost effectiveness (it was a volunteer force) the militia was reliable enough to deal with the mainly agricultural disturbances of pre-industrial Britain.[32]

By the mid eighteenth century the reliability of the militia had been seriously impaired because few of the rising middle class wished to invest their time in non-profitable service with the militia. Consequently it was feared that the militia would soon be largely composed of those whose sympathies might lay with the 'dangerous classes' rather than with their social superiors. In an attempt to stop the rot Parliament introduced in 1757 compulsory service in the militia for those selected by ballot. However, this measure only aggravated matters; balloting itself often resulted in disorder. In 1761, for example, 5,000 Northumberland miners marched to Hexham to stop the ballot for recruits and were fired upon by the Yorkshire militia who killed 42 of them and wounded another 48.[33] Moreover, a reluctant recruit could pay ten pounds to name a substitute and these substitutes tended to be local drunkards and village idiots who had no other way of earning a living. A force composed of such people, although cheap, was hardly reliable and consequently from the mid eighteenth century the public order maintaining role of the militia was taken over by the regular army.

It might be thought that the regular army would provide a completely reliable if not exactly cheap means of dealing with disorder, but the common practice of billeting troops with the very people they might be ordered to fire upon militated against the unquestioning loyalty required by the state. So, in order to distance, geographically and socially, troops and people, strategically placed barracks were built within easy reach of the industrial towns. By the end of the century there were over forty local barracks capable of accommodating approximately 20,000 troops. These regular soldiers were now the costly, but reliable, basis of the state's order-maintaining machinery.

As a cheap complement to the regular army, governments throughout the eighteenth and early nineteenth centuries encouraged members of the upper and middle classes to join the Yeomanry or form private voluntary associations to provide an immediate response to local disorder. This response often involved the enthusiastic application of maximum repression. In 1814, for example, Captain Wiltshire, a troop leader of the North Somerset Yeomanry, shot and killed a miner during a disturbance. He was charged with manslaughter but subsequently acquitted, his defence being that his pistol went off by accident.[34] However, perhaps the most infamous incident involving the Yeomanry was their sabre charge into an orderly crowd at St Peter's Fields, Manchester, in 1819. The consequence of incidents like 'Peterloo' was that the suitability of a middle-class, para-military order-maintaining force began to be widely questioned.

In short, although the Yeomanry were cheap and reliable, both their class composition and their brutality undermined their legitimacy. For this reason, although they were called out on several occasions up until 1867, the general policy from about the mid 1830s was to employ Yeomanry only in cases of extreme need.[35]

But the regular army was relatively small and generally considered inadequate for dealing with widespread disorder on its own. Moreover, although to a lesser extent, the same sort of legitimacy problem that occurred in relation to the Yeomanry also applied to the army. Soldiers were and are the servants of the Crown rather than impartial law enforcers; they tend to be associated with an individual ruler rather than with abstract notions of legality. So a new force was required to enforce the law and to relieve, as much as possible, the army from public order duties.

The Metropolitan Police Act of 1829 established just such a force capable of providing a first line of defence against rioters, revolutionaries and strikers. Moreover, any coercive action taken by this new body was seen to be necessary to uphold the law rather than the Government. The police idea was at first limited to London but eventually extended by the County and

Borough Police Act of 1856 to all other areas of England and Wales. However, prior to the 1856 Act it was quite common for Metropolitan police to be sent to other parts of the country when disorder threatened. For example, from June 1830 to December 1836 approximately 2,000 London policemen were sent to deal with Chartist disturbances.[36]

This policy of sending Metropolitan police to deal with disorder in other parts of the country initially won widespread support. Military men, such as General Charles Napier, who commanded the troops in the North of England during the Chartist disturbances, quickly recognised the value of police in public order situations: '. . . the putting down of one riot by constables has more good effect than putting down ten by soldiers: it also gives the civil powers confidence in themselves, which is very desirable'.[37]

A similar conclusion about the desirability of sending Metropolitan police to the provinces was reached by the Constabulary Force Commissioners and Handloom Weavers Commission which reported in 1840.[38] However, the question of cost reared its head once more; local authorities saw no reason to finance local police forces while the Home Office was prepared to send police from London to deal with disorder. So from the early 1840s the Home Office, in an attempt to pressurise local authorities into establishing their own police forces, became very reluctant to despatch Metropolitan police to other areas.[39] For example, in 1875 when miners in South Wales appeared to be on the point of rioting, the Home Secretary informed the local magistrates that no police aid would be made available.[40] Nevertheless, local authorities remained extremely reluctant to undertake the cost of establishing and maintaining an efficient full-time police force. Instead they tended to comply with the minimum requirements of the County and Borough Police Act and to requisition military aid when disorder threatened. In this way they managed to avoid the full costs of maintaining an adequate police force while still obtaining protection during disturbances. So government policy which was intended to encourage the growth of local police forces and therefore to reduce the need for military intervention had in practice the opposite effect. In the twenty-four years from 1869 to 1893 the army was called out to aid the civil power on no fewer than eighteen occasions.[41]

Sometimes informal arrangements enabled one police force to come to the aid of another thus avoiding the necessity of calling in the military, but mutual aid of this kind was the exception rather than the rule. The Police Act of 1890 attempted to overcome this problem by providing for standing agreements to be made between forces for mutual aid during disturbances. However, these agreements were voluntary and by 1908 only 57 forces out of a total of 192 had made such arrangements.[42] Consequently, military intervention in cases of civil disorder continued; troops were requisitioned six times during the period from 1893 to 1908.[43] It was not until 1925, following a recommendation of the Desborough Committee, that mutual aid agreements became general and the possibility of military involvement in public disorder more remote.

Military intervention in civil disturbances was not an unusual event in the late nineteenth and early twentieth centuries. If local police forces proved inadequate to deal with disorder, if no or only limited assistance was available from neighbouring forces, then, given the Home Office reluctance to send Metropolitan police, a requisition for military aid was likely to be made. The precise manner in which events in the West Riding conformed to this general pattern will now be considered.

In the first place it seems clear that the local police had insufficient manpower to deal with a dispute involving 80,000 miners. The total strength of the West Riding police in 1893 stood at 1,042 men. Moreover, at that time disorder associated with industrial disputes was not likely to be confined, as it was in later years, to the picket line but could occur anywhere in the county. The police had to cover a wide geographical area with their limited manpower. In particular, special events where people were likely to congregate were considered danger spots even though they had no immediate connection with the dispute in progress. This was why it was considered necessary to deploy 259 men, nearly a quarter of the West Riding Force, at the Doncaster Races. Given the scale of the dispute, the commitment at the races and the wide geographical area in which disorder could occur, assistance from other forces or military involvement was inevitable. In the event Captain Russell, the Chief Constable, was unable to obtain aid from neighbouring forces and 200 Metropolitan police were only sent after the military had been requisitioned, deployed and ordered to fire.

Military intervention at Featherstone, then, resulted from a situation where the local police had insufficient manpower to respond to calls made upon them, a situation that could not be rectified by mutual aid from other forces. Of course, this state of affairs was by no means unusual during the late nineteenth and early twentieth centuries; troops were called out to aid the civil power on 24 occasions in the 39 years before 1908. However, the discharge of firearms was unusual, occurring only twice during the 39-year period, and in this respect the events at Featherstone were not typical of military operations in support of the civil power.

Usually, as already observed, the very presence of soldiers, implying as it did the threat of shooting, was sufficient to cause crowds and rioters to disperse. The fact that this did not occur at Featherstone is probably due to three factors. Firstly, the small size of the contingent deployed when compared with the large number of strikers present does not seem to have had the intimidating effect that the presence of a larger body of soldiers would have inspired. Twenty-eight men can hardly have appeared as a very imposing force to more than 6,000 miners. Secondly, the soldiers prior to the arrival of the magistrate seemed unprepared to oppose forcibly the miners; indeed Captain Barker withdrew his men from the colliery premises in order to 'quiet' the situation. It is suggested that the strikers, having succeeded in securing the withdrawal of the troops, must have doubted the credibility of the implicit threat to shoot. In short, the strikers failed to appreciate that the arrival of the magistrate effectively transformed the soldiers from a seemingly compliant force into a killing machine.

The third and final reason why shooting occurred was simply because the absence of cavalry ruled out other less drastic crowd dispersal tactics. It was a long-established principle that cavalry rather than infantry should be used for public order duties. As Wellington said: 'It is much more desirable to employ cavalry for the purpose of police than infantry; for this reason, cavalry inspires more terror at the same time that it does much less mischief.' Initially, the Barnsley magistrates acted in accordance with this principle; their original requisitions specified that cavalry should be sent to the disturbed areas.[44] However, when the Chief Constable telegraphed York barracks on 7 September he requested both cavalry and infantry, only to be told by the Adjunct-General at York that no cavalry were available and that requests for infantry should be sent to Bradford. The Chief Constable then telegraphed Bradford and Captain Barker and 54 infantry were despatched for Wakefield. This force was then divided into two groups – Captain Barker and 28 men eventually being sent on to Featherstone.

Once the mere presence of the infantry proved insufficient to cause the strikers to disperse then the only tactics available were the bayonet charge and, if this did not work, shooting.

There seems no doubt that the soldiers fired to protect property rather than life. Of course, the troops themselves and the magistrate were stoned by the crowd, but it is doubtful if their lives were in danger. Mr Hartley, the magistrate, was struck twice but suffered no injury at all and was unable to name any person who had received an injury.[45] Captain Barker said that stones 'as thick as your fist' and 'bricks' were being thrown, but according to his own evidence more damage seems to have been done to the soldiers' equipment than to the soldiers themselves:

One man had his cheek cut open here and another man was struck on the mouth and his lip cut; another was struck on the ankle and very badly bruised. The damage to their helmets and rifles is considerable. On one rifle the bolt evidently got struck by it; must have been a piece of iron I should think. The bolt of the rifle was smashed through.[46]

Mr Holiday, the pit manager, was not struck by any stones or injured in any way.[47] Moreover, Mr Hartley, the magistrate, somewhat reluctantly admitted that one consideration in giving the order to fire had been to prevent the colliery from being wrecked.[48]

Paradoxically, shooting seems to have been an indiscriminate method of dealing with disorder since both the men killed and some of those injured were not taking part in the riot at all. The coroner's jury returned a verdict at the inquest into the death of James Gibbs:

That James Gibbs was killed by a bullet wound, inflicted by soldiers, fired into a crowd in Green Lane from the Ackton Hall Colliery, after the Riot Act had been read, on Thursday evening last, and that, since James Gibbs was a peaceful man, and took no part in any riotous proceeding, the jury record their sympathy with the deceased's relatives and friends.[49]

The Committee of Inquiry into the shootings also found that Gibbs, a Sunday school teacher, 'was an innocent spectator'. The Committee also implied that the other man killed, James Arthur Duggin, was a spectator, but not an innocent one since he had the 'imprudence' not to move away when he knew that the soldiers had already fired one volley.[50]

Ten shots in all appear to have been fired resulting in two deaths and between eleven and fourteen injuries. The rifles of the soldiers were sighted up to 2,900 yards and had a range of three miles and this meant that people a considerable distance away from the scene of the disorder were at risk. A miner named Oakley, who was standing in another colliery yard a quarter of a mile away, was shot by a bullet that ricochetted and wounded another miner in the neck. Neither of these men were among the rioters.[51] There is some evidence to suggest that several of the other people injured were spectators rather than rioters. One miner told the Committee how he had been shot while watching the rioting and Mr Dyer, the curate of the church at Normanton, sent a letter testifying to the good character of Gibbs and stating that five of the wounded were not taking part in the riot.[52]

It seems then that military intervention during the 1893 strike was hardly an unqualified success. The disorder at Featherstone was probably provoked by the presence of the soldiers in the first place and was only brought under control by the shooting of several innocent people. Moreover, a substantial amount of damage was inflicted on colliery buildings and equipment despite the use of deadly force intended to prevent just that occurrence.

However, the dramatic and in many ways questionable action of the soldiers at Featherstone should not lead us to ignore or underestimate the part played by other agents of social control during the strike. The role of both the police and the justices is worthy of detailed consideration; indeed, as we shall see, the justices controlled to a large extent both the military and the policing operations.

The police

In this section we will consider what attempts the police made to collect intelligence during the dispute of 1893 and what form of public order tactics they used in confrontations with strikers. Police operations in both these areas may seem somewhat unsophisticated and hardly worthy of the detailed consideration afforded to them, but this is to underestimate their value as benchmarks against which subsequent developments can be measured.

One of the notable features of the 1893 strike is the relatively crude and unorganised nature of the attempts to collect information and intelligence that were made. In order to appreciate fully this point it is necessary to consider briefly the state of intelligence collection in the nineteenth century.

Long before the establishment of the Metropolitan police in 1829 the Home Office had been employing spies and *agents provocateurs*. In 1817, for example, a Home Office spy named Oliver persuaded a few hundred Derbyshire working people that a general rising of the whole country was about to take place. Stirred up by Oliver these people set out on 8 June 1817 to join the other revolutionaries and form a provisional government (which some understood to mean a government that would give away free provisions). The little band of revolutionaries were met, not by fellow conspirators, but by the magistrates and soldiers tipped off by Oliver. A cavalry charge into the crowd was made resulting in several injuries, numerous arrests occurred and eventually three people were hung.[53] This sad affair is of interest because it clearly reveals that Home Office agents were active in the provinces during the early nineteenth century.

After the formation of the Metropolitan police, the Home Office was no longer the sole agency concerned with intelligence collection. In 1833 a Select Committee of the House of Commons heard evidence that William Popay, a plainclothes London policeman, had been attending meetings of the National Political Union of the Working Classes. Popay's reports, it turned out, had been forwarded to the commissioners at Scotland Yard and some had been passed on directly to the Home Secretary.[54] It seems then that from about 1829 the Metropolitan police as well as the Home Office were using undercover agents and informers.

In the 1830s and 1840s when the Chartists began to pose a threat to the *status quo* the intelligence system consisting of Home Office and police spies was extended. The Lord Lieutenants in the counties and the magistrates in the towns sent regular reports to London based on information provided by spies and informers under their control. They became in practice 'the confidential agents of the Secretary of State in their localities'.[55] In addition the army had also established its own intelligence network. General Napier instructed all his officers to make assessments 'as to the feelings of the labouring classes in your neighbourhood' based on the reports of 'the most intelligent of your soldiers' who would often be billeted with local people. In this way, commented Napier, 'I make spies of them despite themselves.'[56]

By 1893 there was in existence a relatively sophisticated intelligence network consisting of Home Office spies, plainclothes policemen, the army, and local officials such as magistrates and the Lord Lieutenants.

But there is no evidence that Home Office 'officials' were despatched to the strike areas in 1893, nor is there evidence that the army established an intelligence system similar to that operating in the 1830s and 1840s. Indeed, there seems to have been no attempt by the local police or magistrates systematically to collect information. This was probably because the first month of the strike passed without serious disorder and there was no reason to suppose that the situation would change. A chief constable who, as we have seen, was confident enough to go on holiday during a major industrial dispute would be unlikely to perceive a need for high-level surveillance. Intelligence collection and surveillance of the community, then, tended to be low-level and unorganised during the strike.

What little intelligence the police did manage to collect came from three main sources; informers, plainclothes officers and magistrates. There is no evidence that regular paid informers were at work, but individuals would approach police officers and divulge information about the destination of 'marching gangs'. This kind of *ad hoc* information sometimes enabled the authorities to deploy soldiers before any disorder occurred. The following extract from the report of a police inspector describes just such an incident:

On Friday, 8 September, there was to have been a mass meeting of miners at Featherstone, and large numbers of them began to make for the meeting place, but a heavy storm came on and dispersed them. Afterwards two men came and told me the 'men' were going to march on Glass Houghton Colliery, near Castleford. I reported this to Mr Tempest, the magistrate who was then on duty.

Later, a telephone message came from Glass Houghton that the miners were approaching, whereupon Mr Tempest sent off 50 soldiers, and myself as a guide. I left the soldiers at Glass Houghton, and on my way back I met large numbers of men and youths carrying sticks, and going towards the colliery.[57]

As well as receiving information from informers constables would sometimes go on duty in plain clothes in order to keep the 'marching gangs' under surveillance. For example, Police Constable Frank Wise reported that, while on duty in plain clothes, he had seen a crowd of 200 strikers armed with sticks.

The police also tended to get information from the magistrates; the Deputy Chief Constable, for example, only learnt what had taken place at Barnsley on 5 September when he attended a meeting of the local justices.[58] Some magistrates were also colliery owners and the information they passed on to the police was often designed to secure police or military protection for their property rather than to report actual events. There were numerous cases of magistrates and/or employers requesting military aid when no disorder at all had occurred. Mr Gill, the Deputy Chief Constable, recounted one such incident while giving evidence to the Committee of Inquiry:

'What information or application reached you in the night?' – 'Mr Roberts, a magistrate and pit owner near to Barnsley, requested that soldiers should be sent to protect in addition to the police, and that they should be sent at once, if practicable.'

'What did you do?' – 'I told him that soldiers could be obtained, I thought, from Sheffield, from the barracks, if he would sign a requisition as a justice of the peace for the West Riding, and he said he would requisition them himself.'

'I believe, as a matter of fact, there was no disturbance at that pit?' – 'Nothing of any moment.'[59]

Following the Featherstone shootings, the colliery owners and managers seemed to panic and numerous requests for police and military were made. Indeed, if all these demands for help had been met, 10,000 police and troops would have been required.[60] Yet no further disorder occurred in the West Riding.

Of course, intelligence collection was only one aspect of police work; undoubtedly their main purpose was to deal physically with public disorder when it occurred. One type of tactical intervention was specifically aimed at the prevention of violence. There is evidence that at least on one occasion, local police volunteered to act as guarantors of agreements made between the miners and their employer. The following extract taken from the report of Sergeant Sparrow reveals how he performed this 'bridging' function between the opposing parties:

one of the police constables came up and said to Holiday, 'Your men in Green Lane want to speak to you.' He and I went there. There were several hundred in the lane, and perhaps a few inside the yard. One man said, 'We want to know if you will allow three of our men to remain on the premises tonight to see that no "smudge" is filled or taken away by train?' Holiday said, 'Who are you?' The man said, 'That's my business.' Holiday said, 'Well, if you won't give your name I shall refuse to allow your men to come in.' Another man said, 'Will you take those soldiers away?' Holiday said, 'No I can't do that, but if you'll go away and be quiet the soldiers won't remain long.' He was then hooted. I said, 'You seem to doubt Mr Holiday's word. Will you take mine? I shall be here during the night, and if anything takes place different to what you've agreed to, I'll tell you.' There were cries of 'That will do' and they cheered me.[61]

This sort of police intervention in negotiations between management and workers obviously functioned to reduce the possibility of violence and can be considered a preventative tactic. In later chapters more recent examples of this form of police action will be provided. In many ways the initiative taken by Sergeant Sparrow constitutes in embryonic form a type of police tactic which later became more sophisticated, and generalised. However, in 1893 such preventive measures seem to have been used only on isolated occasions. When disorder occurred the police, although sometimes armed with cutlasses, relied on the baton-charge by foot and mounted men to disperse strikers.[62] Other relatively non-violent tactics, such as the cordon, are entirely absent during this period.

The justices

Perhaps the most notable feature of public order maintenance during the 1893 colliery dispute was the controlling role of the local magistrates. It was they who decided to call in the military. It was they who decided where to deploy the troops once they had arrived in the disturbed area. Finally it was they who decided that the troops should open fire. Compared with the justices, the Home Secretary and the local Chief Constable seem to have been relegated to a very minor role. This, of course, was not specific to the period under consideration, but was common during the nineteenth century.[63] It is only in the early twentieth century that the Home Secretary becomes more directly involved in the policing of disorder associated with provincial industrial disputes (see Chapter 3), while the Chief Constables become more independent of the local magistrates at an even later date (see Chapter 4).

Another remarkable feature is that the justices sometimes had a direct interest in the dispute. For example, Lord St Oswald, the owner of the Nostell Colliery, was also a magistrate who requisitioned troops, directed a detachment to his own pit where he was ready to give them any necessary directions and instructions.[64] Similarly, Mr Roberts, a Barnsley pit owner, was a magistrate who requisitioned troops for his own colliery. It is clear, then, that the military were used very much as the agents of the employers.

The role of the police is more complex. In the boroughs, the Chief Constables were under the control of the watch committees, policing policy would therefore be formulated by the justices and councillors who sat on these committees. In the counties, the Chief Constables were in overall command of the police recognising no higher constitutional authority. However, their social class position and local connections would tend to ensure that they saw eye to eye with the justices and employers on policing policy.

Summary

The strikers' behaviour during the 1893 colliery strike consisted of marching from pit to pit in order to reach agreements with the pit managers about the loading of 'smudge' and similar matters. If agreement proved impossible the 'marching gangs' attempted to destroy colliery property, but usually refrained from personal violence. However, once troops or police arrived on the scene the strikers responded by stoning them. For comparative purposes this entire pattern of behaviour can be characterised as 'stoning'.

The police, because of inadequate manpower, play a relatively minor role in dealing with disorder associated with the strike. Their main tactic was the baton-charge, although on one occasion an individual officer attempted to prevent violence by guaranteeing an agreement made between the opposing parties.

It is the army which assumes the major role in maintaining public order. An escalating series of tactics are adopted by the soldiers. Initially, their mere presence constitutes a dramaturgical display of force incorporating the implicit threat of shooting. In fact this show of force, because in the circumstances it lacked credibility, failed to cause the colliers to disperse. The second tactical stage consisted of both informal and formal (i.e. the reading of the Riot Act) warning and orders to disperse – a form of verbal intimidation ritual. Thirdly, the soldiers attempt to disperse the crowds with a bayonet charge. The fourth stage consists of firing warning shots into the ground and the fifth of shooting to kill. All these stages can be conveniently concentrated under the heading of 'shooting' for comparison with later styles of confrontation.

'Stoning' and 'shooting', then, is a shorthand characterisation of the style of violent action and reaction which occurred during the West Riding colliery strike of 1893.

3

The pivotal period

A miner, Samuel Boyce, lost his life, and hundreds of special constables and mounted hussars, despatched by the Home Secretary, Churchill, patrolled the coalfield. A few months later, two workers were shot and killed during a railway strike in Llanelli. The most violent excesses of industrial America, of the Homestead and Pullman strikes, seemed to have been transplanted to the peaceful Welsh valleys.[1]

For the historian of industrial confrontation the Welsh valleys of the early twentieth century provide a particularly fertile area for investigation. Indeed, two of the industrial disputes that we shall consider in this chapter are specifically Welsh and a third, although more geographically general, resulted in serious violence at Llanelli. But the significance of these incidents lay not in their regional location but in the changing response of the state to industrial disorder. As we shall see, a new policy of sending Metropolitan police to disturbed areas was adopted in 1910 only to be abandoned in 1911 when a return to direct military intervention occurred. A gradual evolution of social control occurs, but reversion to earlier tactics was readily prompted by changes in the general perception, if not the actuality, of the socio-economic climate. It is in this sense that the period between 1909 and 1914 can be considered pivotal.

In marked contrast to advances in order maintenance collective action by strikers evolves in a much more straightforward developmental manner. Throughout all the disputes of the period a new style of behaviour is evident. Strikers are generally no longer concerned with destroying property as they were at Featherstone, but with obstructing, sometimes quite violently, 'blacklegs' or non-unionists.

Industrial unrest 1909–1914: chronology

Tonypandy 1910

The South Wales coal strike of 1910–11 originated in a dispute over the price to be paid for working a new seam in the Ely pit of the Naval Colliery Com-

pany, a subsidiary of Cambrian Collieries Ltd. The owners initially offered a
rate of 1s. 9d. per ton; the miners, on the ground that the seam was particularly difficult to work with many abnormal places, asked for 2s. 6d. per
ton. At this stage only the 70 men who were to work the new seam were
negotiating with the coal owners. On 1 September 1910, in an attempt to
force the issue, the owners locked out all the 800 men employed in the Ely
pit. This lock-out caused widespread resentment and following a ballot of
the coalfield, the South Wales Miners' Federation called a strike of all the
12,000 miners employed by the Cambrian Combine in an effort to '. . . teach
that particular company that tyrannical action over certain men to influence
others was not a paying policy'.[2] The lock-out became a strike on 1 November
1910. By the end of the first week there were 12,000 miners on strike in the
Rhondda Valley and 11,000 in the neighbouring Aberdare Valley; by mid-
winter some 30,000 were locked out or on strike in the South Wales
coalfield.

Some of the coal owners intended from the outset to import 'blackleg'
labour from other districts to break the strike. A clash between the strikers,
who were fully conscious that their right of 'peaceful picketing' had been restored by the Trade Disputes Act of 1906, and the blacklegs was possible.
The owners held a meeting which resolved to take steps for obtaining police
protection for their imported labourers. The Chief Constable of Glamorgan,
Captain Lindsay, after discussions with the local magistrates (some of
whom were directors or shareholders in colliery companies), reinforced his
local police with extra men from Cardiff and Bristol.

On 2 November *The Times* reported some rioting at the village of
Cwmllynfell during which revolver shots were fired. Churchill, the Liberal
Home Secretary, immediately telegraphed the Chief Constable of Glamorgan
requesting a full report of the incident. A telegram was sent in reply stating
that 'no serious damage' had been done. Similarly the Merthyr Tydfil
borough justices had that same day contacted the War Office for information about the regulations concerning the use of the military in support of
the civil power. The War Office informed the Home Office of this enquiry
and Churchill telegraphed the Chief Constable of Merthyr for a report as to
the situation. The Chief Constable replied 'all peaceable and no disturbance
in Borough, all collieries working' and further that 'I have no reason to
apprehend any breach of the peace.'

On 6 November the miners discovered that 'blackleg' labour was to be
imported to work the Glamorgan Colliery at Llwynypia and on the following evening they marched to the colliery which was defended by a large body
of police. It was reported that an attempt was made to reach the pithead, but
was prevented by the police baton-charging the strikers. The strikers were
eventually forced to withdraw and police reinforcements rapidly arrived in
the valley. The arrival of these extra police and the strikers' defeat by the

police guarding the Glamorgan Colliery aroused resentment in the valley. At Tonypandy, a mile or so away from the colliery, there were reports of window smashing and looting between 8.00 p.m. and 1.00 a.m. on the morning of 8 November.

Captain Lindsay, the Chief Constable of Glamorgan, telegraphed to Shrewsbury, Chester and Salisbury Plain for troops to support his police. He also notified the Home Office of the state of affairs:

All the Cambrian collieries menaced last night. The Llwynypia Colliery savagely attacked by large crowd of strikers. Many casualties on both sides. Am expecting two companies of infantry and 200 cavalry today. Very little accommodation for police or soldiers. Position grave.[3]

Churchill immediately arranged a conference between himself, Haldane (the Secretary of State for War), General Ewart (the Adjutant-General), Sir Edward Troup (Home Office Under Secretary), and Sir Edward Henry (the Metropolitan Police Commissioner) and General Macready (a senior army officer). As a result of this meeting the troops requisitioned by Captain Lindsay were stopped *en route* to the troubled area; the infantry at Swindon and the cavalry at Cardiff. It was further decided to despatch 70 (in fact 100 were sent) mounted police and 200 foot police from London. General Macready was placed in charge of the cavalry at Cardiff with orders to take them into the troubled areas if the police proved unable to restore order. A telegram was sent to the Chief Constable informing him of these arrangements and stressing that the military should not be called upon unless it became clear that the police reinforcements were unable to cope with the situation.

The contingent of Metropolitan police was due to arrive at Pontypridd at about 8.30 p.m. on Tuesday (8 November) evening, but their train was delayed for about an hour. At about 8.00 p.m. the Home Office received a telephone message that the situation had become worse in the troubled area. A telegram was sent authorising General Macready to move the cavalry into the disturbed area if the Chief Constable applied to him for assistance. Between 9.30 p.m. and 10.30 p.m. Churchill had further telephone conversations with General Macready and Captain Lindsay. It was decided that, although serious rioting appeared to have stopped, a second contingent of 200 Metropolitan police should leave London at 3.00 a.m. on Wednesday (9 November) for Pontypridd.

Meanwhile, General Macready had, in response to a telephone message from Captain Lindsay, advanced with one squadron of the 18th Hussars to Pontypridd.

The following morning (Wednesday 9 November) Churchill spoke with General Macready and Captain Lindsay on the telephone. They indicated that though the situation was under control, the danger of disorder was not over, and it was agreed that a third contingent of 300 Metropolitan police should be sent that afternoon. This raised the number of police, local and Metropolitan, under the command of Captain Lindsay to 1,400 of whom 120 were mounted. In addition 300 infantry were moved to Newport and 200 to Pontypridd. Churchill also despatched to Pontypridd Mr J. F. Moylan, a 'confidential' Home Office representative, with instructions to collect and transmit in code any information which General Macready or Captain Lindsay could provide for the Home Office.

That evening, following further telephone conversations, Churchill telegraphed General Macready and Captain Lindsay and instructed them to proceed to Tonypandy where it was thought that disturbances would be most likely. Churchill specifically instructed Lindsay to draft the whole of the third contingent of 300 Metropolitan police to Tonypandy. A further force of 300 infantry and 200 cavalry were placed on stand-by to move into the troubled area should their presence be required. However, these elaborate precautions proved to be somewhat unnecessary; that evening the Home Office issued a press communiqué indicating the relative absence of disorder in the strike area.[4] Indeed, only isolated incidents of disorder continued to be reported throughout November and even less frequently until August 1911 when the Cambrian men (who had remained on strike after the Miners' Federation had accepted a settlement in June) returned to work on exactly the same terms as the employers had offered in October 1910.

In retrospect the behaviour of the strikers during the dispute appeared very similar to that which occurred during the West Riding colliery strike of 1893. According to newspaper reports the familiar 'marching gangs' seem to have visited and inflicted damage on those pits that were still working, just as they had at Featherstone:

At an early hour yesterday morning the bugle call was sounded in the district, and by 5 o'clock the strikers had mustered in force at Penycraig, Tonypandy and Clydach Vale. So thorough was the marchers' organization that the police, although considerably reinforced, were only partially able to defeat the plans of the attackers, and very few of the craftsmen succeeded in breaking through the cordon of strikers to the colliery yard.

The wild scenes of the morning developed into an alarming riot in the afternoon. All the engines at the Clydach Vale and Naval Collieries were brought to a standstill, the boiler fires were raked out and a ventilating fan stopped, thus imperilling the lives of a number of officials who were down the mine at the time. The mob marched upon colliery after colliery, the police and officials being quite powerless to arrest their progress. Employees were attacked and frogmarched home, those who resisted being severely attacked.[5]

However, a closer examination of the above report reveals that in many respects the strikers' behaviour was very different from earlier disputes. In the first place the strikers formed a cordon to prevent 'craftsmen' (a term which probably also included officials and imported labourers) entering the colliery yard. A 'cordon', whether used by police or pickets, is essentially a non-violent obstructive technique that bears little relation to the destructive tactics employed in 1893 (see Chapter 2). Secondly, the invasion of the Clydach Vale and Naval Collieries only superficially resembled the attack on the Ackton Hall Colliery at Featherstone. In 1893 the strikers smashed windows, tipped over waggons and set fire to buildings; in 1910 the miners did not damage property at all, but merely prevented the pits from working by raking out fires and stopping ventilation fans. The focus of disorder had shifted from the destruction of property to the obstruction of non-strikers and the immobilisation of pit machinery.

This new type of 'picketing' behaviour was reported on several occasions. Mr Moylan, the 'confidential' Home Office official, sent a memorandum to Churchill noting that:

Difficulties continue with regard to picketing. Several complaints have been made today by men who have been stopped by pickets from going to work. They allege that they have been threatened and intimidated, and that pickets of 12 men have stood in a line across the road and prevented their further passage.[6]

The Times also reported that strikers formed 'cordons' very much in the same way as a 'scrummage is formed in Rugby football'.[7] Of course, attempts to damage property did occur, but both newspaper reports and the coded messages of Mr Moylan indicate that they tended to be limited to attacks on the, usually unoccupied, houses of 'blacklegs'. It was when the police tried to prevent this kind of destruction that they themselves often became the target of stone-throwing crowds and in this respect the behaviour of the strikers had affinities with that of the miners during the colliery strike of 1893.

So far it has been noted that the strikers obstructed non-unionists, attacked the houses of 'blacklegs' and sometimes stoned the police, but they also, on one occasion, rioted, damaging and looting shops in Tonypandy. This isolated incident lasting only a few hours, functioned to concentrate attention on Tonypandy and justify the intervention of troops. It also enabled an extremely long and bitter industrial dispute involving some disorder to be simplified into a law and order issue; a question of anarchy or order. By this means the South Wales Colliery strike of 1910, which lasted nearly twelve months and extended over the entire South Wales coalfield, became known as the 'Tonypandy Riots', on the basis of incidents which occurred on one night in one village. The following discussion is an attempt to place the riots, or more accurately riot, in perspective.

Some accounts[8] suggest that the rioting occurred when the police drove a crowd of striking miners, who had been trying to stop the Glamorgan Colliery from working, over a quarter of a mile to the square at Tonypandy. The strikers, it is argued, then expressed their frustration by smashing shop windows and looting. However, it seems clear from newspaper reports and a statement made by one of the policemen involved that the strikers were not driven back by the police at all, but voluntarily returned to the village having been prevented from stopping work at the colliery.[9] At this time virtually all the available police were on duty defending the colliery so between 8.00 and 10.00 p.m. there was no effective policing of the town. It was during this two-hour period that the worst of the rioting occurred.

Many causal explanations have been put forward for the apparently wanton attack on the shops, including frustration,[10] 'jubilant defiance'[11] and the 'doctrine of extreme socialism'.[12] However, it is possible that the rioting was a ploy to divert the police from the colliery. One senior police officer told a reporter from the *South Wales Weekly Post* that the 'damaging and looting of shops was simply a trap to get us to leave the power station, so that another section of the strikers could have attacked it'.[13]

Just as there is disagreement about the immediate cause of the riot, so too is there over the extent of the resulting damage. The miners, local leaders, British socialists of all persuasions, miners' agents and sympathetic MPs denied that there was any widespread damage at all.[14] The local press painted a very different picture:

From 8 o'clock onwards the town was entirely in the hands of the strikers, who smashed nearly all the windows of the business premises from the Square at Tonypandy to Penycraig, a distance of ¼ mile. With loud shouts the strikers rushed along, hurling huge stones at the plate glass windows and belabouring them with sticks. Terror stricken, the shop owners rushed into their premises and left the contents of the windows to the mercy of the looters who, in many incidences threw the articles in the roadway.[15]

The view that there was widespread damage in Tonypandy is supported by Captain Childs, General Macready's staff officer, who passed through the riot area a few days later and reported that all the shops had been looted.[16] Other eyewitnesses confirm that many shop windows were smashed. Bryn Lewis, who at the time was ten years old, was watching the riot from a side street near the square with a friend:

they started smashing the windows . . . they smashed this shop here, J. O. Jones, a millinery shop that was on the other corner . . . We saw that being smashed and then next door to the millinery J. O. Jones, there was a shop and they smashed the window there . . . on the other side here, there was Richards the Chemist . . . they smashed that. And they smashed the windows of these three small shops here, one was a greengrocer, the other one was fancy goods and the other one was a barber's shop, and I knew the name of the barber quite well, it was Salter, because we used to think it swanky to go to Salter's to have a hair-cut, you see. They smashed Richards the Chemist, then there was the boot shop next door to it . . . and next to that was Watkins the flannel merchant . . . they smashed that and they stole shoes out of the boots, flannel out of Watkins and greengrocery, well they only picked up there. Well next to that there was a few steps up and there was a dentist and one or two private houses. Well, they didn't smash. We didn't see anything that happened below the bridge because . . . we were afraid to go down there in front of the crowd.[17]

On the basis of local newspaper reports and Captain Childs' and Bryn Lewis' eyewitness accounts it is reasonable to conclude that many shop windows were smashed. However, it is argued that Captain Childs goes too far when he states that 'all' the shops were looted. There is evidence to suggest that the strikers engaged in discriminate rather than indiscriminate destruction.

One of the first shop windows to be smashed was that of T. Pascoe Jenkins, the senior magistrate in the Rhondda Valley,[18] who said that the crowd made 'wild threats . . . and then went on with their work of destruction'.[19] It seems probable that the strikers felt a particular grievance against this local representative of law and order. Moreover, there is no doubt that old, and not so old, scores were being settled. J. O. Jones, whose draper's shop was wrecked, obviously felt that a grudge was held against him since he offered to pay £50 to charity 'if a certain statement attributed to me can be proven'.[20] Despite the fact that all other chemists suffered extensive damage one shop in particular was left untouched. This shop belonged to Willie Llewellyn, a former rugby international who had played a part in the historic defeat of the All Blacks in 1905 and who was regarded as a local hero.[21] A total of 63 shops were damaged; chemists, drapers and refreshment houses in particular were ransacked, while other shops suffered less or no damage.[22]

In short, the Tonypandy Riot of 8 November 1910 lasted approximately two hours and followed a logical pattern of its own. In particular it should be noted that no personal violence occurred and that damage to property was limited to window smashing and looting, there being no reported cases of arson or more serious forms of destruction.

The 1911 transport strikes

While the Cambrian coal strike was continuing in South Wales a series of widespread labour disputes occurred during the summer of 1911. In June a seamen's strike commenced in Liverpool and quickly spread to Hull, Cardiff, Manchester, Bristol and Southampton. The strike had an international dimension with Dutch and Belgian seamen also withholding their labour. In Britain dockers and other transport workers came out in sympathy with the seamen and the movement of goods through the docks virtually ceased.

As in the case of the South Wales coal strike the employers resorted to importing labour to break the strike. Some of these blacklegs were literally imported, being Chinese or Finns and were paid at the very rates demanded by the strikers. Given the employers' policy of hiring or coercing blackleg labour the only realistic option open to the strikers was to try to prevent, physically and illegally, the blacklegs from working. Once again the police were used to maintain the law and order that would ensure in effect the strikers' defeat. However, some contemporary press reports indicate that the police exceeded the limits of the law by preventing strikers from trying to persuade 'blacklegs' to join the strike; a right granted expressly by the Trade Disputes Act of 1906. In these circumstances it is hardly surprising that violent incidents, nearly all of them associated with the importation of labour, began to be reported in the press.[23]

In the last week of June more serious disorder occurred at Hull; windows were smashed, flag-stones torn up and police stoned.[24] Five hundred Metropolitans were despatched to support the Hull police who had already been reinforced from Sheffield, Birmingham, Nottingham and York. The second battalion of the South Staffordshire Regiment received orders on 2 July to hold themselves ready to proceed to Liverpool or Hull, but on 3 July the disputes at both cities were settled and the imported police were withdrawn.[25]

Reports of disorder in Manchester, Cardiff, Liverpool and Glasgow appeared in *The Times* during the first weeks of July. On 5 July General Macready and 200 Metropolitan police were sent to Salford and were joined on the following day by two squadrons of Scots Greys and a battalion of infantry.[26] Within days a local settlement had been reached and the police and troops were withdrawn without having come into contact with the strikers. However, disorder associated with the dock and seamen's strike continued to be reported and on 18 July 300 Metropolitan police were sent to Cardiff to reinforce the local police. A week later a further 100 Metropolitan police were despatched to Cardiff.

The dockers at the Port of London also went on strike. Churchill asked Haldane to be ready to move 25,000 troops into the London docks to ensure the movement of essential supplies. The dockers' leaders warned that the use of troops might provoke bloodshed. This explosive situation was defused by the Chancellor, Lloyd George, who, it seems, persuaded the Prime Minister, Asquith, to urge Churchill to moderate his position in case his '... habit of calling in the military to settle industrial disputes should bring open warfare in the streets'.[27] Lloyd George was particularly anxious to avoid any internal conflict that could be interpreted as a sign of weakness abroad in the tense international atmosphere that prevailed after the Agadir incident.[28] Governmental pressure was put on the Port of London Authority and a settlement was reached in early August.

From the beginning of August a series of local disputes involving railwaymen occurred. The railwaymen were striking partly in support of the dockers and partly because the railway companies refused to recognise their unions. In Liverpool, where there was both a dock and a railway strike, there were riots. Police reinforcements were sent to Liverpool from Birmingham and Leeds and Churchill sent two squadrons of Scots Greys, three battalions of infantry, a regiment of cavalry and even a warship.[29] The imported police and military actually clashed with the 'rioters' in Liverpool. *The Times* of 15 August reported that windows had been smashed, shops looted and that the troops had fired on the crowd. Further outbreaks of disorder were reported from Liverpool and elsewhere in the following days and on 16 August the local railway strikes became concentrated into the first British national railway strike. Troops were despatched, not to deal with any actual or threatened disorder but to ensure that the railway system continued to function. However, Lloyd George again used the Morocco crisis to pressure the railway companies and on 19 August the strike was settled. The police and troops deployed at various places throughout the country were withdrawn; the industrial and public order crisis appeared to be over.

The national coal strike 1912

Fears of industrial disorder revived early in 1912 when the Miners' Federation of Great Britain called its first national strike. By Friday 1 March over a million colliers had stopped work and throughout the coalfields of England, Scotland and Wales no coal was being produced.[30] With the possible exception of the 1905 Russian General Strike it was the most extensive stoppage in the history of the industrialised world.[31] Despite, or perhaps because of, the widespread nature of the strike there was hardly any disorder at all. Obviously, the coal owners were unable to recruit enough imported labourers to pose a serious threat to a co-ordinated stoppage by the entire workforce. And since, as we have seen, strikers were concerned with obstructing non-union labour rather than with the kind of destruction that occurred at Featherstone, there was little reason or opportunity for disorder. Indeed, no violent incidents were reported in either *The Times* or the *Daily Mail* during the first two weeks of the strike. In some districts, such as Lancashire, the strike was so solidly supported that there was no need to picket at all.[32] It was only in those few areas where non-unionists or imported labourers were active that isolated incidents of disorder occurred during the third and fourth weeks of March. During March *The Times* reported a mere 11 incidents of disorder associated with the strike (see Table 3), and this of course is persuasive evidence of the general lack of disorder. Even the Home Secretary commented on the essentially peaceful nature of the dispute: '. . . considering the extent and magnitude of the strike, it is remarkable how few and insignificant have been the disturbances accompanying it'.[33] So the miners' strike of 1912 was not only the most widespread stoppage in British history but also one of the least violent.

For their part the Government responded just as they had in 1911 by sending troops to the strike areas even when there was little or no disorder for them to deal with. On 28 March the military were deployed at various collieries, but on this occasion their presence did not provoke rioting as it

Table 3. *Colliery disturbances reported during March 1912*[34]

Place	Date	Nature of disturbance
St Helens	14 March	Crowd of 1,000 dispersed by police 3 police injured
Lanarkshire	18 March	Shops windows smashed, police stoned
Lanarkshire	19 March	Strikers attacked non-unionists
Burton	19 March	Coal cart overturned
St Helens	20 March	Crowd of 300 dispersed by baton charge. No serious injuries
Dumfrieshire	22 March	Strikers stoned police. One miner seriously hurt in baton charge
Huntington	28 March	Police stoned, windows smashed, tubs tipped down pit, numerous baton charges
Mexborough	29 March	Police protecting non-unionists stoned. Baton charge. One miner suffered a broken arm. One policeman cut on head
Sheffield	29 March	Coal cart overturned
Walsall	29 March	Non-unionists and police stoned. One policeman cut on head
Brownhills	30 March	Two policemen stoned – one 'severely' cut about the face

had at Featherstone. Indeed, there were no reports of the military coming into direct contact with the strikers at all. Having been denied the opportunity of employing repressive force against the mass of the strikers the Government decided to take action against their leaders. A series of prosecutions were brought against trade unionists under the Incitement to Mutiny Act of 1797. Tom Mann, the prominant labour leader, was among those arrested. However, the prosecutions succeeded in stirring up a spirit of defiance rather than one of submission. When Mr Justice Horridge passed sentence on the two printers there were shouts of 'Liar' and 'It is our turn next.' In the face of mounting public outcry against the prosecutions the Home Secretary was eventually forced to exercise the prerogative of mercy and reduce the sentences of all five defendants.[35]

Meanwhile, on 6 April, the Miners' Conference had decided on a return to work and by the end of the month all the troops had been withdrawn from the coalfields. Both those who feared bloody repression and those who predicted a syndicalist revolution could breathe a sigh of relief; Britain's most serious industrial stoppage was over.

Industrial unrest 1909–1914: analysis

Government intervention

That the Home Office directly intervened in the South Wales coal strike by stopping the troops requisitioned by Captain Lindsay and by sending Metropolitan police is very surprising. After all, the legal responsibility for maintaining law and order still rested with the local magistrates. Indeed, in the aftermath of the Featherstone shootings the Home Secretary, H. H. Asquith, had at first denied that the Home Office had any responsibility at all for the preservation of public order outside London.[36]

Churchill, then, activated the more interventionist policy of delaying the arrival of troops, sending police reinforcements, obtaining an independent assessment of the situation and finally, if absolutely necessary, authorising the military to move into the disturbed area with instructions to avoid contact with the strikers if at all possible. A memorandum by General Macready clearly sets out this policy:

In accordance with the verbal instructions of the Home Secretary, the general line of policy pursued throughout the strike was that in no case should soldiers come in direct contact with rioters unless and until action had been taken by the police. In the event of the police being overpowered, or not being in sufficient strength to protect a large and intersected area, the military force would come into play, but even then each body of military should be accompanied by at any rate a small body of police to emphasize the fact that the armed forces act merely as the support of the civil power and not as direct agents.[37]

There was, then, a great reluctance to allow the troops to come into direct contact with the strikers. In particular, both the Home Office and the War Office were anxious to avoid the use of firearms.[38] In fact the soldiers only came into contact with the crowd on one occasion when they used bayonets to disperse stone-throwing strikers. General Macready recalls that the troops advanced slowly and were instructed to apply their bayonets 'to that portion of the body traditionally held by trainers of youth to be reserved for punishment'.[39]

Of course, the initial decision to send Metropolitan police was based entirely on information provided by the Chief Constable and also the local justices, of whom some were managers, directors or shareholders in the mining companies concerned in the dispute. The Managing Director of the Powell Duffryn Collieries, known locally as 'P and D' or 'Poverty and Death', was Mr Hann, who was also a magistrate.[40] The Managing Director of the Cambrian Collieries, D. A. Thomas, was the local Liberal MP. It is probable that these local figures would be able to exert great pressure on the Chief Constable and fellow magistrates. So, given the Home Office policy of using police rather than troops, the local magistrates and the Chief Constable could effectively ensure the despatch of Metropolitan police by directly requisitioning troops. However, there is no evidence to suggest that local officials were aware that a request for troops would in fact result in police being sent. Mr Llewellyn, the Manager of the Cambrian Collieries was, to judge from a statement published in the *South Wales Daily News*, rather annoyed that troops had not been deployed:

Mr Winston Churchill's action ... has really made things worse. I applied for military and saw the magistrates on Monday morning, and I told them of the seriousness of the case, and my complaint is that none of this bloodshed would have happened if the military had been here.[41]

Moreover, the local authority would have probably preferred troops, paid for by central government, rather than Metropolitan police for which they had to pay themselves.

Home Office intervention was not limited to sending police; the assumption of overall control of the imported police and the military was a major policy innovation. It has already been noted that in the 1893 West Riding coal strike operational control of the police and the army rested with the local magistrates. In 1910, General Macready was placed in command of both the Metropolitan police and the troops[42] and was himself under the authority of the Home Secretary: 'From the time I started from London I came under the direct authority of the Home Office, except as regards purely military matters connected with the troops.'[43] Moreover, it is clear that central control by the Home Office was actively exercised; General Macready, for one, noted an 'inclination to interfere from Whitehall'.[44]

The new Home Office policy meant that both local officials and employers were excluded from exercising control over the imported police and military. However, it seems clear that employers were still able, to a certain extent, to control the local police. For example, an inspector in charge of police guarding a pit told an army intelligence officer that he had withdrawn his men 'by the kind permission' of the manager.[45] Also there was a close personal relationship between the Chief Constable and Mr Llewellyn, the Manager of the Glamorgan Colliery. Captain Lindsay frequently dined with Mr Llewellyn, shared his horses, and often took his advice on policing matters.[46] In contrast General Macready refused all invitations to his officers and himself to dine with any of the coal owners and described Mr Llewellyn as 'a forceful, autocratic man'.[47] As is clear from the following report to the Home Office, Macready left the employers in no doubt about who controlled the Metropolitan police and the military:

A Meeting with the directors of the colliers was not ... satisfactory, owing to the somewhat dictatorial tone adopted by those present. The idea seemed prevalent among them that the military and police were at their disposal, to be increased to any extent they might demand, and to be allocated according to their advice. I had to point out that the numbers were dependent on what the Government might consider necessary and find available, and that the decision and responsibility for the distribution both of the police and military rested with me.[48]

In short, government intervention in the 1910 coal strike meant that Metropolitan police rather than troops came into contact with strikers and that control of these police rested with the central political authority rather than with the local authority.

At first this policy of using police rather than troops was continued during the transport strikes of 1911. However, as was noted in the case of the South Wales coal strike, intervention of this kind meant that local officials could precipitate the despatch of Metropolitan police by requisitioning troops. For example, Churchill responded to a request from the Mayor of Salford for military aid by also sending London police. Once again, as the following telegraph from Churchill to the King makes clear, troops were only to be used in the last resort:

Mr Churchill has had to authorize the despatch to Manchester of the Scots Greys and an infantry battalion: but 250 Metropolitan police have been sent as well and General Macready who has been placed in general control will not use the military unless and until all other means have been exhausted.[49]

However, the announcement of a national railway strike triggered an immediate change of policy. Churchill suspended the regulation which provided that troops could only intervene if requisitioned by the civil authority. Fifty thousand soldiers were mobilised, issued with twenty rounds each and deployed at various strategic points on the railways. Some districts such as Sheffield, Manchester, Blackburn and Poplar which had not requested and did not want military aid were nevertheless given it.[50]

There seems little doubt that this reversion to a more military response occurred because of a growing sense of extreme unease in establishment circles. For example, the King thought that the situation was 'more like a revolution than a strike'.[51] Similarly, the Mayor of Liverpool told Lord Derby that 'it is no ordinary strike riot'[52] and a Hull councillor remarked that the situation was worse than that prevailing during the Paris Commune.[53] Churchill himself perceived 'grave unrest' and declared that 'the general strike policy is a factor which must be dealt with'.[54] Newspaper accounts reflected and reinforced the general sense of mounting crisis. According to *The Times* the very fabric of society was in danger of disintegrating:

The existing condition of affairs in the industrial world, especially in view of the scientifically organized competition we have to meet, is a cruel satire upon the management of our national affairs. It is a not less cruel satire upon the religion and the morality upon which we pride ourselves. We are assisting at the absolute decomposition of society into its elements, in the absence of settled principles, of sane direction, and of discipline of any shape or form. That decomposition is nowhere more marked than in the trade unions themselves, which flout their own leaders and trample upon their own engagements. There is no King in Israel and every man is a law unto himself.[55]

So, *The Times*, local officials, the Home Secretary and the King all perceived the situation as being critical and it was this sense of mounting crisis that informed the reversion to a more military style of order maintenance. A reversion which, as we have seen, continued throughout the national coal strike of 1912. Of course, this regression to a more primitive form of control meant that overall command of the forces of law and order was exercised once more by local officials rather than the Home Office. Moreover, the Government was unable to establish the kind of highly organised intelligence system which, as we shall see, operated during the South Wales coal strike.

Intelligence collection

In our analysis of the Featherstone disturbances of 1893 we noted that intelligence was collected by local police officers in a very unorganised way and that the Home Office was hardly involved at all, receiving no communications from the strike area. By the time of the South Wales coal strike in 1910 the position had changed somewhat and the Home Office was subjected to a veritable flood of information.

Communications were sent from South Wales not only by employers and local officials, but also by the miners, General Macready and the Home Office official, Mr Moylan. An analysis of the correspondence relating to the disturbances, reproduced in the Parliamentary Paper 'Colliery Strike Disturbances in South Wales', reveals that General Macready and Mr Moylan reported to the Home Office by telegram on 31 occasions in November 1910. Employers contacted the Home Office on five occasions, miners' organisations on four occasions, the Chief Constable on eight occasions and magistrates on two occasions.[56]

The employers proved a particularly unreliable source of information as a memorandum from Mr Moylan to the Home Office makes clear:

At 11.40 a.m. a telephone message was received at Tonypandy Police Station from the Clerk at the Tonypandy Colliery Office of the Cambrian Combine, that a body of 400 armed strikers was marching over the hills in the direction of Nantgwyn Colliery, and that the manager desired police protection. Forty Metropolitan police were despatched in great haste, and arrived breathless on top of a steep slope to find that the armed strikers were the Lancashire Fusiliers taking their walk.[57]

Indeed, in his final report Macready concluded that the information from the managers was 'in practically every case so exaggerated as to be worthless'.[58]

Fortunately, Macready had other more reliable sources of information; Captains Farquhar and Childs were sent by the War Office and an intelligence department was set up in the strike area.[59] Army officers were posted at the various centres to analyse reports, rumours and requests for troops, which could now only be made through them. According to Captain Childs this system worked very well and prevented the 'unnecessary dissipation of troops'.[60]

A second strand of the intelligence network was provided by the presence of two Welsh-speaking CID officers sent from Scotland Yard, at the request of Moylan, to assist in collecting 'accurate information'.[61] It seems that on occasions these plainclothes officers attended strike meetings and reported back to General Macready.[62]

The third and final element of the intelligence system was the presence of a 'confidential' Home Office official in the strike area. According to the Home Office this man's function was simply that of a cipher clerk, but in his memoirs, Captain Childs recalls that he thought Moylan's main function was to provide Churchill with an early warning of any serious military confrontation with the strikers.[63] It is certainly true that Moylan was more than a mere communications officer; he sent thirteen of his own reports and assessments to the Home Office, personally toured the disturbed area and attended meetings with both the employers and the strikers.[64] It is probably the case that Moylan's brief included making his own assessments of the situation and providing Churchill with prior notice of any major military action.

This relatively sophisticated and centrally controlled intelligence network was probably superimposed on the kind of *ad hoc* information collection by local police that occurred in 1893 (see Chapter 2). However, the important point about intelligence collection in 1910 is that compared with earlier industrial disputes, it is both highly organised and centralised.

Strategy, tactics and brutality

Prior to government intervention in the South Wales coal strike the army and the police had often been used to re-establish and sustain the traditional authority of the coal owners.[65] Indeed this, as we have seen, was precisely what happened at Featherstone. However, following government intervention in 1910 the strategy of control became one of impartially maintaining public order. The army and the police were to enforce the rational authority of the law rather than the traditional authority of the employer. Thus, Macready prevented his officers from socialising with the employers and repeatedly stressed to both coal owners and strikers the impartial order-maintaining role of the army.[66]

Certain constraints were imposed on the strikers by means of liaison and negotiation with the strike committees. In particular Macready informed the committees that if more than six men were present on any one picket line this would constitute obstruction and the police would move them on. He also told them that he intended to enforce local bye-laws which prevented the pickets from having a fire within a certain distance of any houses. These measures enabled him to report that by the end of November 'picketing had practically ceased'.[67]

As well as getting the strike committees to agree to the limitation of picketing, Macready also succeeded in persuading them to disapprove publicly of violence and to pass on information to the authorities. The strike leaders held a meeting, passed a resolution and placarded Tonypandy in an attempt to make known their disapproval of rioting.[68] Moreover, at Macready's suggestion, a strike sub-committee was set up to co-operate with the magistrates in 'preventing and suppressing disorder by giving information of any movement or decision of riotous character'.[69] In this way the agents of social control were able to use strike committees to prevent disorder – a major innovation in the history of policing industrial disputes.

General Macready also imposed conditions on the employers which limited the importation of 'blackleg' labour and controlled the use of pumping machinery in the pits. The employers, of course, objected to these conditions and on one occasion D. A. Thomas, the Liberal MP, threatened to go over Macready's head to the Home Secretary:

I was rung up by Mr D. A. Thomas from his private residence, evidently considerably annoyed at some straight talk which had taken place between Mr Llewellyn and myself, when I hinted that if my instructions were not complied with I should withdraw protection from certain mines. Mr Thomas, I suppose on the strength of being a member of Parliament, threatened an immediate complaint to the Home Secretary, and was not at all mollified when he learnt that I had long ago telephoned the incident to Mr Churchill.[70]

The employers were not only prepared to apply political pressure but also to attempt to import secretly labour or commence pumping.[71] Nevertheless, Macready seems to have been ultimately successful in preventing these activities and in this way the conditions imposed on the strikers were balanced by constraints on the employers and the impartiality of the army maintained. Indeed, one striker later described General Macready as 'the fairest and most straightforward gentleman you could meet',[72] while another insisted that 'not one word against the military was ever uttered by the Combine Committee'.[73]

Although the army generally maintained an impartial position there is considerable evidence that the police engaged in indiscriminate violence when attempting to deal with strike disturbances. Newspaper reports, such as the following from *The Times*, suggest that all the members of a crowd became targets for the police batons irrespective of whether or not they had actually committed an offence: 'That the police are using their batons with effect is obvious from the number of bandaged and bleeding ears which are to be seen. They have no time to discriminate and it is a case of "Whenever you see a head hit it!" '[74] One miner, Samuel Boyce (alternately reported as

Royce or Rays) died from head wounds received during rioting on 8 November. The Coroner's jury returned the verdict: 'That we agree that Samuel Rays died from injuries he received on 8 November caused by some blunt instrument. The evidence is not sufficiently clear to us how he received those injuries.'[75] However, since the police, during the riot in question, made 'wave after wave' of baton charges it is reasonable to conclude that Boyce was killed by a policeman.

Many other cases can be cited as examples of police brutality. The following statement was made by the Reverend D. Jones, a baptist minister, and read out in the House of Commons by Keir Hardie:

(1) That a body of policemen, numbering from forty to fifty, were on duty last evening at Penygraig, most of whom were obviously under the influence of drink.

(2) That a body of policemen attacked an old collier without the slightest provocation, and beat him about with their batons so that at 2 a.m. this morning Drs Wishard and Llewellyn, of Penygraig, found it necessary to put in four stitches in attending to the injuries inflicted. I myself had an interview with the above collier, Evan Jones, a quiet, religious, and generally respected man of this neighbourhood. His version was that he, when alone, was repeatedly struck down by two policemen, who, when carrying on this inhuman act, cursed and swore like troopers.

(3) That when Penygraig Road was free from any disturbing strikers, a large number of the above police, without the slightest offence battered in the windows of at least two houses with their batons, and five or six of their numbers rushed into the house next door to Mr Evan Jones at the same Penygraig Road.

(4) That two of the above policemen were seen to fire a pistol into the shop of Mr Locke, grocer, Brook Street . . .

(5) That a number of policemen entered private houses, inflicting serious injuries upon inoffensive occupants – men, women and children – at Bank Street, Penygraig.

(6) Thomas Davies of Bank Street, Penygraig, states that his house was stormed by a number of policemen who hurled stones through the front windows, causing considerable damage without the slightest provocation on the parts of the occupants.

(7) Mrs Francis of Penygraig, returning from shopping at Tonypandy at 8.30 p.m., was knocked down and kicked by the policemen, after which treatment she suffered from convulsive fits.

(8) Policemen were seen to put the street lights out, so that the main street was in perfect darkness.[76]

Hardie cited a further six statements made by merchants and church ministers as well as miners alleging police brutality. The following incidents occurred on the evening of 21 November or early the next day at Aberman where a large crowd had gathered. The police tried to disperse the crowd and Hardie alleged that, among other things, they had pushed an elderly man, who had been collecting coal, and an eleven-year-old boy into a canal.[77] Hardie was supported by other MPs from South Wales such as E. Jones, W. Abraham and G. N. Barnes who also complained of police brutality and called for a public enquiry (which was never granted).

Other complaints and examples of police brutality were made by strike committees, ministers, a local library committee, tradesmen and a local chamber of commerce.[78]

Faced with the cases of brutality which Hardie cited in the House of Commons, Churchill simply replied: 'With regard to the methods of the police, let me say that I must confess I was not convinced by the picture which the Hon. Member for Merthyr Tydfil (Mr Keir Hardie) drew.'[79] Churchill was later able to cite various statements indicating that police behaviour in South Wales had been exemplary in very difficult circumstances. Fourteen of these statements are published in the Parliamentary Paper 'Colliery Strike Disturbances in South Wales'.[80] They are classified into two groups: the first comprises statements relating to the general conduct of the police, the second relates to more specific incidents. One example from each group is reproduced below:

Group 1 From a Methodist Minister
I hereby testify that in my opinion the police during the recent riots at Tonypandy acted with great patience under extraordinary provocation, and this is also the opinion of all persons who have any responsibility whom I have consulted.

The only fault on the part of the police in my opinion was that they refrained for too long a time in using severe measures.[81]

Group 2 From a Railway Official at Tonypandy Station
On the night of 21st November great crowds began to assemble within the vicinity of the station; their manner was of a threatening nature and became worse as time wore on. About 9 p.m. the police who had been sent for dispersed the crowd from the railway bridge. As soon as the police requested the mob to move on, stones began to fly in all directions, some as large as bricks. The police behaved with great forbearance and did not draw their truncheons this time. About 11 p.m. the mob was still in the vicinity of the station; they were booing and shouting, and continued to throw stones. The police had at this time their truncheons drawn, but I did not actually see them strike anyone, as the mob was running in front of them in the direction of Trealaw. I then attended to my ordinary duty. The roadway outside here was littered with stones, bricks . . . which had been used by the rioters. I had ample opportunity of observing the condition of the members of the Metropolitan police, and I can safely say without fear of contradiction that I did not observe any one under the influence of drink, or approaching such. I think the police acted with great forbearance and leniency towards such a disorderly mob, and only acted when it became absolutely necessary.

This is a voluntary statement on my part, and I can swear to anything I have said, as I was a witness of what occurred.[82]

It is difficult to reconcile the statements cited by Hardie with those cited by Churchill, although they are not obviously contradictory. It may be that in one instance, such as that cited above, the police responded to extreme provocation with the utmost restraint while in another instance, such as that cited by Hardie (see p. 41), they brutally attacked an inoffensive child. However, such drastic changes in behaviour seem rather improbable. On

Table 4. *Number and sources of statements cited by Churchill in support of the police action during the South Wales coal strike of 1910*[83]

Source	Statements
Railway officials	6
Colliery officials	2
Religious ministers	2
Tradesmen	4
Total	14

the whole it seems more likely that one set of statements misrepresents the general nature of police behaviour in South Wales.

It is suggested that on a balance of probabilities the statements cited by Keir Hardie present a more accurate picture of police behaviour than those cited by Churchill. The reason for favouring Hardie's statements is that many were made by people who would not normally be critical of the police or ally themselves with the striking miners such as ministers of religion and tradesmen. Churchill's statements, on the other hand, were made by precisely the type of person one would expect to support the police and oppose the strikers (see Table 4). The absence of any statements commending the police from individual miners or strike committees enables less weight to be attached to Churchill's examples than to Hardie's. It seems very likely then that the police, at least on some occasions, acted both brutally and illegally.

There were both tactical and political reasons for the aggressive behaviour of the police. In the first place police tactics were very crude, being limited almost exclusively to the inevitably brutal and indiscriminate baton-charge.[84] Some attempts at less drastic crowd control techniques were attempted, for example on one occasion the Metropolitan police used their rolled up capes to bludgeon the strikers, but the baton-charge remained the standard public order tactic.[85] In fact local supplies of truncheons were completely used up during the South Wales strike and 300 replacements had to be speedily ordered.[86] So, although, as we have noted, there was a strategic commitment to impartial policing the relatively undeveloped state of control tactics militated against its implementation.

There is also evidence to suggest that police violence was related to political influences originating from the Home Office as well as to the tactical limitations of the period. It is difficult to establish a causal link between the political atmosphere at the centre, in the Home Office itself, and repressive police action at the periphery, on the streets of Tonypandy. There is, for example, no evidence of a concerted policy of repression being formulated at the Home Office, but a preference for 'vigorous' police action is unmistakable. This preference can be detected in the following extracts from Home Office telegrams to the Chief Constable of Glamorganshire:

This force (i.e. 500 Metropolitan police) should enable you during the daytime not merely to hold the threatened collieries but to deal actively and promptly with any sign of a disorderly gathering. I am counting upon the action of the police in this respect to avert the necessity for using the military.[87]

Unless you have more serious calls elsewhere you should use the whole of the third contingent of 300 Metropolitan police in Tonypandy to-night and establish a decisive superiority once and for all.[88]

The Chief Constable, Captain Lindsay, replied that he had reminded his men of the Home Secretary's instructions to act with firmness and this seemed to worry Churchill for he sent another telegram urging the police to 'go gently in small matters'.[89]

It is interesting to note that the cases of police brutality cited by the Reverend Jones (see p. 41) occurred merely three days after the instructions to be firm and it is probable that these events were not entirely unconnected.

A similar link between central political influences and police and army behaviour can be detected during the railway strike of 1911. Once a national stoppage had been declared Government spokesmen adopted a very belligerent attitude. The Prime Minister, Asquith, told the railwaymen's leaders that the Government would take any necessary steps to keep the railways functioning and when they refused the offer of a Royal Commission he muttered: 'Then your blood be on your own head.'[90] Similarly, Charles Masterman, Churchill's Parliamentary Secretary, said that Winston was 'longing for blood'.[91] Indeed, when he heard that the strike was finally settled Churchill telephoned Lloyd George and told him 'I'm very sorry to hear it. It would have been better to have gone on and given these men a good thrashing.'[92] The Home Office certainly prepared for such a 'thrashing'; 50,000 troops were mobilised and a circular urging a more repressive interpretation of the picketing law was sent to Chief Constables.[93] The Mayor of Liverpool was even promised a Bill of Indemnity for any illegal action he might take to ensure that ships were unloaded.[94] Home Office circulars and instructions of this kind probably functioned to encourage a more aggressive approach to the strikers. In any case, there is little doubt that in some instances the police and army behaved in a very repressive and brutal manner.

Many complaints were made to MPs; Ramsay MacDonald received letters alleging police brutality in Liverpool and Cardiff, T. P. O'Connor also received complaints about the police action in Liverpool and Carr-

Gomm obtained information about the ill-treatment of women and children in Horsley Down in London.[95] As in the case of the South Wales coal strike, many complaints against the police were made by people who would not normally be expected to ally themselves with the strikers. For example, J. Ward MP received letters of complaint about the Liverpool police from a doctor and several traders. A stipendary magistrate, Mr T. W. Lewis, was reported to have held the view that on at least one occasion in Cardiff the police had gone beyond the limits of the law. He maintained that they had usurped the legal authority of the magistrates by deciding for themselves that it was not necessary for the Riot Act to be read prior to dispersing a crowd.[96] It is improbable, then, that all the accounts of police misconduct, relating to the 1911 strikes, were fabricated; particularly since some originated from people who would not normally be sympathetic to organised labour.

Although on some occasions the police were unnecessarily brutal at least they were not equipped with firearms. Of course, the same cannot be said of the army which opened fire on strikers at Llanelli ultimately resulting in six people losing their lives. This occurred when a train was stopped near Llanelli station by strikers sitting on the line; a man then boarded the engine and put out the fire, effectively preventing further progress. Some troops, under a Major Stuart, arrived on the scene together with three magistrates. The Chief Constable of Carmarthenshire reported the subsequent events to the Home Office:

Troops attacked on both sides by crowd on embankments hurling stones and other missiles. One soldier carried away wounded in head and others struck. Riot Act read. Major Stuart mounted embankment and endeavoured to pacify crowd. Stone throwing continued, crowd yelling at troops. Shots fired as warning, no effect, attitude of crowd threatening and determined. Other shots fired, two men killed, one wounded, crowd fled.[97]

Later in the same day a crowd at Llanelli attacked the house and business premises of a Mr Jones, one of the magistrates who had been present at the earlier incident, and the police made repeated baton-charges to protect his property. At about the same time some railway trucks containing detonators were set on fire. An explosion occurred which caused the death of four people and injured many others.

There is evidence to suggest that the Chief Constable's account of the Llanelli shootings (above) was inaccurate and distorted the reality of the situation. Official accounts such as the Chief Constable's paint a picture of train and troops being subjected to a shower of stones from the rioting strikers. Although there is little doubt that some stoning occurred the fact that not one carriage window was broken and that none of the passengers were hit or molested suggests that the 'attack' on the train was not as serious as was alleged. Moreover, the strikers had no logical reason to continue the attack; the fire had been drawn and the train was already effectively prevented from proceeding. At the inquest into the deaths of the two men shot by the soldiers several witnesses gave evidence that few stones were thrown and none at all from the garden of the house where one of the men was shot.

The inquest proceedings also revealed that most of the people fired upon by the troops were in their own gardens overlooking the railway cutting. The Riot Act which authorises the police or, as in this case, the troops to use as much violence as is necessary to disperse a riot, specifically orders the rioters to 'depart to their habitations or lawful business'. As the people killed were already in their 'habitations' it can be argued that they had complied with the Riot Act and that the use of force by the troops was without lawful authority. In view of the fact that no evidence was given at the inquest that the shot men had actually thrown any stones a verdict of murder or at least manslaughter might have been expected. The Coroner summed up in the following manner:

it was immaterial whether these young men were rioters or had thrown any stones or not. They were in the direction from which the stones came, and as there was no evidence that they actually threw the stones it was just unfortunate that they were present.[98]

The jury returned a verdict of justifiable homicide and added the rider: 'We think it would have been better if other means than the order to fire had been adopted by Major Stuart for the purpose of dispersing the crowd.'[99] It is difficult to see how this verdict can be justified on the basis of the evidence. Keir Hardie argued that the rider was incompatible with the verdict;[100] if other means could have been used to disperse the crowd (and the rider clearly implies that they could) then the shooting was not justified. Moreover, Major Stuart said he had 'explicit' orders that he was, under no circumstances, 'to allow a train to be held up'.[101] These orders to Major Stuart and his order to fire can be seen as a result of the Government's policy of using the police and army not merely to maintain order but to ensure the uninterrupted working of the railways.

It seems, then, that both acts of police brutality and the Llanelli shootings by the army were conditioned to some extent by political influences. In 1910 the Government encouraged vigorous policing in an attempt to avoid the necessity of more repressive measures, while in 1911 the atmosphere of crisis functioned to promote repression in order to put down a strike perceived as neo-revolutionary.

Summary

Collective action, during the period under consideration, generally consisted of violent picketing – the active obstruction of 'blackleg' labour –

rather than the kind of destruction which occurred in earlier times. Indeed, in those rare instances when the employers made no serious attempt to import outside labour, as in the coal strike of 1912, there was virtually no disorder at all. The strikers' concern with obstruction rather than destruction also meant that confrontation tended to be more confined, both geographically and temporally. Disorder now typically occurred at the factory or colliery gate and only at the time when imported labourers attempted to enter or leave. But, despite this moderation and confinement of collective action, strikers were still sometimes subjected to harsh repression. One miner was killed at Tonypandy, probably by a police baton, two strikers were shot dead at Llanelli and another two were killed by troops in Liverpool. Not a single fatality was suffered by either the police or the military during the same period. Clearly, the degree of violence employed by the agents of social control was far in excess of that resorted to by the workers.

Nevertheless, it is too simplistic to describe the policy of social control as consisting of mere repression. On the contrary, the Liberal Government, at first, adopted a relatively progressive approach by intervening in the South Wales coal strike precisely to avoid the sort of incident that occurred at Featherstone. It is somewhat paradoxical that, although committed to the impartial maintenance of public order, the Government in their anxiety to prevent military involvement seem to have actually encouraged a more repressive style of policing.

In any event, the reliance on the police and the emphasis on impartiality did not last for long. As we have seen, in 1911, when the Government perceived the national railway strike as a virtual revolution, something of a reversion to a Featherstone-style of order maintenance occurred. Once again troops were deployed, not as a last resort to reinforce embattled police, but as an immediate response to disorder. Moreover, the Government seem to have gone out of their way to encourage repressive action by both police and military. Indeed, it is difficult to escape the conclusion that it was only the restrained action of the strikers which prevented more extensive bloodshed.

The six years prior to the First World War constituted a pivotal period in the evolution of social control. A new policy of impartially maintaining order during industrial disputes involving the use of police rather than troops was adopted in 1910 only to be abandoned the following year. The period thus provides us with the first glimpse of a control strategy that was to predominate in later years.

4

The decline of violent labour protest

'If there's any trouble here', said Edwards to Bevan, 'we'll have the place running with blood.' Bevan replied that no police officer had any right to use such language and that the matter would be raised in the right quarter when time was available. Meanwhile, if the police behaved themselves, there would be no violence. The prophecy was fulfilled; self-discipline in Tredegar worked so well that Superintendent Edwards could find no excuse for the stern counter measures he was eager to employ.[1]

It was not only at Tredegar that strikers behaved in an orderly manner. Indeed, one of the significant changes relating to industrial conflict during the period from 1915 to 1945 was the decline of violent labour protest. Despite numerous and often large-scale industrial stoppages there is no evidence during this period of the generalised 'stoning' and 'violent picketing' that, as we have seen, went on during earlier disputes. The police, however willing they were to baton-charge strikers, had few opportunities for such repressive action. Of course there were isolated incidents when these earlier forms of behaviour occurred, but on the whole the period is notable for the orderly manner in which strikes were conducted.

Significant developments also took place in control strategy. In particular, the centralisation of order maintenance which first occurred during the South Wales coal strike of 1910 was extended and continued on a permanent basis. In a very real sense there was a state take-over of responsibility for controlling industrial disorder from local officials and political élites.

Industrial unrest 1915–1945: chronology

For those who feared that the strikes of 1910 to 1912 were the harbinger of class war the first two years of the Great War must have been immensely reassuring. No major industrial disputes occurred and the whole country seemed to be united in the war effort. Even in 1916 when brief stoppages took place on Clydeside and in Lancashire there appeared to be a certain lack of concern in government circles. For example Basil Thomson, at this time head of the Criminal Investigation Department (CID), dismissed these

48

strikes as a 'holiday' necessitated by 'war-strain'.[2] However, in the following year strikes by engineering and bus workers threatened to disrupt the war effort; munitions workers were unable to travel by bus to Woolwich and work on artillery shells at Ipswich and Chelmsford was held up. This time the Government took action; nine strike leaders were arrested with the intention of intimidating other workers from joining the stoppage. Eventually, an agreement was reached that the men would return to work provided no more arrests were made. The year 1917 passed without further industrial unrest.

In the summer of 1918 when the war was at a critical stage and the Government's attention was focused on events in France, another wave of industrial unrest swept the country. There were strikes by munitions workers in Coventry, by cotton workers in Lancashire and, more seriously from the Government's point of view, by police in London. Some members of the Cabinet favoured adopting a policy of outright repression; Churchill, for example, wished to draft all the strikers into the army.[3] However, Lloyd George's more subtle appreciation of the situation led him to settle these disputes with some concessions. No public disorder occurred although the military were called in during the police strike to guard buildings in Whitehall.[4]

The most critical year for the government was probably 1919. In January a general strike occurred in Glasgow which culminated in a running battle in St George's Square between police and strikers. Troops were sent, but in the event order was restored without a direct confrontation between strikers and military. During February and March all three unions of the newly formed Triple Alliance had grievances and were threatening strike action. However, these threats were postponed or resolved through negotiation and the threat of a co-ordinated strike receded. Miners in some areas did strike in July and naval personnel protected by troops were sent to man pumping machinery in the pits.[5] There were no reports of any violence associated with the strike although examples of alleged intimidation appeared in the press.[6] The strike ended in late July, but the industrial peace was broken again when, in the following month, the police went on strike for the second time in two years. Looting and rioting broke out in Liverpool and troops supported by tanks and even a battleship moved in. Several bayonet charges were made, occasional shots were fired and some bloodshed occurred.[7]

However, it is worth emphasising that these measures were not taken in response to industrial disorder *per se*, but to deal with those who might take advantage of a police strike to commit criminal acts.

More germane to our theme is the Government's reaction to a national railway strike which lasted for seven days in late September and early October. In marked contrast to the railway strike of 1911 (see Chapter 3) there was no disorder and although troops were deployed they never came into contact with the strikers at all.[8]

In 1920 there was only one major industrial dispute, a national coal strike which started on 16 October and lasted until 3 November when an interim pay award was agreed. Yet again there was an almost complete absence of disorder, only two very minor incidents being reported during the entire strike.[9]

In March 1921 the interim pay award, granted at the end of the 1920 strike, ran out. At the same time the control of the mines which the Government had exercised during the war was handed back to the private coal owners. The employers immediately set about implementing their policy of cutting wages. Notices were posted throughout the coalfields that all contracts of service would end on 31 March; new contracts of course were to be offered at much lower rates.[10] Not surprisingly the miners reacted by calling a strike for the end of March and the employers retaliated on 1 April by declaring a general lock-out in all the coalfields. The Triple Alliance (of transport workers, railwaymen and miners) originally formed in 1916 had not engaged in any specific action till this time apart from taking part in the negotiations which ended the 1919 railway strike. But now it seemed likely that the dockers and railwaymen would strike in support of the miners. However, on 15 April – 'Black Friday' – the Triple Alliance called off its proposed national strike and the miners were left to fight on alone.

There were some relatively violent incidents during the miners' strike which continued until June. Windows were smashed by angry pickets at the Broidwood Colliery near Motherwell and at Sheffield three 'blacklegs' were injured.[11] In Thornton there was even a 'Tonypandy-style' riot with shop windows being broken and looting taking place.[12] Indeed, it seems clear that the three forms of behaviour that we have found in early disputes – stoning, violent picketing and rioting – all occurred during the 1921 strike. However, equally clearly it is the case that such forms of behaviour were now exceptional rather than general. There is considerable evidence to support the view that even this strike was generally conducted in a non-violent manner. According to many newspaper reports the striking miners were interested in gardening and football rather than picketing.[13] Even the Prince of Wales commented on the 'calm and steadiness' of his fellow countrymen,[14] while an editorial in the *Police Review* observed that 'the workers proved themselves by their patience and their law abiding demeanour to be self respecting citizens of a great country'.[15] Similarly, the Chief Constable of Bristol, speaking at the Chief Constables' Annual Conference, paid tribute to the 'good order' that the miners had maintained during the strike.[16]

Overall, then, order rather than disorder characterised the miners' strike of 1921, despite the fact that this long dispute, for all the initial hopes of the Triple Alliance (now known as the 'Cripple Alliance'), eventually ended, like many of the others we have considered, in defeat for organised labour.

For the next two years, in conditions of economic decline, a demoralised trade union movement concerned itself with unemployment and job security rather than with industrial action.[17] However, in 1924, with a Labour Government in power for the first time, a number of major industrial disputes again occurred. In January the Transport and General Workers Union led by Ernest Bevin called a strike of 110,000 dock workers. Although the dispute was settled within three days without any disorder occurring, it is clear that the Labour Government was prepared to use troops if necessary to keep food supplies moving.[18] Ernest Bevin ruefully wished for a Tory Government since the unions would 'not have been frightened by *their* threats'.[19]

A strike by London tram and tube workers in March similarly involved no disorder and was settled within a week. Other strikes in 1924 by building, shipyard and market workers followed the same non-violent pattern. Indeed, no serious disorderly incidents associated with industrial disputes were reported until the General Strike of 1926.

The events leading up to the General Strike can be briefly stated. In 1925 the mine owners again proposed severe cuts in wages, but this time, unlike in 1921, the miners were able to threaten strike action with the unwavering support of the TUC.[20] The prospect of a miners' strike combined with a TUC embargo on the movement of coal frightened the Government into making concessions. A temporary subsidy was granted to enable wages to be maintained until an official enquiry – the Samuel Commission – reported on the coal industry. This apparent victory for the miners was known, in contrast to the 'Black Friday' of 1921, as 'Red Friday'. However, jubilation in the coalfields was short-lived. When the Commission reported in March 1926 it recommended the same sort of wage cuts as had been demanded by the employers in the first place. In April the state subsidy agreed on 'Red Friday' ran out and at midnight on 3 May, despite last minute negotiations between TUC and Government, the General Strike began.

Not surprisingly perhaps the General Strike was a more disorderly industrial dispute than any other that occurred during the period under consideration. In Leeds strikers smashed shop and tram windows before rushing at the police who defended themselves with batons.[21] Similar disturbances in Newcastle and at Chester-le-Street, near Durham, were firmly dealt with by the police. 'Despite rough play', noted the *British Gazette*, 'the crowd showed a sense of humour';[22] but it is unlikely that many of the 41 people taken to hospital in Hull following police baton-charges were particularly amused.[23] Similar violent clashes between police and strikers were reported in Southsea, Swansea, Nottingham and Preston. In Scotland disorder occurred in Edinburgh and Glasgow. However, *The Times* reported that in Glasgow iron bars, pickheads and hammers were used as missiles against the police, but the aim of the strikers must have been extremely defective since the same article noted that no police had been injured.[24]

At Crewe shots were fired at a passing train while at Sidcup eleven strikers were injured in clashes with the police.[25] In London the police baton-charged strikers in Wandsworth, Lambeth, Deptford, Paddington, and Camden Town. One example of the sort of incident which occurred is provided by a report published in the *Daily Mail*:

At the mouth of the Blackwall Tunnel the crowd numbering several thousand attempted to stop every vehicle leaving the tunnel. A big force of mounted and foot police was stationed at the spot and made baton charges every few minutes to keep the crowd on the move.

Bottles and other missiles were thrown at the police. The ambulance men were kept employed dealing with the casualties, chiefly head injuries from police batons.[26]

However, incidents such as those mentioned above should be kept in proper perspective; some four million people were on strike yet in most areas for most of the time order prevailed. In Derbyshire there was so little disorder that the chairman of the local magistrates commented on the 'exemplary' conduct of the miners.[27] Newspapers noted that the situation was 'generally quiet' and 'disturbances few',[28] while the editor of the *Police Review* drew attention to the 'tact and common sense displayed by both sides'.[29]

Although several disorderly incidents occurred during the strike it was still generally perceived as a relatively non-violent affair. To those who could remember Featherstone, Tonypandy and Llanelli, the General Strike symbolised order and tranquillity rather than chaos and social disintegration. It says much for the lack of industrial violence during this period that the most disorderly dispute was noted for the law abiding behaviour of those involved.

From the end of the General Strike until the Second World War there were relatively few major industrial disputes. This was partly because the Labour movement was seriously weakened by what many regarded as a betrayal by the TUC leaders in 1926; but also because the industrialised world was entering a major recession. Unemployment rose to around the three million mark in the early 1930s and public disorder when it occurred was associated with hunger marches and fascist meetings rather than industrial disputes.[30]

Of course, there were some violent incidents associated with industrial disputes between 1926 and 1945. For example, baton-charges were made against strikers during both the Monmouth coal strike of 1929 and the Lancashire weavers' strike of 1932.[31] However, probably the most violent dispute of this period was the Harworth Colliery strike of 1937. Much of the disorder took the same form as the 'violent picketing' that we noted during the South Wales coal strike of 1910. When police intervened to protect 'blacklegs' they were roughly handled themselves and on two occasions rioting occurred. The worst disorder took place when police raided a hall, where the strikers were holding a dance, in order to arrest several men against whom warrants had been issued. A police car was overturned, windows were smashed and several baton-charges made.[32] During these riots 34 people were arrested, some of them receiving relatively severe prison sentences which caused anger and alarm throughout the Labour movement (see Chapter 6).

However, we should remember that, generally, order rather than chaos characterised industrial disputes during the thirty years between 1915 and 1945. Even in those exceptional cases when violence did occur, namely the miners' strike of 1921, the General Strike and the Harworth Colliery strike, it tended to be short-lived and on a relatively small scale. Given both the number and size of the industrial disputes during this period the absence of violent labour protest is particularly noteworthy.

Industrial unrest 1915–1945: analysis

The Government's strikebreaking organisation

In our consideration of the 'Featherstone shootings' it became apparent that central government played virtually no role at all in controlling or organising the various social control agencies who responded to the disorder. By contrast the police and army operations in relation to the South Wales coal strike of 1910 were to a considerable extent controlled and co-ordinated from the Home Office. Of course, this was a relatively unplanned and spontaneous sort of control; there were no contingency plans for dealing with industrial disputes and no Cabinet committee with sub-committees to implement and co-ordinate them. It was only in the years immediately following the First World War that contingency planning in relation to industrial disputes became a permanent function of central government.

The process of establishing a centralised strikebreaking organisation was set in motion by the Lloyd George Coalition Government which appointed a special committee, the Industrial Unrest Committee (IUC), in February 1919. This Cabinet Committee, chaired by the Home Secretary, met throughout the year to draw up plans for countering a major industrial dispute, possibly involving co-ordinated action by the Triple Alliance. In late summer, when it became apparent that a national railway strike was going to take place, several last-minute changes were made to improve the efficiency of the IUC. Eric Geddes, an ex-railway manager and wartime Minister of Transport, was considered the ideal choice to head the Committee whose name was now changed to the succinct Strike Committee.[33]

Under Geddes' direction arrangements were made for the road transport of essential supplies and for the recruitment of volunteers to drive lorries. Despite the fact that no disorder whatsoever occurred during the strike it was also considered necessary to recruit a 'Citizen Guard' to help maintain order in London. General Macready, who by this time was the Metropolitan Police Commissioner, thought this an 'idiotic proposal'.[34] However, the various plans of the Strike Committee, including the 'Citizen Guard' idea, were not fully tested because the strike was settled within seven days, but the strategy of using volunteers to combat any disorder associated with industrial disputes was firmly established.

The Strike Committee had, of course, been mainly designed to deal with the railway dispute and now that a settlement had been reached there was some suggestion that it should disband. However, the Committee had proved itself to be so useful that at its last meeting, on 6 October, it was decided to keep 'a nucleus of the existing organisation'[35] in existence. The new organisation was known as the Supply and Transport Committee (STC); a name designed to give the body a more neutral identity and to reflect a concern with industrial disputes in general rather than with one particular strike.[36] This new Cabinet Committee had of course a number of sub-committees for dealing with matters of detail and mainly concerned itself with organisational and policy matters.

One of the first tasks of the STC was to try to establish precisely what legal powers government departments and agencies would need to cope with a major industrial dispute. By June 1920 the STC had presented a shopping list of requirements for Cabinet approval which eventually formed the basis of the Emergency Powers Act of that year. The Act enabled the Government to declare a 'state of emergency' and then to issue virtually any 'regulations' it liked. In effect the executive would be able to suspend or amend all existing law as well as introduce any new measures in the form of regulations. The only regulations not permitted were those that would introduce compulsory military or industrial conscription, those that would make striking an offence and those that would alter existing criminal procedure.

In addition to this legal framework for emergency planning the STC also drew up a detailed administrative framework. The country was to be divided into sixteen districts each under the command of a Junior Minister who would have the title of District Commissioner. In fact this plan was slightly amended and eleven districts were eventually established to co-ordinate the military, the police and the provision of essential services during a strike or other emergency. The District Commissioners were also to be responsible for organising the recruitment of volunteers for the Special Police or Citizen Guard.[37]

Indeed, the STC quickly realised that it would have to rely on recruiting volunteers during a strike to provide the necessary manpower to implement its plans. This was because the large wartime army was being demobilised and the regular army was considered too small to cope alone with a major emergency. However, these volunteers could not be recruited in antici- pation of a major strike because this might antagonise labour, precipitate a strike and alienate public opinion. Volunteers would, therefore, have to be enrolled once a strike had begun rather than in advance of it. Nevertheless it seems clear that accepted STC policy at this time was to use volunteer special constables rather than the military to support the police whenever possible.[38]

Although volunteers were only to be recruited during a strike the organisation for recruitment could be prepared in advance. The STC set up strategically located recruitment offices and local and national volunteer committees to administer and co-ordinate recruitment. These committees were known as units of the Volunteer Service Committee (VSC) and were centrally co-ordinated through the Civil Commissioner's office in co- operation with the eleven district commissioners.[39]

These counter-strike preparations were put into practice when the miners were locked out in April 1921. The STC met on the eve of the lock-out and arranged for coal exports to be stopped, troops to be put on alert, and for a 'state of emergency' under the Emergency Powers Act to be declared. Four days later, on 4 April, the Government issued 'Emergency Regulations' under the Act authorising troops and naval personnel to take up positions in the coalfields and other strategic points.

All military and naval leave was cancelled, reservists were called up and troops were hurriedly brought back from Ireland, Malta and Silesia. In ad- dition the contingency plans for recruiting special constables and a volun- teer defence force were activated. Over 70,000 men had enrolled in the defence force within fourteen days of it being formed and many others had joined the special constabulary and transport volunteers.[40] Of course all this mobilisation was designed to combat strike action by the Triple Alliance in support of the miners, but this sympathetic action, as we have seen, never materialised as a result of 'Black Friday' (see p. 50). There was no need, therefore, to activate fully the STC's contingency plans and the defence force was disbanded just two weeks after it had been formed. The Govern- ment's strikebreaking organisation was not subjected to a prolonged test, but there seems little doubt about its efficiency; the Chief Civil Com- missioner, L. S. Amery, for one, thought that it had 'gone off like clockwork'.[41]

Although the STC's anti-strike planning had worked very well it had proved extremely costly. For example, the costs of the STC for the year ending 31 March 1921 (which did not include the expenses incurred in relation to the miners' strike) amounted to £776,262.[42] The economy was in a depressed state, government departments were having to make cuts and since the Triple Alliance was no longer a serious threat the axe fell on the STC. Its budget was reduced to a mere £2,000 a year[43] and only a nucleus of the old organisation continued under the general supervision of the Home Office.[44]

However, when the Conservatives were returned to power in 1922 it was decided to appoint a special committee under John Anderson to review the Government's counter-strike organisation. Anderson reported to the Cabinet in July 1923 and several changes were made. Baldwin's friend J. C. C. Davidson was appointed Chief Civil Commissioner and given the job of simplifying and streamlining the whole STC system. He had only just completed this task when the first Labour Government was elected in 1924.

The revitalised organisation now consisted of two sets of institutions, one for normal times, consisting of a simple standing committee, and one for emergencies, consisting of four specialised sub-committees.[45] Davidson thought these new arrangements, which he had worked so hard to implement, were threatened by the new Labour administration. When he discovered that Labour MP Josiah Wedgwood was to replace him as Chief Civil Commissioner, he went to Wedgwood and told him '. . . it was his duty to protect the constitution against a Bolshevik inspired General Strike . . . I begged him not to destroy all I had done and not to inform his Cabinet of it.'[46] Davidson need not have worried; on leaving office Wedgwood told him his plans were safe and confessed 'I haven't done a bloody thing about them.'[47]

In fact Labour used the strikebreaking machinery twice; in the dock and tram strikes called by the Transport and General Workers' Union. But, as we have noted, these strikes were quickly settled and other than the declaration of a state of emergency during the tram workers' strike in March there was no public indication of Labour's readiness to use the STC's plans.

The Conservatives, under Baldwin, were returned to power in October 1924 and responsibility for emergency planning was handed to the Home Secretary; John Anderson remained as Chairman of the STC.[48] The strikebreaking organisation updated by Anderson and Davidson in 1922 had survived intact eleven months of Labour administration and was shortly to be used during the General Strike.

The Government used the nine-month interval between 'Red Friday' and the General Strike to complete its contingency plans. The eleven Civil Commissioners were all appointed by the end of 1925 and a circular outlining their powers and duties was sent to all local authorities. At the end of September a supposedly independent body – the Organization for the Maintenance of Supplies (OMS) – began to advertise in the press for volunteers to maintain essential supplies in the event of a general strike. It seems probable that this body was government instigated – a solution to the problem of advance recruiting without alienating public opinion. The central council of the OMS included Lieutenant-General Sir Francis Lloyd, the food commissioner for London from 1919 to 1920, Major General Lord Scarborough,

Table 5. *Number of volunteers recruited during the General Strike*[49]

Force	Number
Special Constabulary	240,000
OMS	100,000
Civil Constabulary Reserve	140,000

director of Territorial and Volunteer Forces from 1917 to 1921, and Admiral of the Fleet Lord Jellicoe. Its Chairman was none other than Lord Hardinge, a former Under-Secretary of State for Foreign Affairs and ex-Viceroy of India. The involvement of such high-ranking establishment figures clearly suggests that the OMS was not quite the unofficial body it appeared. Moreover, the Home Secretary made it plain that he wholeheartedly approved of the OMS and also that he had been 'consulted' about its formation.[50]

By May 1926, then, the Government could rely not only on the official strikebreaking organisation established and co-ordinated by the STC, but also on the 'unofficial' OMS. Once the strike had started a state of emergency was declared, a series of Regulations passed and contingency plans put into effect. The basic policy was to use police supported by the various volunteer organisations to maintain public order. Neither the Reservists nor the Territorials were to be mobilised and regular troops were only to be used for policing duties in the last resort.[51]

Perhaps the most important decision taken by the STC during the strike was to use, contrary to the accepted policy, troops rather than police to escort a convoy of lorries out of London docks. The docks had been at a standstill for some days as traders were reluctant to drive their lorries through the crowds of pickets that surrounded the area. The situation became so bad that Lord Winterton, the Civil Commissioner for the South Midlands, threatened to resign unless his lorries were guaranteed protected access to the docks. Moreover, in London itself certain supplies, such as flour, were running dangerously low. The STC seemed to accept that any attempt to use police would be violently resisted. However, the Committee was not completely swayed by Churchill's argument for machine guns to be placed along the route of any food convoy from the docks to Hyde Park and for tanks to patrol the roads. Nevertheless the STC did conclude that in this particular instance troops rather than police should be used. A convoy consisting of 105 lorries loaded with Guardsmen and escorted by twenty armoured cars were driven into the docks at 4.30 a.m. Meanwhile, 500 volunteers headed by Lord Burghley, Master of Magdalene College,

Cambridge, were towed along the river from Westminster Pier to the docks. Once inside the docks the volunteers under the direction of their rather academic foreman began to load the lorries with flour and other supplies. At about 10.40 a.m. the convoy with its military escort left the docks and made its way through the East End to the Hyde Park depot.

The protection provided for this food convoy seems in retrospect to have been somewhat excessive. The journey into the docks in the early hours of the morning took place without a single striker being present and on its return trip the convoy was 'received with enthusiasm and cheering' by those lining the route.[52]

The above incident seems to have been the only occasion on which the military were placed in a position where confrontation with strikers was possible. In all the violent clashes reported during the strike it was the police and the specials who were used to maintain orde.r Even the Civil Constabulary Reserve does not seem to have seen 'action' during the strike. The navy and RAF also played a role, though not a combative one, during the stoppage. Marines guarded certain waterside installations and warships were sent to several ports, while the RAF flew copies of the *British Gazette* to distribution centres far from London. It seems then that the contingency plans involved the armed services in a logistical rather than a public order capacity.

The General Strike ended on 12 May and, although the miners continued their industrial action for another six months, the danger of serious industrial disorder was over. As we have already noted, public disorder became associated with hunger marches and fascism rather than with industrial disputes in the following years. The growth of fascism in Germany and Italy during this period was of particular concern to the Government. Emergency planning during the 1930s concentrated on civil defence in response to external military aggression rather than on establishing a strikebreaking organisation.[53] Nevertheless, the Government had clearly demonstrated that in the event of major industrial action it now had the necessary machinery to organise and co-ordinate a centrally controlled response.

Intelligence and surveillance

Just as there was a centralisation of contingency planning in relation to industrial disputes during the period in question so too was there a centralisation of intelligence gathering. This process began during the 1914 war when 'every new Ministry almost inevitably formed an Intelligence Section'.[54] The Ministry of Munitions, for example, set up a 'directorate of intelligence' to watch and report on industrial unrest in the arms factories. Moreover, it seems that the army was also collecting intelligence in relation to industrial matters during this period. Sir Basil Thomson, then head of the

CID, thought that this sort of thing could 'raise a cry of military dictatorship and provoke strikes' and it seems probable that military intelligence gathering was curtailed after 1916.[55] Nevertheless, there was still a multiplicity of intelligence departments set up by the various Ministries and of course the CID itself. Indeed, Thomson sometimes had more than one CID officer infiltrate the same body:

Yesterday there was a meeting of the Central 'Stop the War' Committee. The only attendants were two lady police spies, who entered into conversation, neither knowing the other's occupation. At a subsequent election for vacancies on the Committee both these ladies were elected, so I shall not be without information.[56]

Given the independence of the intelligence organisations it is not entirely inconceivable that, unknown to Thomson, yet other members of this Committee were undercover agents. As Thomson himself commented 'there was overlapping and waste of energy, to say nothing of the inevitable waste of money'.[57] The inefficiency of these arrangements became apparent to the Government who decided to give Special Branch a co-ordinating role in relation to intelligence collection in May 1919. Thomson was given the title of 'Director of Intelligence' and was appointed head of the Special Branch which was now completely independent of the CID. From this point onwards information collected by uniformed police, plainclothes police, CID officers, agents of various government departments and military intelligence would be passed on to and assessed by Special Branch. In addition to their co-ordinating and assessing roles Special Branch officers would themselves be engaged in operational intelligence matters. Moreover, from about 1924 there is evidence that MI5 became involved in industrial intelligence collection.

It is, of course, difficult to cite specific examples of intelligence-gathering in relation to industrial disputes as these matters tend to be kept secret. Nevertheless, some information is available about the activities and methods of the various organisations whose existence is noted above. For example, the policy of arresting strike leaders during the 1917 munition workers' dispute was only possible because the CID kept a list of 'the most dangerous men' and 'accumulated' evidence against them.[58] We also know that during the 1919 railway strike General Macready, the Metropolitan Police Commissioner, took certain steps to obtain and verify information:

I took the precaution, having in mind my previous experience of railway strikes, of sending a selected officer to each of the large railway termini to keep in close touch with the management, in order to check and verify all reports that might come in before they were passed on to the Yard.[59]

The police historian T. A. Critchley informs us that a 'particularly distasteful feature' of the 1919 police strike was that Special Branch officers reported on the activities of their uniformed colleagues.[60] Moreover, the Home

Office, in an answer to a parliamentary question, admitted that the Special Branch was expanded in 1920 so that it could cope with the increase of work resulting from the industrial situation.[61]

In 1923 Sir Wyndham Childs, who had by this time replaced Thomson as head of Special Branch, revealed that during the dock strike of July and August an unofficial strike committee had been created by the Communist Party. The evidence on which he based this accusation was contained in correspondence between the Strike Committee and the London Communist Party District Committee which had been intercepted by his officers.[62] Similarly, in 1924 Childs provided the Prime Minister with details of Communist involvement in various strikes.[63] Childs seems to have regarded fighting Communism as his *raison d'être*, not surprisingly, perhaps, since he had been told by a 'representative of the Government' that this was the 'most important' part of his work.[64] However, a contemporary Cabinet committee concluded that there was 'little evidence' of Communist involvement in industrial disputes and paradoxically much of the evidence submitted to the committee consisted of Special Branch reports and assessments.[65]

There is also evidence that several intelligence-collecting organisations were active during the General Strike. For example, soldiers in plain clothes were sent to some areas to mingle with the strikers and report on 'what these chaps are saying and thinking'.[66] Indeed, the army's intelligence section was strengthened by twelve 'highly trained' officers from MI5 who proved 'of the greatest assistance during the emergency'.[67] The Special Branch was also active during the strike. Sixty officers raided the premises of the *Daily Herald* and many members of the Communist Party were arrested by Branch officers.[68]

As well as raiding the premises of publishers and arresting Communists there is some suggestion that Special Branch officers acted as *agents provocateurs*. For example, a mysterious sympathiser seemed rather anxious to supply the Westminster Strike Committee with ammunition. The Committee was convinced that the man was a police agent.[69] Similarly Lewisham Council of Action suspected a man called Johnstone, who was the local secretary of the Unemployed Workers Committee Movement, of being a police informer. Their suspicions turned out to be justified for when Johnstone committed suicide shortly after the strike both his wife and his mistress admitted that he had been in the pay of Scotland Yard. His mistress revealed that Johnstone had occasionally invented the reports he had sent to his masters and that once the police had challenged the authenticity of the information he was providing. After this incident Johnstone, not unreasonably, became convinced that there was at least one other police informer in the London District Council whose reports were being compared with his.[70]

Both individual trade union leaders and the TUC itself seem to have been under surveillance during the strike. Arthur Cook, the miners' leader, returned to his London hotel room on one occasion to be told by the chambermaid that two men claiming to be detectives had searched it while he was out.[71] The TUC accumulated considerable evidence that letters addressed to their Ecclestone Square headquarters were being opened and suspected that telephone calls were being tapped.[72] On the basis of the above evidence, it seems clear that the various intelligence-collecting organisations were particularly active during the General Strike.

During the period between the end of the General Strike and 1945 there is little evidence of intelligence and surveillance in relation to industrial disputes. This is probably due to the fact that the Labour movement, weakened by the defeat of 1926 and the severe economic recession that followed, concerned itself with unemployment rather than with industrial action. This change of emphasis was mirrored by the intelligence organisations who now concentrated on the National Unemployed Workers' Movement rather than on the trade unions.[73] However, a centralised and co-ordinated intelligence system had been established and, as we have seen, activated during industrial disputes. The important point to note is how sophisticated and organised intelligence collection became during this period compared with earlier times.

Crisis and brutality

The establishment of centralised intelligence and contingency planning was accompanied by a general perception of crisis in government circles. This sense of crisis was engendered, as was the case in 1911, by the fear of revolution. But this time foreign affairs, in particular the Russian Revolution of October 1917, affected the Government's perception of and reaction to domestic industrial disputes.[74]

The first period of crisis occurred early in 1919 when to many people revolution seemed a distinct possibility. Basil Thomson, at Scotland Yard, thought the strikes on the Clyde were 'of a revolutionary rather than an economic character',[75] while C. E. Penney, one of the key members of the STC, perceived an oncoming 'battle between loyalists and revolutionaries'.[76] By early 1920 many Cabinet Ministers seemed to be in a state of near panic. Sir Maurice Hankey, the Secretary to the Cabinet, reveals, in a note sent to his deputy marked 'Personal and Secret', the extent of Ministers' fears:

The ministers who have come over here seem to have the 'wind up' to the most extraordinary extent about the industrial situation. CIGS [Commander in Chief of the General Staff] also is positively in a state of dreadful nerves on the subject ... From a meeting yesterday evening I came away with my head fairly reeling. I felt I had been in Bedlam. Red revolution and blood and war at home and abroad.[77]

So great was the fear of industrial action leading to revolution that a special conference of Ministers was held on 2 February to consider the situation.

Lloyd George started the meeting by trying to establish the number of troops in Great Britain and Ireland that could be immediately deployed in case of disorder. Churchill and the Chief of the General Staff argued that the country was virtually defenceless. At this point Lloyd George asked: 'How many airmen are there available for the revolution?'[78] and when told that the pilots had no weapons for ground fighting he 'presumed they could use machine guns and drop bombs'.[79] Roberts, the Food Controller of the STC, observed 'there are large groups preparing for Soviet government'; Eric Geddes, the Minister for Transport and member of the STC, thought the power stations would be put out of action, and Bonar Law, the Lord Privy Seal, advocated making all weapons available to the 'friends of the government'.[80] These sorts of comments reveal just how seriously Ministers viewed the situation.

If anything, the sense of crisis intensified during the summer of 1920 following a threat of widespread industrial action for political purposes. The National Council of Action, a body set up to campaign against possible British aid to Poland in that country's war with Russia, promised that 'the industrial power of the organized workers will be used to defeat this war'.[81] In fact hostilities soon ended and the Council was disbanded. However, the threat of an overtly political strike further alarmed the Government. The Treasury was given instructions to regard the industrial crisis 'as comparable to a state of war',[82] and Basil Thomson told the Cabinet that 'hot heads dream of seizing the government through a coup'.[83] This sense of alarm was also transmitted to the police. Colonel Anson, the Chief Constable of Staffordshire, appealed for volunteer policemen 'to counteract the machinations of those who aim at nothing less than revolution and the subversion of all law and order'.[84]

Although, as we noted, the miners' strike of 1920 was called off when interim pay rises were awarded, the 'threat to the constitution' manifested itself again in April 1921 when miners, apparently supported by the Triple Alliance, were locked out. Once again there was considerable alarm in establishment circles which only subsided after 15 April – Black Friday – when the Triple Alliance called off its proposed sympathy action and left the miners to struggle on alone.

The next four years were peaceful if not prosperous; there was no serious industrial unrest and no one spoke of revolution any more. This tranquil period came to an abrupt end in July 1925 when the miners, this time supported by the TUC, threatened strike action. Once again alarm and panic emanated from government circles. However, the panic of 1926 was in some respects different from the panic of 1921. All the available evidence suggests that in 1921 Ministers really did perceive a threat of revolution whereas in 1926 there is evidence that alarm about the usurpation of constitutional authority was deliberately fostered. For example, Churchill, who was now Chancellor of the Exchequer, told the House of Commons:

In the event of a struggle, whatever its character might be, however ugly the episodes which would mark it, I have no doubt that the State, the national State, would emerge victorious in spite of all the rough and awkward corners it might have to turn. But if you are going to embark on a struggle of this kind, be quite sure that decisive public opinion is behind you ... As the struggle widened, as it became a test of whether the country was to be ruled by Parliament or by some other organization not responsible by our elective processes to the people as a whole – as that issue emerged more and more, and with every increase in the gravity of the struggle, new sources of strength would have to come to the State or some action, which in ordinary circumstances we should consider quite impossible, would, just as in the case of the Great War be taken with general assent and as a matter of course.[85]

In other words a panic about revolution would legitimise any necessary coercive action. So by May 1926 the Government had not only established an efficient strikebreaking organisation but had also manufactured a panic which functioned to legitimise its use.

Government spokesmen and sympathisers lost no opportunity to emphasise the constitutional rather than the economic nature of a general strike. For Wyndham Childs, who had by now replaced Basil Thomson as head of Special Branch, the General Strike was a Communist plot,[86] while Stanley Baldwin, the Prime Minister, declared the strike to be unconstitutional.[87] The voice of Sir John Simon, the Attorney General, joined the finely tuned chorus by declaring the stoppage illegal; a view promptly endorsed by Mr Justice Astbury in the High Court.[88] However, the strike was not merely depicted as illegal but also as immoral; Cardinal Bourne decreed it 'a sin against the obedience we owe to God'.[89]

Between 1915 and 1945, then, there were two distinct periods of crisis. The first period lasted from the last few months of 1918 until 15 April 1921 – Black Friday – while the second period occurred just before and during the General Strike of 1926. Both periods of crisis probably functioned to legitimise and encourage repressive measures taken by the agents of social control. In addition to the general political atmosphere created by these periods of panic there were sometimes more explicit attempts to encourage an aggressive response. For example, during the 1921 miners' strike an editorial in the *Police Chronicle* urged every police officer to 'devote himself to a hunt for the Communists and other extremists' who were organising the 'colossal strikes'.[90] Moreover, on 8 May the following announcement was made in the *British Gazette*:

All ranks of the armed forces of the Crown are hereby notified that any action they may find it necessary to take in an honest endeavour to aid the civil power will receive both now and afterwards the full support of His Majesty's Government.[91]

Indeed, it is not unreasonable to interpret this statement as constituting an indemnity for even the most ruthless of repressive measures. George V was so worried by its implications that he took the trouble to inform the War Office that he thought it an 'unfortunate announcement'.[92] In addition, the

Government directly instructed the police not to co-operate with the strikers: 'The police of His Majesty's Government is in every sense to refuse co-operation from those who are organizing the General Strike, and it is recommended that this attitude should be maintained by all authorities.'[93] It seems probable that many police officers would interpret this statement as a call for a 'tough' approach when dealing with strikers. Explicit statements such as these in the context of an atmosphere of crisis would, it is suggested, increase the likelihood of repressive measures being adopted.

At this point in our argument an apparent contradiction has been revealed. Why, if the political atmosphere of the times engendered a repressive police response, was there relatively little violence during the strikes of this period? After all, we have already seen that a perceived crisis during 1911 was related to acts of brutality (see pp. 44–7). Yet many commentators have stressed that the strikes of the inter-war years are notable for the restraint and good sense demonstrated by both police and strikers.[94] How, then, can we equate a sense of crisis on the one hand with 'good humour' and 'forbearance' on the other? The solution is simple. There was indeed 'forbearance' but it was virtually all on one side. Too much credit has been given to the police for the general lack of violence when it should really be given to the strikers. When violence did occur the evidence suggests that it was the forces of law and order who were responsible. For example, it seems clear that the police were responsible for the disorder during the Glasgow general strike of 1919. On Friday 31 January a large, but orderly, crowd of strikers had assembled in St George's Square outside the City Chambers. The police decided to clear a path through the crowd, by mounting a baton-charge on the strikers and spectators in the way. This police action was carried out, according to the *Glasgow Herald*, with:

a vigour and determination that was a prelude to the extraordinary scenes which the Square was afterwards to witness, and to which the city, with all its acquaintance with labour troubles, can happily offer no parallel. A strong body of police . . . swept the crowd in front of them, raining a hurricane of blows which fell indiscriminately on those actually participating in the strike and on those who had been down to the scene merely through curiosity.[95]

This account constitutes particularly impressive evidence of police brutality since it appears in a newspaper that was very unsympathetic towards the strikers. Indeed, the editor described the formation of the Strike Committee as 'the first step towards that squalid terrorism which the world now describes as Bolshevism'.[96] An editor with such a viewpoint would hardly be likely to overemphasise indiscriminate violence on the part of the police.

Moreover, aggressive police behaviour also occurred during the General Strike. Walt Dodsley, a retired miner, provides an account of how the police attacked an orderly procession of strikers near Mexborough:

we'd heard on Wednesday when it was the General Strike, we'd heard there was some blacklegging on Hatfield Road, carting coal . . . and all that. We'd had this meeting and decided to go and talk to these people who were doing the blacklegging like. We went up Dunscroft from picture house up Broadway to top of Broadway . . . We were all in orderly fashion, like, we weren't shouting or owt, we weren't singing. There were as many women, following us like, but when bobbies came – there was a little bus come down, it were one of them pit buses that used to take us to Thorne Colliery and it were loaded with police. And then there were these six police mounted, come from Cuckoo Lane Road somewhere . . . And they just, ooh!, didn't they swoop down on us and they got their sticks out. One of our blokes got a clout on back of head and we think it were that that killed him. When we came out . . . of prison we went to bury him like . . . Anybody that were there they were just picking up and chucking into bus. (General Striker)

In a report submitted to the National Union of Railwaymen W. Wright, a Branch Secretary, described how in London the police, 'without the slightest provocation', baton-charged and 'unmercifully belaboured men, women and children, injuring many'.[97] On another occasion, J. Withers, a printer, heard a police officer call out 'charge the bastards – Use everything you've got' and saw 'men, women and even youngsters knocked over and out like nine pins'.[98] Some reports indicate that many strikers and even a priest were struck down by police batons outside Poplar Town Hall.[99]

The Special Constabulary, in particular, did much to provoke violent clashes with the strikers. The Tilbury Strike Committee reported that 'these police flourished revolvers and sticks, accompanying these acts by unseemly gestures' all of which, not unreasonably, aroused resentment.[100] The Stanford-le-Hope Strike Committee noted that Specials had 'made grimaces and held up truncheons' and drove at the pickets.[101] Similarly, a local official of the National Union of Railwaymen complained to the TUC that 'irresponsible youths called specials jump out of motor cars and thrash about with their batons without any discretion whatever'.[102] Even the regular police, who as we have seen were none too gentle in their confrontations with strikers, on at least one occasion actually had to restrain the Specials from batoning an orderly meeting of strikers outside Paddington Station.[103]

It seems then that many of the violent clashes that occurred during the General Strike were provoked by the police or the Specials. Of course there were occasions when police officers sought to avoid confrontation with tact and good humour, but on the whole they adopted a very aggressive approach. The discipline and restraint of the strikers ensured that relatively little disorder occurred. For example, only 18 out of the 60,000 special constables were assaulted during the entire strike.[104] This restraint is all the more remarkable when one considers that the strikers were not only subjected to harassment on the streets but also to the possibility of arrest.

Indeed, the police made numerous arrests often for very trivial reasons. Of the 3,149 prosecutions arising out of the strike, 1,760 related not to offences under the normal law but to infringements of the Regulations made under the Emergency Powers Act.[105] Many arrests were made for relatively minor matters. At Accrington a small boy was arrested for throwing orange peel at a charabanc,[106] a Heath woman was fined 40s. for chalking 'Don't be a scab' on the road[107] and a striker at Farnworth was sent to prison for tearing down a government poster.[108] However, the majority of the prosecutions brought under the Regulations concerned the production and distribution of 'seditious' literature. A glance at contemporary newspaper reports reveals numerous examples of police action against printers and publishers. Many of those arrested were Communists, some sources suggest that as much as 20% to 25% of the entire party were arrested during the nine-day General Strike.[109]

Summary

Several major industrial disputes occurred during the period from 1915 to 1945, but they were characterised by order rather than disorder. On the whole strikers refrained from rioting, destroying property and even the kind of violent picketing that took place before the war (see pp. 25–47). Many of the relatively few violent clashes that did occur were provoked by the police or the Specials. Aggressive policing of this kind was, it is suggested, engendered and justified by the general political atmosphere of panic that existed in the early 1920s and during the General Strike.

At the strategic level there was a centralisation of order maintenance and intelligence gathering, while at the tactical level few changes occurred with the baton-charge remaining the stock response to disorder.

By the 1940s this pattern of non-violent picketing and repressive police reaction had in many ways become unsuited to changing social and political conditions. Industrial disputes after the Second World War, particularly in the late 1960s and 1970s, were policed in a very different way from those that we have considered so far.

5

Pushing and shoving

> At Hadfields it was rough, but I would say it was what you would call pushing and shoving. (Jack Taylor, President of the Yorkshire Miners)

Since 1945 no fewer than nine states of emergency have been proclaimed in response to strike action by dockers (3), power workers (1), seamen (1), miners (2) and other public service workers (2). During many of these 'emergencies' military personnel have been employed to carry out a wide variety of tasks – to unload ships, to move petrol, to collect garbage and to fight fires – but they have not been used directly to confront strikers as they were in the past. Indeed, until the late 1960s, post-war industrial disputes were generally very orderly and consequently required little police let alone military intervention. Picketing in the late 1960s and 1970s certainly involved illegal behaviour – obstruction, intimidation and the immobilisation of vehicles – but recourse to actual violence – beyond, that is, the mere pushing and shoving described above – was comparatively rare.

In this chapter we will examine six industrial disputes which involved allegedly 'violent' clashes between police and strikers. These case studies are by no means exhaustive of major industrial disputes involving large-scale picketing, but have been selected simply because the disorder associated with them is generally considered excessive.

Industrial unrest 1946–1984: chronology

Roberts–Arundel 1966–1968

In July 1965 the Roberts Company of Sanford, North Carolina, took over the textile machinery manufacturing company Arundel–Coulthard of Stockport. A new management team was appointed to increase the profitability of the firm (now registered as Roberts–Arundel Ltd.) by introducing new work methods. Studies in the sociology of organisations have often shown that the introduction of new work practices tends to cause resentment and resistance among employees unless their agreement and co-

67

operation is first obtained.[1] Unfortunately the management team at Roberts–Arundel do not seem to have been aware of this research since in their enthusiasm to end tea-breaks and install vending machines they appear to have resorted to such insensitive actions as smashing workers' mugs, confiscating kettles and ripping out power points.[2] The resentment caused by this kind of behaviour was aggravated when 51 men were made redundant. However, it was not so much the actual redundancies which caused trouble as the management's refusal to accept the traditional 'last in, first out' principle in deciding who should go. The workers retaliated by imposing a four-day week and overtime ban which speedily forced the management into making a compromise agreement. Clearly industrial relations at Roberts–Arundel were becoming very strained.

Shortly after the redundancies were made the company began to advertise in the local press for female machine operators. To the shop stewards it seemed obvious that the management was deliberately making men redundant so that their jobs could be filled by women employed on much lower rates of pay. Moreover, the company refused to negotiate with the unions over the wages and conditions of the new female workers. The patience of the workforce finally ran out on Monday 28 November when they 'clocked-on' to find that a total of five women had been employed. The men downed tools and walked out.

The rather insensitive management at Roberts–Arundel now succeeded in escalating this dispute which was initially about wages and conditions of women workers into a conflict about the principle of trade union recognition. They did this by sacking all those on strike and by advertising in the *Manchester Evening News* for non-union replacements.[3] Not surprisingly this action provoked the trade union movement. The Amalgamated Engineering Union (AEU), the Transport and General Workers, the Sheet Metal Workers, Plumbers, Joiners, Foundrymen, Electricians and Draughtsmen declared the strike official and 'blacked' all goods and materials destined for Roberts–Arundel. Picketing began outside the factory and a few minor clashes between the strikers and the newly recruited labour force occurred.[4] However, it was on 22 February during a half-day token sympathy strike that the first serious disorder took place. Workers from all over the Stockport area had been asked to finish work at lunch time and to proceed to the Roberts–Arundel factory for a meeting and demonstration. More than 1,000 pickets, many of them building workers, were expected from the Shell Chemical plant at Carrington alone. By midday about 600 men had gathered outside the factory and when the Shell contingent arrived stones and bottles were hurled at the factory, smashing 20 windows, and a total of £4,000 worth of damage was done.[5] Four police officers were injured including the Deputy Chief Constable who suffered a fractured wrist and chest injuries.[6] According to Mr D. W. Hay, the Town Clerk, the situation became so bad that some consideration was given to the idea of reading the Riot Act (last read in 1919) and on the following day all demonstrations in the vicinity of the factory were banned under the Public Order Act.[7] Normal picketing, punctuated by occasional clashes between police and pickets or pickets and 'blacklegs', was resumed.

On the picket line the tension was not eased by Managing Director John Cox who would drive in and out of work at top speed, scattering the pickets in all directions. Indeed, on one occasion he collided with a placard wedged in a grid, swerved and crashed into a lorry. He was subsequently found guilty of driving without due care and fined £15.

But despite the tense situation, made more uneasy by allegations of unnecessarily rough treatment at Stockport Police Station, no serious disorder occurred until 1 September when another one-day sympathy strike was organised.[8] Some 40 factories and building sites in the Stockport area stopped work and more than 3,000 workers from 20 different unions held a meeting on waste ground near the Roberts–Arundel factory. The police had banned any demonstrations outside the factory and tried to prevent a contingent of strikers from Reddish who were marching to the meeting from walking past the factory with their placards. Some fighting took place during which individual policemen drew their truncheons. Union officials rushed to the scene and together with the Chief Constable managed to calm the situation. The meeting was resumed and it was agreed that no demonstration ought to be held but that the right to picket would be maintained by marching round the factory. As they passed the building some of the pickets hurled stones and bricks at the windows and scuffles broke out with the police. However, there is little doubt that this violence was directed at property rather than persons as the factory was closed, 'blacklegs' and management having taken the day off.

Picketing continued with occasional arrests and allegations of police brutality until the end of the dispute on 13 May 1968. One incident, in particular, was the cause of some controversy. John Tocher, the District Secretary of the AEU, has argued that the violence which occurred on 22 November, when six pickets were arrested, was instigated by the police rather than the strikers. There is considerable evidence to support Tocher's allegation that the police were unnecessarily aggressive. In the first place two shop stewards, B. Frayne and Harry Smith, had asked the Superintendent in charge to restrain his men. He replied: 'Never mind that, there were three policemen injured last Thursday.'[9] This statement together with an increased police presence suggests that following earlier incidents the police had come prepared and possibly looking for trouble. Moreover, there is no doubt that the police were prepared to use violence against pickets, as three of the six men arrested appeared in court the next morning with broken noses, severe bruising and in one case a neck injury. One of the pickets was

Table 6. *Disturbances, arrests and police injuries during the Roberts–Arundel dispute*[10]

Date	Nature of disturbance	Size of crowd	Number of police	Arrests	Police injuries
22 Feb. 1967	Missiles thrown at factory, 20 windows smashed, £4,000 worth of damage	1,000	200	9	4
1 Sept. 1967	Missiles thrown at factory, 40 windows smashed	3,000	70	12	–
17 Nov. 1967	Scuffles between pickets and police	120	24	2	3
22 Nov. 1967	Scuffles between pickets and police	100	90	6	–

Total number of arrests during entire strike – 50

so badly injured that he collapsed outside the court and had to be taken to hospital.[11] The men alleged that they had been beaten at the police station and told to shout 'Mercy, mercy'. Although an enquiry conducted by an officer from another force concluded that three Stockport policemen had a case to answer for 'assault occasioning actual bodily harm' no criminal or even disciplinary charges were brought. Nevertheless, £2,280 agreed damages were paid to the men by the police.[12] Altogether there were four incidents of serious disorder and numerous scuffles associated with this long-drawn-out dispute (see Table 6). This violence was hardly on the same scale as that which occurred at Featherstone, Tonypandy, Llanelli or even during the General Strike, but in post Second World War terms it did constitute something of a reversion to a more disorderly form of picketing. However, no serious violence associated with industrial disputes was reported for another four years until the miners' strike of 1972.

The miners' strike of 1972

At Aberdeen in July 1971 the National Union of Mineworkers' (NUM) annual conference passed a resolution calling for wage increases of up to £9 per week. The resolution also required the Executive to consult the membership 'with regard to various forms of industrial action' if there was no satisfactory response from the National Coal Board (NCB).[13] By October the NCB had offered £1.80 for surface men and £1.75 for underground workers; to the union negotiators this was 'insulting and disgusting' rather than satisfactory. A special conference of the Executive was called and it was decided to implement a national overtime ban from 1 November and to ballot the membership on whether or not to call an all-out strike. On Thursday 2 December, the result was known: 58% had declared themselves in favour of strike action and the first national coal strike since 1926 was called for 9 January 1972.

Coal stocks were very high before the overtime ban with the NCB holding 10 million tons and their biggest customer, the Central Electricity Generating Board (CEGB), holding over 17 million tons at power stations throughout the country.[14] Although the ten-week overtime ban had undoubtedly reduced these stockpiles the Government was confident that the coal would outlast the miners and took no action to limit consumption until 10 February, when a somewhat belated state of emergency was proclaimed.[15] By this time, however, skilfully organised picketing had largely prevented the movement of coal and indeed other commodities to and from coke depots and power stations.

From the start of the strike picketing was intended not only to prevent the production of coal but also its distribution from NCB to CEGB stocks. Pickets were sent to coal and coke depots, power stations, steel works and ports throughout the country. Initially, small groups of 'flying pickets' were sent to assess the situation and establish picket lines at the key 'points of energy'.[16] Where drivers, usually non-union private contractors, insisted on crossing these picket lines a mass picket would be organised. This happened during the first week of the strike at Grimethorpe where 300 pickets tried to prevent the movement of fuel from a Coalite plant and at Kincardine when a similar number stopped lorries delivering slurry to a power station.[17] Although angry words were exchanged between the miners and those wishing to cross their picket lines no violence occurred during the first eight days of the stoppage.[18] The first violent clashes were reported on 18 January; in Nottinghamshire a shop selling prepacked coal had its windows smashed and in Staffordshire two pickets were arrested for using threatening words and behaviour with intent to provoke a breach of the peace.[19] Further disorder occurred at Dover Docks where a miner was injured and two others arrested following a confrontation between lorry drivers and pickets.[20] On the same day at Calverton Colliery in Nottinghamshire two policemen were slightly injured. These injuries were accidental rather than intentional, one policeman was crushed against a car bonnet and the other slipped on ice.[21] Nevertheless the NUM leadership were becoming increasingly alarmed by the publicity given to such incidents and when three pickets were arrested following a clash with lorry drivers at a coal depot in Kent, Joe Gormley appealed for peaceful picketing.[22] But, although subsequent picketing was generally peaceful, reports of violence continued to appear in the press. For example, on 20 January the *Daily Mail* reported that 'policemen wrestled with banner waving pickets' and that lorries trying to break through the picket lines were met with 'a hail of anthracite'.[23] But it was an incident outside the NCB's Doncaster area headquarters that attracted most adverse publicity. For several days a mass picket had been called to prevent office workers, many of them women, from entering the building. The situation was particularly tense as some of the office staff belonged to the Colliery Officials and Staffs Association (COSA), the clerical branch of the NUM (which naturally supported the strike), and others to the Association of Professional, Executive and Computer Staff (APEX) which did not call on its members to observe picket lines. Moreover, there was some suspicion that a number of office workers had deliberately left COSA and joined APEX in order to carry on working. The climax came on 21 January when 50 girls had to pass through a corridor of angry pickets. An eyewitness account sent by the NCB to the NUM describes what happened:

As they proceeded through the picket-lines they were kicked, punched, spat upon. This treatment was given to all irrespective of age, sex or any apparent union membership. Once inside the building almost every female of the staff collapsed in tears, were hysterical or otherwise physically distressed. They were given first aid and treatment. They cleaned up, for many had been spat upon and bore the marks of tobacco juice, and went to their desks. An hour later, many were still in tears.[24]

Having treated the office staff in a way which, as *The Sun* alleged, 'shocked the country' the pickets turned on BBC and ITN cameramen accusing both organisations of distortion.[25] According to one miner both the police and some of the office staff were very provocative:

I saw some booting at Coal House, I saw some booting but it were indiscreet [sic], it were under cover like, they were putting the boot in, like. You see they didn't do it for the cameras to see, and I'll tell you something, this situation that evolved, the news media, television cameras never recorded this, or if they did record it they didn't show it. But they showed incidents at Coal House where they alleged that miners were spitting on girls, but they didn't show the treatment we had from Coal House occupants when they were emptying tea leaves and hot tea on us from top. (NUM picket)

Another picket, who is also a magistrate, confirmed the above version of events:

When we gets to Coal House we sees these APEX lasses up there going like that [makes V-sign] and chucking bloody tea out, that were the first day. There would be about 60 of us. Second day there were 200 there and a lot of lasses were with us. And then police came. These women up there were going like this [makes V-sign] and shouting and telling us 'Take yer hook and go down the hole where you belong, you rats' ... The third day it got really rough, there were about 1,000 there ... Police escorted them through but they did push, they did spit and they did kick. (NUM picket)

So it seems that the miners, having been provoked by the office staff, did spit on, jostle and verbally abuse female workers. This behaviour undoubtedly lost the strikers some public sympathy and caused NUM headquarters to issue a circular stressing the need for peaceful picketing.[26] However, on 1 February 20 pickets were arrested at Clipstone Colliery, near Mansfield, and at Kilnhurst Colliery five were arrested for breach of the peace and obstruction.[27] Outbreaks of violence, it appeared, were going to continue.

On 3 February an event occurred that significantly contributed to the tension in the coalfields. Fred Matthews, a 37-year-old miner from Yorkshire, was killed by a lorry outside Keadby power station near Scunthorpe. Matthews had been picketing when an articulated lorry driven by a non-unionist forced its way into the station where the power workers refused to unload it. The driver took off his load by himself and then drove out through the picket line at high speed scattering both police and pickets. The rear of the lorry mounted the pavement and hit Matthews, killing him outright. The police borrowed one of the pickets' cars and chased the lorry, which had not stopped, finally catching up with it about a mile from the power station.

The death of Fred Matthews undoubtedly increased the feelings of anger and determination in the mining community. In the House of Commons Tom Swain, an NUM-sponsored MP, declared: 'This could be the start of another Ulster in the Yorkshire coalfield. I warn the Government here and now that if there is not an immediate statement from a responsible minister, I shall go back to my constituency tonight and advocate violence.'[28] The Home Secretary, Reginald Maudling, expressed his sympathy for Mr Matthews' family and said that the police would investigate the incident. However, the conciliatory tone adopted by Mr Maudling was not shared by the local coroner who told the jury to return a verdict of accidental death and who commented that the driver's action had shown him 'doing his best by his employer and if I may say so by his country'.[29]

The day after Fred Matthews' death picketing began in earnest outside the Saltley Coke Depot in Birmingham. The depot was the only major distribution point still operating and it contained a massive stockpile of 100,000 tons. Moreover, its normal outflow of about 400 lorries a day had almost doubled during the strike; clearly Saltley would have to be closed for the strike to be really effective. So far picketing involving only a dozen men had not been very effective; only about one in a hundred drivers was turning back. On 4 February mass picketing began when 200 reinforcements arrived from Stoke-on-Trent. However, this intensified picketing proved equally ineffective with some 596 vehicles going through the depot gates. An article in *The Miner* blamed the police for this lack of success and claimed that they were 'not inclined to allow the pickets their constitutional rights'.[30] This allegation is hardly substantiated by the fact that the police were stopping lorries so that pickets could speak to the drivers even though they had no legal entitlement to such communication.[31] On the other hand, once a driver had indicated that he wished to cross the picket line the police made sure he was able to. As one police spokesman put it: 'If the lorries wish to go in we have given instructions that the entrance must be cleared. If the pickets bar the way they are causing an obstruction.'[32] It seems that the police, far from being biased, were trying to balance the driver's right to proceed through the picket line if he wished with the pickets' right to persuade peacefully which was being frustrated by moving vehicles. Of course, these legal rights are all very well in theory but bear little relation to the reality of a strike situation. A non-union driver being paid high bonuses precisely to drive through picket lines is hardly likely to listen to peaceful persuasion, while picketing entirely within the law is likely to be wholly ineffective. At this stage of the conflict at Saltley it seems that any bias lay in the law itself rather than in its enforcement.

On Saturday 5 February picketing continued and two arrests were made. The NUM Midland Area Secretary Jack Lally called for reinforcements and the message went round the coalfields that 'they're beating hell out of our lads'.[33] At Barnsley, Arthur Scargill received a telephone call for assistance at 4.00 p.m. and within five hours he had sent off 400 men and was making his own way to Birmingham. Other pickets set off from South Wales and from all over the Midlands. The Communist Party, the Labour Party, local students and the Transport and General Workers Union (TGWU) hurriedly organised accommodation and meals and the next day picketing began in earnest. An agreement had been negotiated with the police that only one of the depot gates would be used by lorries and 200 to 300 pickets congregated outside this one entrance. They met with initial success as several lorries turned away. However, their early jubilation turned to anger and frustration when a long string of lorries insisted on crossing the picket line. Several of these drivers made threatening gestures and uncomplimentary comments about the NUM. One had an Alsatian dog in his cab, another clutched an iron bar. Tension inevitably began to mount. The President of the Midlands Area of the NUM alleged that the police had gone back on their agreement and were allowing lorries to use another gate at the depot. The police strongly denied this suggestion but feelings were obviously running high.[34] Matters came to a head when a lorry driver drove through the crowd at speed, forcing both police and pickets to quickly jump out of the way. This incident was immediately likened to that which had resulted in the death of Fred Matthews and the miners became very hostile.[35] At 10 o'clock Gas Board officials decided to close the gate for the rest of the day to allow tempers to cool down.[36]

The fourth day of picketing was also the most violent to date. By the time the gates opened at 10.00 a.m. there were about 800 pickets outside the depot, by 11.30 the number had swollen to 2,000. As the number of pickets increased so did that of the police. Initially 220 policemen were deployed but reserves, kept out of sight a few streets away, were summoned by radio in batches of 34 until about 400 were in place. According to most reports the day started peacefully but when lorry drivers insisted on entering the depot disorder ensued. A report in *The Miner* provides a graphic description of these events:

Coal lorries turned up by the score, and their drivers, owner drivers they said they were, inspired by greed, displaying iron bars and sticks, insisting on forcing their way through the pickets, who were surging forward from behind the police ring, rocking these giant coal carriers.

More policemen were hurriedly called up and as they hastened to the fray it could easily be seen that they now outnumbered the pickets. Arrests were being made indiscriminately it appeared, the black marias roared their way up the hill to the police station, and quickly returned for another load. Nor were the policemen tender in their treatment of our men. I have signed statements by witnesses, of police kicking pickets who had been knocked down.

These incidents inflamed the situation and the miners retaliated. Vehicles continued to drive through the crowd of fighting jostling pickets and policemen, some panicked and drove dangerously, knocking over both sides together, arrests continued to take place, and gradually the police gained control and the pickets returned to their places on the footpath, licking their wounds, their numbers depleted by arrests and injuries.[37]

During the day 21 people were arrested and 44 out of 91 lorries turned away. Two policemen were injured by lorries and the entire Birmingham police force of 3,000 men put on special alert. The relationship with the police seemed to take a turn for the worse; allegations were made that special 'heavy squads' had been sent in from other areas to sort out the miners. Moreover, it was claimed that the police had been unnecessarily aggressive and on one or two occasions resorted to unprovoked violence.[38]

On Tuesday 8 February yet more pickets arrived from South Wales, Yorkshire, Derbyshire and the North Midlands. Once again the pickets attempted to break through the police cordons and swarm around any lorry that attempted to enter the depot. During the day 18 arrests were made and 18 people were injured, six of them police. A Chief Inspector received a fractured thigh when a lorry accelerated towards the depot gates and following this incident the police themselves began to advise drivers not to attempt the passage.[39] Only 50 lorries tried to cross the picket line and of these 39 were successful. For the first time the tide seemed to be turning in favour of the miners. Moreover, the strained relationship between the police and the pickets of the day before had eased when both sides had co-operated in helping injured men.[40]

On Tuesday night Scargill made an emotional appeal to the District Committee of the Amalgamated Union of Engineering Workers in order to get more reinforcements for the picket line:

We don't just want your pound notes. Will you go down in history as the working class of Birmingham who stood by while the miners were battered, or will you become immortal? I do not ask you – I demand that you come out on strike.[41]

Later that same night Scargill also obtained promises of support from the TGWU and unofficially from the GMWU. In addition the Birmingham Trades Council put an advert in the *Birmingham Post* asking for everyone to support the miners outside the depot gates on Thursday. On Wednesday there were a further 25 arrests and four injuries, but the climax was to come on Thursday when the massive reinforcements were due to arrive on the picket line.

By ten o'clock on Thursday 10 February about 3,000 miners had gathered outside the coke depot for what was to be the last mass picket at Saltley. There were 800 police on duty, the largest number deployed so far, and no sign of the promised union reinforcements. To the miners it must have seemed as if they would never succeed in closing the gates. Indeed, Arthur Scargill has noted both how dispirited the miners were and the boost to morale provided by the eventual arrival of the additional pickets:

Here we had a situation where miners were tired, physically and mentally des-perately weary. They had gone through nearly six weeks' strike action, they had gone through the worst battling encountered in strike action in any time in recent years. Their comrades had been arrested, one of them had been kicked to bits and yet they were still battling on. I readily concede that some of the lads were feeling the effects and were a bit dispirited that no reinforcements were coming. And then over this hill came a banner and I've never seen in my life as many people following a banner. As far as the eye could see it was just a mass of people marching towards Saltley. There was a huge roar and from the other side of the hill they were coming the other way. They were coming from five directions, there were five approaches to Saltley; it was in a hollow, they were arriving from every direction. And our lads were just jumping up in the air with emotion – a fantastic situation. [42]

By 11 o'clock about 15,000 people were blocking the entrance to the coke depot; a roar of 'Close the gate, close the gate' was taken up and it was apparent that no lorry would have a chance of getting through. At 11 o'clock the Chief Constable of Birmingham, Sir Derrick Capper, announced that, in the interests of public safety, the gates would indeed be closed.

The police asked Arthur Scargill to disperse the crowd and he agreed on condition that he could make a speech using their public address equipment since his own was 'knackered'. So the final, rather incongruous, scene out-side the Saltley Coke Depot was of Arthur Scargill standing on an old urinal addressing the crowd through a police loud hailer. [43] By 2 o'clock the only people in Nechells Place were two policemen standing guard outside the locked gate.

On 14 February, four days after the gates had closed at Saltley, the NUM announced plans to reduce the numbers on picket lines to a mere token pres-ence. This step was taken not because of adverse public comment about mass picketing but because the strike was now almost totally effective. [44] Ironically, on the same day the last serious disorderly incident of the strike occurred at Longannet in Scotland. A mass picket of 2,000 miners tried to

Table 7. *Numbers, injuries and arrests at Saltley*[45]

Date	Pickets	Police	Injuries	Arrests	Lorries entering
4 Feb. 1972	200	48(est.)	–	–	596
5 Feb. 1972	130	48	–	2	320
6 Feb. 1972	200	48	–	2	–
7 Feb. 1972	2,000	400	9(8 police)	21	47
8 Feb. 1972	2,000	400	18(6 police)	18	39
9 Feb. 1972	2,000	400	4(2 police)	25	43
10 Feb. 1972	15,000	800	1(1 police)	8	10
Total			32	76	

prevent workers entering a power station and there were scuffles with the police; thirteen strikers were arrested and charged with 'mobbing and rioting'.[46] These serious charges, together with the fact that the men appeared in court wearing handcuffs sparked off a wave of protest in the Labour movement and there were rallies and demonstrations up and down the country. In the event all thirteen men were acquitted.[47]

The day before the gates had closed at Saltley the NCB made a new offer to the NUM of £3.50; this was rejected but the NUM modified their demand from £9 to £7. By now the extent of the crisis facing Mr Heath's government was clear. Only six million tons of coal were left, drastic steps had to be taken to reduce energy consumption. A state of emergency was declared on 9 February and on the 11th a three-day week was imposed with restrictions on office heating and display lighting. However, it was clear that the Government had miscalculated; the miners were united and determined. By 18 February 1.6 million workers had been laid off and there were only about two weeks of electricity supply left. The Government did the only thing it could; a Court of Inquiry under Lord Wilberforce was appointed 'to inquire into the causes and circumstances of the present dispute'. It eventually recommended £6 a week for underground workers and equivalent agreements for surface workers. These recommendations were rejected by the NUM who now had the Government where they wanted it. Several improvements on the Wilberforce offer were negotiated and the strike ended on 25 February.

As we have seen, there were several disorderly incidents during the strike, but in the words of Reginald Maudling, the Home Secretary, 'the bulk of the picketing that has taken place has certainly been peaceful'.[48] Even in those exceptional cases where scuffles occurred between police and pickets little more than spirited pushing and shoving seems to have taken place. In particular the picketing at Saltley – often presented as an extreme example of industrial violence – consisted of large numbers of strikers pushing against smaller numbers of police. Such behaviour is hardly the ultimate manifestation of anarchy that it is often depicted to be.

The Neap House Wharf industrial dispute 1972

Mass picketing similar to that which had been successfully used during the miners' strike of 1972 was also resorted to during the dock strike of that year. But this time, the police seemed determined not to be seen to lose as they had at Saltley. The conflict began on 20 July when warrants were issued in the National Industrial Relations Court for the arrest of five London dockers. The response to the arrest of the men now known as the 'Pentonville Five' was immediate; all registered dockers in the Humberside region walked out in protest. However, six small Trent-side wharves that were not registered under the National Dock Labour Scheme continued to function normally. The strikers held a series of meetings over the next three days and it was decided to commence picketing the unregistered wharves on 24 July.

Initially a small party of 18 pickets visited each of the six wharves and attempted to persuade the men still working to withdraw their labour. This picketing was observed by a police contingent made up of one inspector, six sergeants and 18 constables who reported that no incidents had occurred and that no intervention was necessary.[49] However, this picketing had not only been entirely peaceful but also totally ineffective; none of the unregistered employees was prepared to strike and work continued as normal.

On the following day a mass picket of 800 visited each of the unregistered wharves in turn. Each wharf, except Flixborough, closed down when the pickets arrived. At Flixborough, which was well protected by perimeter fencing, the management were determined that work should continue whether pickets arrived or not. However, when peaceful persuasion failed, the strikers, despite the presence of 53 police officers, forced their way through the gates and entered the wharf whereupon work stopped. Although the pickets had undoubtedly acted illegally they had not resorted to any physical violence, nor had they damaged any property.

Further picketing took place on 1 August when 35 strikers again visited Flixborough, but this time work continued behind locked gates. A mass picket was called for the following day and 400 strikers managed to stop work at both Neap House Wharf and Flixborough, the only two wharves still functioning. Once again no physical violence seems to have occurred, although some dock workers were undoubtedly intimidated and obstructed. In particular there was no physical contact between the strikers and police.

By this time the strike had been made official and various agreements were negotiated between the dockers' shop stewards and the managements of most of the unregistered wharves. Consequently no picketing took place on Humberside on 3, 4, 5 or 6 August. However, at a meeting of lorry drivers and wharf workers held at the Worltey Hotel, Scunthorpe, it was decided that Neap House Wharf would, from 7 August, operate normally come what may. Just as the miners had concentrated on picketing the Saltley Coke Depot, so the registered dockers now turned their attention to Neap House Wharf.

By 10.00 a.m. on 7 August 100 pickets had gathered outside the wharf and police intelligence reports suggested that another 200 could be expected within an hour.[50] The 100 police officers on duty were reinforced by three Police Support Units (102 men) from within Lincolnshire itself and by all available officers from the nearby Scunthorpe Division. It seems that there was a policy of trying to match picket strength with an equal number of police.

The first hostile confrontation occurred when an empty lorry attempted to enter the wharf. A description of what happened is provided in a 'confidential' police report:

Up to this time, pickets had lined up on the road immediately opposite the gateway, but as the lorry slowed down near the entrance, it was swamped by pickets and the driver had to stop to avoid colliding with them. Some pickets climbed between the lorry cab and articulated trailer and turned off the air supply, effectively setting the brakes on the trailer. Others removed blocks of wood and chains from the rear of the trailer and wedged them firmly underneath the wheels, preventing the vehicle from moving backwards or forwards. At this point the cab door was opened and the opening shouts of 'Get the bastard out' gave every indication of what was to be expected in the days ahead. A wedge of police officers moved forward, forcing themselves between the pickets and the lorry as a hail of stones came from the back of the crowd, breaking a side window. The wedge turned into a cordon and the pickets were forced back far enough for other officers to remove the obstruction from the wheels, and the lorry moved into the wharf with the trailer wheels still locked.[51]

After this determined attempt by the pickets to prevent access to the wharf the Divisional Police Commander following consultations with the Deputy Chief Constable requested five Police Support Units (PSUs), each consisting of 34 men, from various other forces. However, additional pickets were also arriving and by 12.45 p.m. some 350 strikers had collected outside the wharf. Several individual and small group efforts were made to break through the police lines guarding the wharf but all were repulsed and a few arrests were made. The police had also arranged for no lorries to attempt to leave until the PSUs arrived, but by mid-afternoon the wharf had become increasingly congested with laden lorries as more and more ships were unloaded. It became obvious that some lorries would soon have to leave whether or not the police reinforcements had arrived.

Under police guidance lorries were started up at different times in different parts of the wharf and the crowd of pickets moved from one gateway to another in an attempt to anticipate the point of egress. The lorries were about to try and slip out when the first PSU, from Nottingham, arrived. The considerable effect on the strikers of these and later reinforcements was noted in the police report:

Having de-bussed several hundred yards from Sector 4 the new contingent marched smartly into position. At first the pickets were taken aback, but they then cheered, laughed and shouted derogatory remarks at the new unit. Within minutes, another PSU arrived, this time from Derbyshire. The pickets fell silent and when they saw wave after wave of light vans with 'Police' markings moving towards the wharf, all hope of holding up the lorries failed. By 5 p.m. the area was clear of all pickets and the loaded lorries left the wharf. It was becoming abundantly clear that the pickets respected nothing but strength.[52]

So it seems that the pickets gave up when they realised the full extent of the police strength. However, it was not merely the number of reinforcements but also their appearance and behaviour that overawed the strikers. A Chief Inspector commented:

Our lot were really struggling on one occasion at Neap House and the Nottinghamshire men drove in a bus and they got out, and they were all six foot men and they marched up and they changed the whole complexion of the situation because they were a smart body of men who appeared to know what they were doing. Now whether they did know what they were doing we don't know, but they appeared to, and it changed everything. (Chief Inspector)

On this occasion, then, a show of force was sufficient to cause the strikers to disperse without any disorder taking place. However, the situation was not so easily dealt with on the following day.

The police reinforcements were given overnight accommodation and by 9 o'clock the next morning they were again deployed at the wharf. A total of 425 officers were given the twin tasks of preventing the strikers from entering the wharf and of ensuring that lorries could enter and leave at will. A mass picket of 400 dockers gathered with the specific intention of preventing lorries from leaving the wharf; in this situation violent clashes were inevitable.

Early in the day, before all the pickets arrived, the police developed a deliberate 'cat and mouse' game, whereby lorries were despatched at one gate when pickets moved to the other. But soon there were enough strikers to cover both gates and other tactics had to be employed. When a group of three lorries prepared to leave the police cordon stretched across the entrance suddenly pivoted from one end forcing the pickets back out of the road. The lorries quickly drove out along the cleared road the police cordon hinged back into position. A shower of stones flew from the rear of the pickets; the windscreen of the first lorry was smashed and several policemen hit.[53] More seriously some of the dockers, obviously frustrated by these tactics, attacked some of the officers in the cordon. One constable lost his grip on his colleagues and was grabbed by two dockers who held him while a third hit him in the face causing a wound requiring stitches. Another officer in the cordon was kicked in the face and several arrests were made. However, the man who had struck the constable in the face had not been arrested for fear of escalating the situation at the very time when the lorries were trying to get away.[54]

During a period of inactivity following the successful departure of the lorries the pickets placed a telegraph pole on the roadside opposite the gateway. The police not unreasonably assumed that this would be used to block the road if any more vehicles attempted to leave. At this point four police officers tried to arrest the picket who was wanted for the serious assault on the constable; but a large group of dockers ran to his assistance and surrounded the four men. Two PSUs were deployed to rescue their colleagues and recover the telegraph pole. Fighting broke out, but the PSUs eventually returned with six prisoners, including the wanted man, and the telegraph pole.[55]

By 4.15 p.m. more lorries were ready to leave the wharf. Once again the police managed to fool the pickets into collecting around one gate while several vehicles quickly slipped out another. In order to allow the last lorry to leave the police cordon across the gate again hinged from one end pushing the strikers out of the road. The lorry sped out making a tight turn which caused a 7-ton pack of wood to slide off and burst open on the road. A long police cordon was immediately formed to keep the pickets back while a chain of police and wharf workers moved the wood into the wharf. As they worked stones were thrown from the crowd and two policemen were knocked unconscious. However, once the wood had been cleared the strikers left the area having achieved very little.[56]

On the following day, 9 August, some 700 dockers arrived at Neap House to face just over 500 police officers. Similar police tactics were used as previously when pickets massed at one gate. Lorries were sent out of alternate exits thereby forcing the pickets to split into two groups so both gates could be covered. Some steps had also been taken to combat stone throwing. Early in the morning before the dockers had arrived a team of police had sifted the area surrounding the wharf and had removed anything that could be used as a missile. Moreover, squads of 12 officers, under the leadership of a sergeant, were positioned behind the picket line at each gate. These officers took no direct part in moving the pickets out of the road, but when the cordon began to hinge round the squads watched the pickets and moved in to arrest the 'militant trouble-makers'. These tactics proved very successful; despite the large number of pickets all the lorries were able to enter and leave when required and no police injuries were sustained.[57]

The next day only 100 pickets arrived at the wharf and no violent incidents were reported. On 11 August rather more pickets turned up but they were matched by the PSUs who were summoned as required from the nearby North Lindsay Technical College where they had been provided with temporary accommodation. By 5.00 p.m. all the pickets had dispersed and once again no violence had occurred.

Another mass picket was called for Monday 14 August. By early afternoon some 900 dockers had congregated outside Neap House Wharf. Only 335 police were on duty and further reinforcements were hastily summoned. In order to gain time the police gave orders that no lorries should attempt to leave, although unloading continued and laden lorries were 'stock-piled' on the wharf. By 2.30 p.m. the reserve PSUs began to arrive and at 4.00 p.m. fresh PSUs from Nottingham, Leicester and Rutland marched into position. Almost immediately a confrontation occurred between these units and some of the pickets during which five arrests were made.[58]

The next clash took place when a stone was thrown at the strikers from behind the wharf fence. The pickets surged forward and grabbed the specially constructed wire fence and tore it from its concrete support posts; one post crashed over narrowly missing several strikers. Some men then tried to enter the wharf over the flattened fence but were pushed back by the police. According to the police report there was a brief pause followed by another attack culminating in an assault on a police officer:

Following the physical effort involved in this episode, the situation again became calmer, but minutes later the whole incident erupted again and appeared to be caused by the heat of the afternoon and sheer frustration of the dockers because of lack of progress in their aims. They again rushed the wire ... but before any entry could be gained to the wharf, a large group of police officers reinforced the line at that point and were able to force their way between the pickets and the fence. During this confrontation, one police officer found himself isolated between the police and picket lines. He was immediately dragged into the crowd of dockers and kicked unconscious. A police cordon moved forward and pushed the pickets back far enough to recover the injured officer, but as he was being carried away by colleagues, a docker kicked him again.[59]

However, this account can be contrasted with that provided by Michael Parkin of *The Guardian* who saw a single policeman 'rush into a group of dockers with his arms flailing'.[60] The dockers also seem to have been provoked by the way in which the police were treating prisoners; some were roughly handled and one was seen with his trousers round his ankles. This does not, of course, excuse the attack on the unconscious officer, but it does make it more understandable. No further violence occurred and once again the strikers dispersed without having had the slightest effect on the working of the wharf.

The attack on the unconscious policeman proved to be the last violent incident associated with the strike. A mass picket of 500 gathered outside the wharf on the 15th without any disorder occurring at all. Similarly a smaller

Table 8. *Numbers, arrests and police injuries during the 1972 Neap House Wharf industrial dispute*[61]

Date	Pickets	Police	Arrests	Police injuries (necessitating hospital treatment)
24 July	18	25	–	–
25 July	800	53	–	–
26 July	–	117	–	–
1 Aug.	35	–	–	–
2 Aug.	400	84	–	–
7 Aug.	350	400	9	1
8 Aug.	400	425	12	10
9 Aug.	700	500	22	–
10 Aug.	100	120	–	–
11 Aug.	160	160	–	–
14 Aug.	900	800	9	3
15 Aug.	450	400	–	–
Total			52	14

group picketed on the 16th and again on the 17th, even though the strike was now officially over, but no more violence occurred. The police operation finally closed at midday on 21 August when it became apparent that no further picketing was going to take place.

Indeed, no more mass picketing was to occur for the next four years – until the dispute at the Grunwick Processing Laboratories in North London.

Grunwick 1976–1978

On Friday 20 August 1976 a young Asian, Devshi Bhudia, was sacked from the mail order department of Grunwick Processing Laboratories for working too slowly. Five other workers, including Mrs Jayaben Desai and her son Sunil, walked out in sympathy. So began a dispute that was to culminate in mass picketing involving more people, police, arrests and injuries than the incident at Saltley in 1972. The events which led to this escalation have been well documented and need only be briefly stated.[62]

On Monday 23 August the workers who had walked out on Friday positioned themselves outside the factory gates with placards urging those going to work to sign a document supporting a union. Several signed and a walk-out was arranged for that afternoon. In the event some fifty workers walked out and after an angry exchange with management representatives they marched to a neighbouring Grunwick works in Cobbold Road where some windows were broken. The police were called and the strikers quickly dispersed without any physical violence occurring.

The small group of strikers sought advice from the Brent Trades Council as to which union to join so that they could be represented in their dispute with management. They were advised that the Association of Professional, Executive, Clerical and Computer Staff (APEX) was the most appropriate union and a strike committee consisting of Jack Dromey, Secretary of the Brent Trades Council, Len Gristey, APEX area organiser, and Mrs Desai was formed.

Within a week there were 137 on strike (comprising 91 permanent staff and 46 vacation workers) out of a total workforce of 490. The 91 permanent staff who walked out all joined APEX. Naturally APEX requested recognition by Grunwick but, having no success, applied to the Advisory, Conciliation and Arbitration Service (ACAS) for assistance. ACAS approached Grunwick on numerous occasions during the remaining months of 1976 but to no avail.[63]

For the first 40 weeks of the strike, right through the winter, picketing remained non-violent and totally ineffective. By May 1977 the Strike Committee, the Brent Trades Council and APEX itself had come to the conclusion that both attempted negotiation and normal picketing were achieving very little. It was decided that a mass picket should be called for Monday 13 June and maintained for several weeks. The object of this mass picketing was, according to Roy Grantham, the General Secretary of APEX, to publicise the dispute rather than to obstruct those still working. He told the Scarman Inquiry on 14 July that:

The industrial justification for the kind of picket that we asked for on the original day was, first of all, to impress upon the people inside that we were concerned about the fact that this issue was going on for a long time and, secondly, to draw the attention of the public authorities to the fact that we had a strike that had been running then for over forty weeks, which we had attempted to resolve by all the legitimate available means to us and upon which there was no prospect of making any progress unless somebody came along and said 'This is an issue that has to be resolved.'[64]

It seems then that the mass picketing at Grunwick was organised for a very different reason from that at Saltley. In the former case the objective was to draw attention to the fact that the dispute existed, while in the latter case it was simply to obstruct lorries going in and out of the coke depot. It is somewhat ironic that a mass picket called for publicity purposes actually resulted in more disorder than one called specifically to break the law. Of course Grantham's statement to the Scarman Inquiry could have been a retrospective justification of the mass picket rather than an accurate account of why it was called, but this is unlikely. There is no convincing evidence that the 'scenes of confusion, shoving, thumping and an apparent breakdown of general law and order' were anticipated by the organisers.[65] In any event,

Grantham was certainly worried about some of the organisations that were supporting the call for mass picketing.[66] The Socialist Workers Party (SWP) urged its members to join the Grunwick picket line and pointed out that 'aggressive picketing can close the factory'.[67] Moreover during the first ten days of June the SWP issued 22,000 leaflets and put up 2,000 posters publicising the mass picketing.[68] Both the Communist Party of Great Britain and the Communist Party of Britain: Marxist–Leninist supported the call for a mass picket. The supporters and members of these organisations were not of course in any way connected with the trade dispute at Grunwick and were demonstrators rather than pickets. Their presence can hardly have been welcomed by the rather right-wing leadership of APEX.

Monday 13 June witnessed the first of the mass picketing outside the Grunwick factory. Around 700 people turned up and crowded into the narrow streets next to the factory near Dollis Hill underground station. Many spread out across the factory gates blocking the way for those who wished to enter. The police warned that they were obstructing the highway and ordered them to move onto the pavements. When the pickets refused to move the police cleared the road and established a cordon to keep people on the pavements; scuffles took place, numerous arrests were made and 84 people eventually appeared in court.[69] Allegations were made against the police of 'unnecessary brutality' and 'aggressive and provocative tactics' but these were denied by both the Home Secretary and the police.[70] Superintendent Hickman-Smith who was in charge of the operation told reporters:

Everyone who wanted to go into work was being called a 'scab' and shouted at. There were about 200 people massing outside the gates and we had to put a cordon on to allow free access to the premises. I do not think there was any over reaction at all. We were quite impartial. We are put in situations like this and we have a duty to keep the highway clear and allow peaceful picketing. I thought people got over excited and the police simply reacted to the circumstances. Police helmets were knocked off and eggs and flour bombs were thrown at the police.[71]

Once the police had cleared the factory entrance they agreed that an official picket of six APEX strikers could stand in front of the cordon to try to persuade people not to go to work.[72] It seems then that the police were trying to balance the workers' right to enter the factory free from obstruction or intimidation with the pickets' right to persuade peacefully. However, there is evidence to suggest that when obstruction did occur the police resorted to very aggressive tactics. For example, Stuart Weir writing in *New Society* described how the entrance to the factory was cleared on one occasion:

Two phalanxes of police began to make a series of charges against the crowd and we, in turn, pressed back. The pressure in the midst of the picket grew as the police charged and eased as we regained our ground. Even so, it was surprisingly intense at times – much worse than in any football crowd I've been in – and people began to shout and scream in panic. I was particularly worried for a short, slight young woman behind me, but I could do nothing; I was quite unable even to move my arms in the crush.

The police tactics changed. A file of policemen threw themselves at us from the front and began to drag pickets out one by one. I can still see in my mind's eye the first man to go. A policeman plunged down on him, made a two-handed grab at his hair, and threw him out. Behind the first file of assault troops, a second line of police mopped up. People who had been thrown out of the picket, usually onto the ground, were then punched, pushed or kicked right [out] of the way. A few were pulled away, presumably arrested. [. . .]

We fell apart under the police assault. I felt my heart pounding and tensed myself to be hit. Steve was grabbed, thrown and punched in the face, breaking his glasses. As he stumbled away, another policeman grabbed at his glasses, which were hanging away from his face, but missed.

Suddenly I found myself, irresistibly and sickeningly, thrown forward through the air, smack into the chest of a large middle-aged copper. And in the split second as our eyes met I heard myself saying, incongruously, 'Sorry'. He pushed me on.[73]

On the following days of mass picketing there seems to have been rather less violence. The police established their cordons and generally the pickets waited more or less peacefully behind them until the workers, now transported by bus, attempted to enter the factory. Then the strikers would surge forward in an effort to break through the police lines and obstruct the bus, the police for their part would push back hard to hold their position.[74] Sometimes police 'snatch squads' would enter the crowd to make arrests and scuffles would occur, also a certain amount of back-heeling and elbowing took place as the police and pickets pushed against each other. Nevertheless, the general pattern of picketing was one of relatively non-violent pushing and shoving. Stuart Weir notes that violent confrontations were 'outside the direct experience of the vast majority of pickets'[75] and goes on to describe more typical behaviour:

We normally join the mass picket outside the front gate and stand with several hundred others on the pavement behind a dark-blue cordon of police. Anyone who stands in the road to talk is quietly asked to 'move on' or 'stand on the pavement' [. . .]
As the time for the doubledecker bus's arrival draws near, the tension grows, and the chat begins to dry up. But the surge forward from behind the linked ranks of the police which accompanies it is usually halfhearted, though we shout 'scabs' fiercely enough. The police hold the surge off capably enough, the bus rolls serenely through the open gates, and it's usually all over again bar the shouting.[76]

Newspaper reports confirm that simple pushing was the main tactic used by both the police and the pickets. For example, *The Times* reported that:

In order to get the bus in the police have to push back the pickets who are at that moment pushing forward. If the pickets continue to grow in numbers, we may reach the point where the police can only get the bus in by clearing and closing the roads for some way round the factory. As they push the pickets back in order to clear the way the police inevitably become involved in direct physical contact, and that inevitably leads to fights between the pickets and the police.[77]

It is worth noting that there is no evidence of the use of weapons or hard projectiles by the demonstrators or the use of truncheons by police. As Joe Rogaly in his book *Grunwick* points out 'what actually took place was less threatening than the rhetoric used to describe it'.[78]

Of course, occasionally more dramatic events occurred outside Grunwick and at least some of these ought to be noted. On Tuesday 21 June several Labour MPs joined the picket and one of them – Audrey Wise – was arrested on an obstruction charge. She was alleged to have grabbed the arm of a policeman who was dragging off a girl by the hair whereupon the officer, who obviously believed in discretionary law enforcement, spun round and arrested her with the words: 'Never mind, love, you'll do instead.'[79] On 23 June, Mick McGahey, having stated his intention of 'doing a Saltley', arrived outside Grunwick with 12 Scottish miners thus demonstrating touching faith in the prowess of his countrymen.[80] Arthur Scargill appeared with a more credible force of 150 Yorkshire pit men, but ended the day in a police cell rather than on a urinal as he had at Saltley.[81] However, the arrest of Scargill was by no means the most significant event of 23 June. During scuffles a young policeman, PC Trevor Wilson, was struck on the head by a bottle and severely injured. Newspaper photographs and television news showed him lying on the pavement with a pool of blood seeping from his head.[82] The injury inflicted on PC Wilson and the publicity given to it had a dramatic effect on both the Government and the Grunwick Strike Committee. A Court of Inquiry headed by Lord Scarman was set up in an obvious attempt to take the heat out of the situation and to remove the struggle from the streets.[83] Meanwhile, the Strike Committee made it clear that it was totally opposed to violence on the picket line and Roy Grantham tried, not entirely successfully, to limit the number of pickets to 500.[84] It seems that these measures had their intended effect; the number of pickets declined and the only serious violence occurred on 11 July which had been designated as a 'national day of action' and on 7 November during the last mass picket.

Many of the organisations involved in the picketing disagreed with Grantham's attempt to reduce the numbers picketing. For example, the SWP called on its members to step up the picketing and to make a special effort on 11 July.[85] Similarly, 'The Marxist paper for Labour and Youth' produced by the Young Socialists described the limitation of picketing as 'disastrous' and advocated a mass picket of 20,000.[86] Arthur Scargill took the same line and promised support from the Yorkshire miners.

In the event some 18,000 people turned up to picket outside Grunwick on the day of action.[87] Initially the pickets succeeded for the first time in preventing the bus from entering the factory, but later when the mass of demonstrators had moved away to attend a march and rally it was able to drive through the gates virtually unopposed. Thirty people, including 18 policemen, were injured and 70 arrests were made.[88] There were some violent clashes: Arthur Scargill said he had seen one policeman punching a picket in the face, cans and paper cups were thrown at police horses and policemen and demonstrators 'lay groaning on the ground'.[89] However, in the following days there was a rapid reduction in the numbers picketing and no further reports of violence. Indeed by 22 July the number of demonstrators had dwindled to 100, fewer than the workers still employed at Grunwick.[90] A proposal for another mass picket on 8 August caused a split between the Strike Committee which felt that this tactic was the only alternative to conceding defeat and APEX who opposed any more mass demonstrations. In the event Roy Grantham, after threatening that APEX would stop paying strike money if the mass picket went ahead, succeeded in getting the Strike Committee to reject the proposal. Nevertheless, the SWP urged its members and supporters to picket and 2,800 people turned up only to be told that they had no right to take over the dispute from those who had been involved for 50 weeks. There was no violence and the workers' bus entered the factory without difficulty.[91]

No further mass picketing occurred until 17 October when about 4,000 pickets met outside Grunwick for the first of four once-weekly demonstrations. This course of action had been organised by the Strike Committee without the approval of APEX and was intended to culminate on 7 November in a peaceful rally. The demonstrations held on 17, 24 and 31 October were relatively peaceful involving few arrests and no injuries. However, the last mass picket held at Grunwick on 7 November did involve some of the most violent clashes of the entire dispute. Approximately 4,000 pickets collected in Chapter Road and there were clashes with the police that resulted in 113 arrests and 42 police injuries.[92] Many of those present thought that the police themselves had caused most of the trouble and a deputation of 3,000 people marched to Willesden Green police station in protest.

In view of the fact that relations between the police and pickets were severely strained following these clashes it is perhaps fortunate that no further mass picketing took place at Grunwick. The dispute finally ended in July 1978 when all but two of the remaining strikers voted to seek jobs elsewhere.

The steel strike 1980

On 2 January 1980 workers in the public sector of the British steel industry went on strike for the first time since 1926. The dispute centred upon the British Steel Corporation's (BSC) offer of a basic 2% pay award which was unacceptable to the Iron and Steel Trades Confederation (ISTC) who were seeking increases of around 20%.

From the start of the strike ISTC pickets attempted to prevent the production and distribution of steel not only from BSC plants but also from private steel makers and stockholders. During the first few days picketing was not particularly well organised but by the end of the week a strike head-quarters had been established at Rotherham and thereafter the strikers were more co-ordinated. A number of disorderly incidents were reported on 7 January; there were scuffles at Port Talbot when non-striking craftsmen, white-collar workers and managerial staff tried to walk through a picket of 200 strikers and a steel worker was arrested at Corby.[93] On the following day six arrests were made outside Hadfields, a private steel works, when police used a wedge to clear pickets away from the factory gates. This confron-tation seems to have followed the pattern of pushing and shoving which, as we have seen, occurred during the miners' strike, the Neap House Wharf dispute and at Grunwick. All the arrests were for the non-violent offence of obstruction and resulted in conditional discharges.[94] Nevertheless, this relatively minor incident received national news coverage and made Hadfields the focal point for picketing in South Yorkshire.

A similar incident occurred on 11 January in Strathclyde when nine strikers were arrested for obstruction; once again there was no violence and no one was injured.[95] No further disorderly incidents were reported until 16 January when three pickets were arrested at Walsall; one for damaging a lorry and the other two for obstructing the police.[96] However, the first serious clashes of the strike occurred at Corby Steel Works on 22 January when 14 pickets were arrested. More scuffles occurred on 29 January when 39 pickets were arrested in South Wales at two private steel works. Thirteen arrests were made at Pontypool when, according to the police, 60 men blocked the gates of Walker Steel Ltd. and refused to allow lorries to leave while another 26 were made at Newport in similar circumstances.[97]

Relations with the police also deteriorated at Sheerness in Kent where two flying pickets from Scunthorpe were arrested outside a private steel works following unsuccessful attempts to stop lorries entering the plant.[98]

Missiles were thrown for the first time during the dispute on 31 January outside the private steel firm of Hall and Pickles at Payton, Cheshire; ten lorries were 'pelted' with stones, one windscreen was smashed and a driver was hit in the face.[99] On the following day scuffles occurred between 150 pickets and 70 police at Templeborough Rolling Mills in Rotherham during which a brazier was knocked over and eight arrests were made.[100] Another three arrests were made at the same venue the next day but this time for non-violent obstruction. No further disorder occurred until 7 February when 200 flying pickets from South Yorkshire attempted to stop lorries leaving British Leyland's car body plant at Castle Bromwich in Birmingham. An official of the ISTC said that the trouble started when police tried to push strikers out of the way. He alleged that pickets had been forced to the ground and kicked by the police. Similar allegations were made about police behaviour at the

Pressed Steel Fisher factory, also in Birmingham, after a brick had been thrown through the windscreen of a lorry.[101]

There were no more reports of disorder until 11 February when mass picketing began at Hadfields in Sheffield and Sheerness Steel in Kent. Four strikers were arrested at Sheerness when they attempted to push their way past police cordons and two were arrested at Hadfields for similar behaviour.[102] However, more serious disorder occurred at Hadfields on the next day when strikers tried to break through police cordons on two separate occasions, there were scuffles, flying helmets, and five arrests.[103] Similar events took place on 13 February at Hadfields when ten pickets were arrested, while in Telford 11 lorries used for transporting steel had their windscreens smashed, fuel and brake pipes cut and wiring ripped out.[104]

On Thursday 14 February 1,500 pickets including a large contingent from the NUM made a determined attempt to halt steel production at Hadfields. Nevertheless, the police were able to contain the situation and all those who wanted to get into work were able to do so, although some were undoubtedly intimidated. Despite the large number of determined pickets there was no serious violence; a contention supported by the fact that all the 22 arrested were charged with threatening behaviour rather than more serious offences such as assaulting the police.[105] Moreover, only one police officer was injured and that according to an eyewitness account appears to have been accidental.

During the same day union meetings were taking place inside Hadfields and a decision was finally reached for those still working to withdraw their labour in support of their public sector colleagues. It should perhaps be emphasised that this was a decision of the union representatives to support their National Executive's call for all ISTC members to strike and was not influenced by the mass picketing.[106] Although the Hadfields workforce returned to work on 25 February they did so with ISTC approval and no further large-scale picketing or disorder occurred outside their factory.

The next disorderly incidents to be reported occurred on 20 February during mass picketing of the Shearness Steel works in Kent and two stockholders' yards in Lanarkshire. According to newspaper reports the picketing at Shearness was relatively non-violent, the 'atmosphere was nearer that of a football match',[107] while in Lanarkshire, although there were 30 arrests, no serious violence occurred.[108] On Saturday 23 February the ISTC headquarters at Rotherham was deliberately set on fire and a member of staff had to jump from the first floor of the building in order to escape.[109] This arson attack, not surprisingly, angered the strikers who by this stage of the dispute were severely frustrated and could see no immediate solution. Nevertheless, no disorder occurred in South Yorkshire until 12 March when 400 pickets marched from one steel works to another in what may now be described as a final attempt to gain solidarity for their cause. Although 75 arrests were

Table 9. *Numbers, arrests and injuries at the Hadfields factory during the 1980 steel strike*[110]

Date	Pickets	Police	Arrests	Strikers' injuries	Police injuries
8 Jan.	150	–	6	–	–
12 Feb.	620	150	14	–	–
14 Feb.	1,500	680	22	–	1

made no violence other than the usual pushing against police cordons seems to have occurred and only one constable was slightly injured.[111]

Meanwhile on 6 March, in South Wales, another 36 steel workers were arrested for various relatively minor public order offences. Three policemen and two pickets were injured when an articulated lorry crossed a picket line at Gowerton Iron and Steel Suppliers near Swansea. The tail end of the vehicle hit both police and pickets, one constable suffering a fractured pelvis.[112] No further incidents of disorder were reported and the longest national strike since 1945 ended after 13 weeks on 1 April 1980.[113]

Industrial unrest 1946–1980: analysis

The pickets

Picketing in the late 1960s and 1970s certainly involved illegal behaviour – obstruction, intimidation and the immobilisation of vehicles – but recourse to actual violence – beyond, that is, the mere pushing and shoving described at the head of the chapter by Jack Taylor – was comparatively rare. Indeed, when asked about their most violent experiences most union officials described what amounted to no more than aggressive pushing. For example, an NUM branch secretary who had previously likened the 1972 miners' strike to the Vietnam war said the worst 'battle' he had seen involved 'hundreds of miners and police shoving against each other'.[114] Similar descriptions were given of the picketing outside Grunwick:

the SPG lined themselves up at the side of their buses with their backs towards their buses facing the crowd, and the crowd by this time – we're talking of mid-morning period, 11 o'clock – were really chock-a-block in the street from end to end, and they then started to try and push the crowd back into walls and this again provoked the situation – it could have been nasty. It may have been so in certain areas but in the particular place that I were in, what happened was that the crowd was such a mass of number that it ebbed and flowed. The police would push and then it would just be a movement like a wave where they would be just pushed back and you'd got scenes where it seemed as though the sides of the buses were almost bellowing in – because of the size of the crowds the police were pushed. (Grunwick picket)

Even during the largest mass picket at Hadfields, considered to have been very disorderly by some sections of the press,[115] nothing more serious than pushing seems to have occurred:

At that particular day when Hadfields were closed, the incidents of violence actually were minimal, nothing of a very serious nature. A bobby crushed his arm against a bloody lamp post – only by the way that they'd linked up arms – anyhow, there were very few incidents, certainly not violence. Pushing, more than 'owt else. We were pushing against police, that's all. (ISTC shop steward)

Indeed, all but four respondents thought that picketing in relation to people ought to be limited to obstruction and verbal abuse but that it was all right to damage lorries. This position is particularly well illustrated by the following comments of a NUM officer:

I'm against violence anyway. I don't think it does anything for the picket. I think it only causes bad feeling, bad publicity and difficulties ... If you mean violence towards movement of materials and people, then I think, yes, a certain amount of violence is justified. Not against individuals, you can't get hold of a bloke, beat him up and say 'You're not going to work.' To stand in front of him and stop him going in, yes. Like he says, pull the wheels off the lorries, nails in the lorries, all that stuff, yes. I think it's obviously not justified legally, but if it's the only way to stop them then you use it ... Violence to people doesn't really get you anywhere; then again, it depends on your classification of violence. Shouting at people, waving at them, and to some extent spitting on them, although I don't agree with that, just making a noise trying to upset or frighten them, yes, but not physical violence. (NUM officer)

Two of the four union officials who disagreed with this position thought that picketing should be contained strictly within the law and were opposed to even relatively non-violent obstruction and the immobilisation of lorries. The other two dissenters were on the other extreme and advocated more violent means:

I'd throw a bomb at 'em [i.e. the police], it's as simple as that with me, because same as I've said, it's my livelihood [...] ... if you've got to prove a point you can go through it peacefully or you can go through it very violently. That's me anyway, it's as simple as that; I've only got two ways. (NUM picket)

In particular one NUM official admitted to a rather violent method of stopping lorries:

We were very good, we used to vie with one another as to who shall do a lorry. The police quickly found out that if we could get behind them and a lorry, what you do is shove them under the bugger. The quickest way to stop a lorry is to shove a policeman under it. (NUM Branch Secretary)

However, it should be emphasised that these were exceptional views. The vast majority of respondents were prepared to sabotage lorries in various ways and to obstruct police and 'blacklegs' but they did not favour more violent picketing methods.

Various methods were used to immobilise lorries. Respondents admitted smashing headlights, tampering with brakes and removing windscreen wipers.[116] Not surprisingly, attempts were made to puncture tyres:

We were at Thorpe Marsh one particular night and an oil lorry went through, 'cos police got it through like, and we appealed to driver and driver's mate to turn back. 'No', he says, 'It's my money, I've got to live' and all this stuff, and there were a kid there and he said, 'Can I get a car, I want to go back to pit.' He were blacksmith at pit. He came back about four hours later. He'd been in pit yard in forge and he'd made some things which you throw on floor and chance which way you throw them there's a spike stuck up to throw under wheels. He'd made about a dozen at pit yard, that was to defend the principle of stopping these lorries going in. (NUM Branch Secretary)

Only two officials said that they would be prepared to throw bricks at windscreens of lorries that attempted to cross a picket line. Nevertheless, both stressed that this course of action would only be adopted after other less violent methods had failed.

It seems clear, then, that although most strikers have or are prepared to damage lorries very few have experience or advocate personal violence in excess of mere pushing and shoving. Moreover, it is equally clear that pushing and shoving only tends to occur during *mass* picketing; the vast majority of picketing is carried on by relatively few pickets and involves hardly any disorder at all. Often this form of picketing, which can be called 'symbolic confrontation', was the result of an informal agreement negotiated between the police and the pickets. For example, one ISTC official described how such an agreement was reached during the steel strike:

In the mining strike there was an unfortunate incident near Scunthorpe at a place called Keadby where a miner was run over by a lorry and killed and prior to the steel strike coming off we were requested to go see Superintendent Allcock at Scunthorpe. There was myself, one or two other senior trade union officials in the town, and he explained that if possible he didn't want a repetition of such large numbers, people jostling and inevitably fatalities or serious injuries. So he gave us his assurance that if we were to minimize the pickets on any particular gate then in turn his men would stop the lorries so that we could talk to them, but he reserved the right to uphold the law and if the driver wished to proceed then he, at the end of the day, would ensure that he did do so. So we put this to the Strike Committee and it was agreed that we would co-operate down the line; have four or five pickets on each gate, locally in Scunthorpe. Fair to their word, the police did just that. Any lorry that came along or any vehicle that came along the police flagged them down and lads spoke to them and everything worked well. (ISTC official)

Indeed, all the union officials reported that relations with the police during normal as opposed to mass picketing were usually very good. Numerous examples were provided of friendship and sympathy on the picket lines:

We were camping out all night sometimes. I went down one night, half-past three in the morning. Policemen were stood there and they'd got bloody frying pan on with bacon and eggs in, did lads, with tea, about bloody eight of them. They said 'Do you want a bit cock?' 'Ay, that would be nice', said bobby. 'Get yourself sat down, get a bacon sandwich' and that's how they treat them, you know. I've had that two or three times, bobby's come up aside you and said 'That smells bloody good'. We took it all in good part; they'd a job to do, we'd a job to do, as long as they did theirs right, as long as we did ours right. (NUM Branch Secretary)

At one colliery the village policeman even gave the strikers lifts in his police car to and from the picket line.[117] On another picket line the strikers had set up a tent complete with heater, cooker and portable television; the lone representative of law and order frequently took advantage of these facilities to indulge his predilection for 'Z-cars' and toasted cheese sandwiches.[118] In South Yorkshire during the steel strike several pickets were so impressed with the behaviour and, no doubt, pay of their local police that they applied to join the force.[119] However, perhaps the most remarkable example of co-operation occurred during the miners' strike of 1972 when the police, albeit from self-interest, provided the pickets with certain information:

initially during the '72 strike they were giving us a bit of information on the side to avoid trouble, as to when certain private miners were intending getting the men to work and things like that. Because he knew if we knew we could stop it and it would be no trouble. Instead if it developed there would be trouble. We got information on the side from the police inspector, purely from his own point of view. He knew that we would stop it anyway. (NUM Branch Secretary)

Of course even on small picket lines vehicles were occasionally damaged or immobilised but these incidents do not seem to have destroyed the very good relationship that had been built up with the police.

this driver came through this particular day, and we stopped him and we said 'Don't go in, it's a little bit naughty' and he says, 'I'm going, I've come so and so', and he'd got his steel on the back, and we said, 'If you go in, love, you'll not come out'. Anyhow, he still said he were going in so they just dealt with his waggon accordingly and when he came out the police weren't there 'cos we'd got there about 4 o'clock in the morning, and then the police arrived and this three pipper came and he says 'He says you've done some damage, you've damaged his vehicle', and I said, 'No, I don't think so' and all the glass what had been under the vehicle it were all in the water, the lads had dispersed it, and when he came out I said to this three pipper, I said, 'You're never going to allow him on the road like that', I says, 'He's had an accident on the way in.' He knew I was probably joking, because he'd no wipers and he'd no headlamps and he'd no indicators and no rear lights or anything like that and the police officer wouldn't let him out. He said 'I've got to come and take some statements because he says you lot have damaged the lorry' and I says 'No!' and he looked and he says, 'Well, I can't see any evidence of any broken reflectors or anything like that' and he just took a couple of statements and the lads got a warning, but the kiddy called me on one side then. He said, 'Look, that's enough now, you've made your point, let's have no more. I wasn't going to, but I've now got to put some police officers on' and he did. He put two young women on with us . . . in another area they'd have just lifted the whole picket line. (ISTC official)

Contingency planning

In the last chapter we noted that emergency planning following the defeat of organised labour in 1926 was mainly concerned with civil defence in the face of external military aggression. This preoccupation with the external threat to established order continued until the late 1960s when internal social and political pressures once again came to the fore.[120] Two states of emergency were declared in 1970 in response to strikes by dockers and power workers and in the following year the first steps were taken to up-date industrial contingency plans.

In February 1971 a committee consisting of officials from the Home Office and Ministry of Defence and Sir Robert Mark, who was then the Deputy Metropolitan Police Commissioner, was set up to co-ordinate the use of police and troops in the event of civil disorder.[121] At the same time a working party of the Defence Scientific Advisory Committee was given the task of reviewing available intelligence-gathering and crowd-control equipment.[122] Following strikes by dockers and miners in 1972 yet further changes were made to the Government's strikebreaking machinery. A National Security Committee (NSC) was appointed under the chairmanship of Lord Jellicoe to prepare contingency plans for similar strikes in the future. By early 1973 the NSC had drawn up new plans for the maintenance of supplies and services during a major industrial dispute and these were put into effect in December of that year in response to an overtime ban and threatened strike by the NUM. Regional Commissioners were appointed from government Ministers, and the police, military and civil service were placed on stand-by.[123]

Several other measures were taken to combat any repetition of the kind of mass picketing which had closed the Saltley Coke Depot during the 1972 strike. In particular a new intelligence unit was established at Scotland Yard which, according to a report in *The Times*, was 'a clearing house for information so that provincial forces can be alerted in advance of possible trouble. A support system has also been devised so that a large concentration of officers in any one area does not denude other regions of police cover.'[124] This unit, which later became known as the National Recording Centre, as we shall see, played a key role in co-ordinating the policing of the 1984–5 coal strike. However, back in 1974 all these measures proved unnecessary; no mass picketing occurred and only one or two minor disorderly incidents were reported. The strike was eventually ended very much on the miners' terms and resulted in the fall of the Heath Government.[125]

The succeeding Labour Government under Harold Wilson changed the name of the NSC to the less controversial Civil Contingencies Committee (CCC), but retained the same organisational structure.[126] In addition it was suggested in 1975 that a new centralised intelligence agency should be created to co-ordinate police, Special Branch, MI5 and various other intelligence operations. It is not known whether this new agency was shelved because of rivalry between various agencies or whether it is now fully operational;[127] in any case it certainly seems clear that a Labour administration was prepared not only to retain but also to extend this sort of strike-breaking organisation.

During their period in opposition the Conservatives, now led by Mrs Thatcher, conducted a review of contingency planning. A group of senior party members headed by Lord Carrington spent two years considering what a future Conservative Government could do to combat industrial action. The group reported in 1978 that there were certain key sectors of the economy where strong unions and/or advanced technology made it virtually impossible for the Government to win an all-out confrontation. Moreover, the group suggested that any military involvement on a large scale would alienate the unions and some sections of the public from the Conservative Party. The implications of the group's report were that the army should only be used to replace small unskilled workforces in situations where such intervention could be justified in terms of public safety.[128] Of course any government could reject this advice and use the armed services to confront pickets or to replace any group of strikers, but it is interesting to note that recent military intervention in industrial disputes has conformed to the Carrington group's recommendations. The armed services have not been used in a direct public order maintaining role and have only replaced strikers when such intervention can be justified on the grounds of public health and safety. For example, 21,000 troops were used to replace 32,000 firemen in 1977, while in 1979 police, army and airforce personnel were employed to drive vehicles during strikes by ambulance drivers.[129] The police, it would appear, are now the sole agency for dealing with disorder associated with industrial disputes.

Police strategy

The formulation of police strategy in relation to industrial disputes depends to a considerable extent upon the availability of good intelligence. As a Superintendent said 'As long as you know, as long as you've got good intelligence, you can make plans accordingly.'[130] Some of this intelligence is collected in a way that is reminiscent of the techniques used by General Napier in the nineteenth century. It will be remembered that in those days soldiers billeted with the civilian population passed on any information they picked up to military intelligence officers (see p. 20). A somewhat similar system of surveillance seems to be operated today by junior police officers reporting on the activities of their families and friends. For example, a

Superintendent implied that intelligence was collected in this way during the steel strike:

you need intelligence and to gather it. Also you get it, of course, from bobbies who live at home. I mean it was one of their mums and dads in the steel strike. They talk between bobbies, and mum says, 'Just a minute, they're all going to concentrate at so and so.' Well, that may well be intelligence coming in that way. (Superintendent)

The same officer also pointed out that a certain amount of information was collected by constables simply reporting on what was happening on the ground: 'Bobbies walking the streets see pickets going to a place or coming from a place and identify the fact.'[131]

It seems, then, that by simply reporting back what they see and hear on the streets and in the home, constables provide an important source of information. However, they are by no means the only source of industrial intelligence. In particular, widespread use seems to be made of informers of various kinds. Indeed, another Superintendent implied that there were many people prepared to provide information in this way:

we have a Special Branch which works very hard and as not only a sort of under-cover function but also as a collating centre where people will inform with great enthusiasm – who are also in the unions. There are informants in all walks of life. (Superintendent)

Sometimes the police have directly contacted a union official and asked for certain information. A NUM branch secretary recalled that this happened to him during the 1972 miners' strike:

we just talked down there [i.e. on the picket line] and they [i.e. the police] took my name and address and that sort of thing but now I seem to have it in my mind that they did 'phone me later and were asking me different things. They weren't asking me what colour underwear did I wear, they were asking me how long had I been an official at the Branch, had the Union appointed me to be the co-ordinator in charge, the leader, down there, how did I envisage that it would go and this type of thing. And later there was another call from an 'high up there' that never moves out of an office. 'We've been speaking to Superintendent Blogs and he said that you were the man to contact. Could you just give us one or two details' and we got talking that way. (NUM Branch Secretary)

Information about the movement of flying pickets is obtained not only from union officials and informants but also by consulting the management of those bus companies providing transport for the union concerned. For example, a Chief Superintendent, with considerable experience of policing industrial disputes, said:

we try to get details of such things as buses which are hired; for instance if you're getting a large crowd here, and I was talking about 1,700 here on one day, these people come from Birmingham, Manchester, Scotland, Liverpool, London, Oxford, all over the place, South Wales. If you have reason to believe people are coming from a particular place, you can ring the police force concerned and say, 'Can you make some enquiries at bus companies, to see how many have been hired for . . . about 7 o'clock on such and such a morning?' That's the type of intelligence we do, so that we know how many people to expect. And this is again basically a question of knowing how many men you want on duty yourself, again to try and save the taxpayer's money. (Chief Superintendent)

However, some union officials realised that the police were collecting intelligence in this way and tried to take evasive action by ordering a coach for a particular journey and then changing the required destination *en route*. [132] The police, it seems, responded to these tactics by following coaches hired by the union. [133] Indeed, one police officer admitted that not only would he have his men follow coaches but also that they would stop the coach and find some reason to delay it:

I would trail them, yes. And the trick is to stop them before they get there, and go through all their documents, and that's a good thing with public service vehicles because there's an incredible list of documents they've got to have and then we can always say this vehicle is unfit. (Superintendent)

Moreover, several union officials suspected that the police asked coach firms to insist upon prior notification of true destinations. Whether this was true or not is difficult to substantiate, but it was certainly the case that some coach firms instructed their drivers only to travel to previously agreed destinations. [134]

Of course, the police also use more controversial methods to obtain information such as the deployment of Special Branch or plainclothes officers on picket lines or at strike meetings. For example, James Brownlow, the Chief Constable of South Yorkshire, revealed in his evidence to the Employment Committee, that on at least one occasion plainclothes officers were used during the steel strike. Similarly, a report in *The Times* noted that 'plainclothes officers mingled with pickets' [135] during the Roberts–Arundel dispute. Special Branch officers were active during the Neap House Wharf industrial dispute, as is made clear in a confidential report by Chief Superintendent Cranidge:

Most mornings the dockers held mass meetings in their respective towns. Special Branch officers attended all such meetings and from these assessed the likely number attending the wharves that day. Information gathered in this way was passed through the officer's own Force Headquarters to the Police Control at Neap House, and there was constant interchange of information between the Special Branches of all Forces concerned.

Usually the function of Special Branch and plainclothes officers is to provide information about the probable number of pickets so that an adequate police presence can be planned. They are also used to establish whether the police need to continue an operation or not:

We did use plain clothes officers after the demonstration because we didn't know whether they were going to picket the employees going out as well as going in, and we didn't know whether to keep our main body of men on duty or not, so we did have some officers in plain clothes who mixed with the strikers after the demonstration to ascertain whether they were going to picket the exit of the power station. They chose not to and we learned that and we were able to dismiss our men as it were. (Superintendent)

Sometimes plainclothes officers are used to identify who is in charge of a group of flying pickets. One Chief Superintendent recalled how he had met with little success while engaged on just such a mission:

I've had this experience standing in shop doorways in the background watching. They come very well organized . . . I approached the – this is extremely confidential isn't it? – I approached the President of the National Union of . . . 'No, I'm not responsible'. I approached the Regional man, no, he wasn't responsible, and I didn't know these people from Adam. This is the first day, and I don't know Dick, Tom or Harry. I didn't know who was who, and I made numerous enquiries. The first man I went to said he thought I'd come for a different purpose, when I asked who he was and he said, 'Well, would you like to join the Socialist Workers Party?' and he gave me a red and white document and asked me to send £1 to a certain address in London! (Chief Superintendent)

There is some evidence to suggest that occasionally plainclothes officers take a more active role in picketing situations. For example, during the Grunwick dispute the *Socialist Worker* published pictures of two roughly dressed men, one of whom it was alleged had been accused by pickets of throwing bottles. On being challenged this man had punched a woman picket in the face and had run off down the road. Another picture showed the same man sitting in a police van happily chatting with several uniformed officers.[136] A similar accusation was made by Roy Grantham of APEX who told *The Guardian*:

Union officials had photographed four men, two of whom had hurled milk bottles at the coach bringing workers to the Grunwick plant in the morning. One of our officials, Mr John Wall, interviewed the people concerned. He elicited that they were not unionists. They claimed to be students but didn't appear to know which college they were at. Subsequently, one of them ran away and jumped into a police van – we don't think pickets would do that.[137]

Of course, one would hardly expect senior police officers to admit that this sort of thing went on, but a Superintendent did say that he would have plainclothes officers in a mass picket not only to collect intelligence but also to make arrests.[138] It is not beyond the bounds of possibility that officers deployed specifically to make arrests would on occasions deliberately provoke illegal behaviour in the manner suggested by some of the above reports.

Perhaps the most controversial method of collecting intelligence involves tapping telephones at union offices and strike headquarters. In a well-documented article published in *New Statesman* Duncan Campbell not only pointed out that a tapping centre in London had the capacity to tap 1,000 lines simultaneously but also that 'union leaders and others involved in major industrial disputes are frequently, even routinely, tapped'.[139] In particular, Campbell noted that not only were the telephones of the Grunwick Strike Committee tapped, but also that Special Branch officers used long-range microphones to monitor conversations through windows.[140]

Not surprisingly, most of the senior police officers interviewed tended to deny that much telephone tapping went on during industrial disputes. As one Superintendent put it:

Absolutely not. That's out of the question. You appreciate that we need a warrant signed personally by the Home Secretary whenever a 'phone is to be tapped, and it's for much more serious things than this type of thing.

It is interesting to note that the system of control outlined by this officer has itself been found by the European Court of Human Rights to be an inadequate safeguard.[141] Two senior police officers did imply that strikers' telephones were sometimes tapped. A Chief Superintendent requested the interviewer to turn off his recorder and said: 'We use all possible means to gather intelligence, I won't say anything else; we gather intelligence in every way possible.'[142] Another officer cryptically commented: 'I think telephone tapping is a lot wider than people believe it to be.'[143] Moreover, several officers pointed out that information was passed to them by Special Branch and they did not know how it was obtained.[144]

All but three of the union officials interviewed thought that their telephones were tapped. In most cases their suspicions were based on 'funny noises' and 'clicks on the line' which, of course, hardly constitute convincing evidence. However, in one or two cases there were more concrete reasons for their fears. One NUM Branch Secretary was told that his telephone had been tapped by a friend who happened to be a Post Office engineer who worked at the local exchange.[145] But perhaps the most telling evidence was provided by the ISTC South Yorkshire Strike Committee who, in order to test whether their telephones were tapped, arranged a fictitious picket at a certain location. Within four minutes of the call pickets observed a police car and two vans full of policemen arrive at the address of the false disturbance, Granelli's Ice Cream factory.[146]

A similar event occurred during the 1972 miners' strike when a telephone request for pickets to go to a certain location was made to the Barnsley offices of the NUM. Within a few minutes police had arrived at the scene of the alleged picket – a turnip field.[147] It seems that either a sudden enthusiasm for vegetable gardening simultaneously swept over several officers of the West Yorkshire Police or the NUM telephones were being tapped.

Once the police have obtained accurate information about the number of people likely to attend a mass picket they can then decide how many men to deploy and whether assistance will be required from other forces.

The problem of having sufficient manpower at hand to deal with industrial disorder has been solved in different ways in different historical periods. As we have seen in the late nineteenth and early twentieth centuries the army was often used to confront strikers when the police response proved inadequate. During the inter-war years reliance was placed on various volunteer forces such as the Special Constabulary to fulfil this important support function. But in the post-war period it has become politically more difficult to justify the intervention of military forces or middle-class volunteers in an industrial order-maintaining role. The police, as representatives of the law rather than as agents of a political élite, are now the only force that can maintain legitimacy in the industrial context. Of course the police have not always had the resources or administrative organisation to perform this order-maintaining function. For example, it seems clear that had there been large-scale industrial disorder in the 1950s or 1960s the police would simply have been unable to cope. One Superintendent recalled that at that time 'the thin blue line was a bloody thin blue line'[148] and if widespread disorder had occurred the force would have been stretched 'beyond breaking point'.[149]

Although the manpower problem was eased by the creation of traffic wardens and the greater use of civilian staff it nevertheless became acute during the miners' strike of 1972. Indeed, following the evident inability of the police at Saltley to prevent large numbers of pickets from effectively closing the coke depot it was decided to review the mutual aid system whereby one police force can be reinforced by officers from another area.

Since 1880 police authorities and later Chief Constables have had the power, in certain circumstances, to reinforce their police with members of other forces. Originally mutual aid agreements were voluntary and relatively few forces entered into them but in 1925 they were made compulsory in the face of the impending General Strike.[150] A further refinement of the system was put into effect after the Second World War when it was decided that Police Support Units (PSUs) should be formed to provide mobile squads of men for civil defence purposes.[151] Following the defeat for law and order at Saltley the function of the PSU system has changed from wartime civil defence to peacetime public order and it has become the basis of the mutual aid system.

Each PSU unit consists of 34 officers; an inspector, three sergeants and 30 constables who train together about once a month for public order operations. The rest of the time they spend carrying out normal policing duties and it is in this respect that they differ from Special Patrol Groups (SPG) who constitute a permanent mobile reserve. Following their successful use at Neap House Wharf in 1972 it was suggested that all PSU members should be volunteers, physically fit and under 35 years old. [152] It is thought that most police forces have implemented these proposals so now trained, fit reinforcements can be rapidly deployed to combat mass picketing.

As a picketing situation escalates so the police can respond by increasing their manpower. Initially officers from different divisions within the same force would reinforce the division in which the dispute occurred, secondly the permanent mobile reserve (i.e. the SPG) would be deployed and finally, if necessary, PSUs from neighbouring forces would be requisitioned. This system has enabled the police to deploy far more men in picketing situations than was previously possible and many forces have a policy of matching pickets man for man.

Police tactics

As a preventive measure the police often make contact with both employers and union leaders at the beginning of a strike. For example, James Brownlow, the Chief Constable of South Yorkshire, did precisely this during the national steel strike:

Before the national strike began, my Assistant Chief Constable (Operations) spoke to employers and trade union leaders alike and the dialogue was extended as more firms and other sections of the unions became involved. The law on picketing and public order was explained along with the duties and responsibilities of the police – and also how we intended to approach our task. During the ensuing weeks the establishing of these contacts proved invaluable and it is an interesting fact that when these contacts were maintained on a daily basis, no trouble ensued but when the strike leaders became unavailable, trouble followed. [153]

These contacts sometimes enable the police to reduce tension between employers and strikers and so decrease the likelihood of disorder occurring. Sometimes the police have been able to prevent an employer from taking action that would undoubtedly provoke the strikers. In one case a Chief Superintendent prevented a Managing Director from having the fenders of his delivery vans sharpened so that the strikers would 'cut their fingers off' if they attempted to lift the rear wheels off the ground. [154] The same rather reactionary employer hired security men with alsatian dogs only to be told by the police 'For God's sake, keep those bloody dogs out of sight or I'll do you for breach of the peace.' [155]

The police also try to prevent disorder by maintaining only a token presence on picket lines while at the same time making clear what the strikers can and cannot do. As a Chief Superintendent put it:

I would only have one policeman there. I would not have so many policemen there that I was threatening the pickets. I would make it very apparent that the pickets were the overpowering thing . . . and I would have talked to them, to tell them this,

'Because we've got a strike here, there will be a policeman.' There would be one small bobby, I wouldn't pick a big fellow, and he would be there and 'He will be the law and order here. What I want from you blokes is your co-operation, because I'm giving you mine. Christ, I'm giving you mine. I'll go out on a limb here with one bobby and you won't have any more than one bobby at all. But don't you let me down by doing the wrong thing. You can use all the verbal that you want on anybody that crosses through here but if you overstep the mark, then I shall get a call from my policeman that I don't want to get. But if I do get it, he shall be supported and you'll know it then.' I shall try to lean on them heavily to not cause me hassle. (Chief Superintendent)

Indeed, most officers said that these token police would be encouraged at briefing sessions to be friendly with the pickets and to try to establish a degree of rapport. According to a union official this approach was successfully tried in at least one area during the miners' strike:

I shall always remember Jack Wood who were Chairman of the Watch Committee. He said that when the Chief Constable, he had all the police out in the station yard and he marched them up and down in front of them and he said, 'Look chaps, you're going to deal with men, you're not going to deal with students, you're going to deal with men who have nothing in their pockets, half of your fathers work in the industry and you know how they feel. I want you to humour them rather than aggravate them.' And we found that in '72 picketing at my own colliery, we had a marvellous relationship with the police. I even sent him a letter after 1972 thanking him for all they'd done. Because make no bones about it, tempers did get frayed on all sides, especially early in the morning, but they were marvellous. They'd rather come and give you a good ticking off rather than – they could have thrown me into black maria. (NUM Branch Secretary)

It seems possible then that the friendly relations that, as we have seen, generally exist on small picket lines are to a certain extent consciously created by the police. In a sense this deliberate fraternisation constitutes a subtle form of social control, as another union official was well aware:

When people are, like you said, sharing soup and sharing a fire and all this, we found when we came back in this area we went rough and the first thing we did were to put all the fires out, because people would stop picketing. There were a game of football or a game of cricket and traffic were moving freely, so you can understand why there were a fair relationship. As soon as we went and kicked fire out and told police 'If you don't mind please' and started stopping the vehicles again, then everybody said, 'Well it's marvellous, I've been coming through for last week' and we said, 'Well, we'd prefer it if you didn't go through today' and then the atmosphere changed. I think atmosphere, with its friendliness, was the fact that the pickets were being ineffective anyhow. (ISTC official)

So far we have noted several tactics that the police use to prevent disorder – liaison, token policing, verbal warnings, the establishment of rapport – but it is now necessary to consider what happens when obstruction or violence occurs. In a normal picketing situation involving a dozen or so people the initial police response is to arrest as many strikers as is necessary to restore order. As one Chief Superintendent made clear, the person in charge of the picketing is likely to be among those arrested:

The next step is to arrest, isn't it? The next step is that I would stand a fair bit of truck, I would stand it more than I ought to stand it [. . .] I am trying hard not to make arrests, I am trying hard to reason, I am trying – it goes back to the general philosophy – I am trying to get both sides of the dispute to act reasonably with good intelligence so I would be trying as hard as hell not to arrest. But if they keep on pushing me, that is the situation that I won't back off from, I will make arrests. The first man I will arrest, of course, is the man in charge because he's the man that's causing it. I will lock him up right away. And I would tell him that I am locking him up because he is causing the problem. 'Would someone else like to take charge and command this so that you are within the law?' and see what happens then. I should probably also get on to the union organizer and get all the power out there to make them come within the law. But so it goes on, I shall just arrest and arrest. (Chief Superintendent)

Of course, this policy of making arrests works very well in a normal picketing situation involving relatively small numbers where the entire picket line can be removed if necessary. However, in a mass picketing situation other tactics are required and it is to a consideration of these that we now turn.

Intelligence usually provides at least several hours', sometimes several days', warning of a mass picket and this time will be used to prepare the police response. Senior officers will visit the site of the proposed mass picket to make various assessments. According to a paper presented to officers attending a special two-week course entitled 'Public Order – The Industrial Perspective' at Bramshill Police Staff College, visiting officers will:

Reconnoitre scene to see:
(a) What points will need protection.
(b) Problems of getting workforce in and out.
(c) How much room can pickets be allowed to move around in. Obviously the more they can be spread out the better.
(d) Are there any objects at the scene which should be removed, e.g. piles of bricks, rubble, etc.
(e) Is there a high vantage point for observation by the police and for police CCTV [Close Circuit Television].[156]

An example of the type of action that might follow from such a site visit was provided by one Inspector:

There were precautions that we took that day . . . when we visited the site before the main day, there was a shingle path at the main gate, pebbles, and we pointed this out to the management, pointed out the dangers, and they came out and concreted those paths to remove that danger before the day. Because we foresaw that could be used for throwing at people. (Inspector)

So the physical layout of the probable area of confrontation will be assessed and possibly modified in order to assist the police operation. The next step recommended by lecturers on the Bramshill course is to:

Contact Management to ascertain:
(a) Whether normal working is to be maintained.
(b) Whether it is intended that deliveries and collections should be made.
(c) What is the attitude of the workforce to the dispute.
(d) Will there be any advantage in providing buses for employees temporarily.
(e) Identification marks for employees' vehicles.[157]

It seems, then, that in addition to physical layout, methods of entry into a factory and even working arrangements themselves may be modified or suspended. Several officers were able to provide examples of these tactical changes. One Chief Superintendent recalled how, during a strike by journalists, he had altered the way in which the local paper had been distributed:

On this occasion I had regular meetings with one person who was the Circulation Director, who was responsible for getting the paper away, and he and I and my Deputy, we formulated plans weekly, depending on what was going to happen, and instead of the . . . 'Evening Post' say, being circulated from this office block here which is just round the corner, we had perhaps half a dozen very large vehicles going to various points on the perimeter of the City, and the small vehicles distributed them from there. This is just one of the things we did. We used various entrances and various methods. (Chief Superintendent)

Perhaps the most frequent measure that senior officers mentioned was the provision of buses to transport workers through the picket line.[158] It is obviously easier from the policing point of view to shepherd one large vehicle through than a multitude of individual cars, motor-cycles, push-bikes and pedestrians.

Other logistical preparations were outlined on the Bramshill course:

Warn surrounding forces that assistance may be required. Select sites for Main and Forward Controls. Contact Operations Department to arrange communications and supply staff.
Designate:
(a) Staff Officer
(b) Officer i/c [in command] Main Control
(c) Complaints Officer (at main 'charging' station)
(d) Admin. Officer and Staff
(e) Inspector to log incident
(f) Press Liaison Officer and photographer
(g) Federation representative
On information available decide:
(i) How many officers will be required
(ii) Prepare plan of action either:
    (a) to be dealt with as a single incident, or,
    (b) to be divided into separate sectors
    (c) appoint as appropriate either *Unit* or *Sector* Commanders and deputies
Procure accommodation for rest, recreation and refreshment. Consider tea bar close to scene. Order transport – with hired transport remember drivers' hours of work and possibility of Union interference with drivers. [. . .]
Do not use facilities which may be offered by firm involved in dispute.

(i)   Arrange for charging and documentation of prisoners – preferably at a station at least five miles from scene. If many prisoners are expected warn stations that they may be used as 'back-ups'.

(ii) Request Training Department to provide staff for charging rooms and prepare likely charges.

(iii) Arrange use of several prisoner vans. Polaroid cameras to be used for photographing arresting officer and prisoner.

Arrange for 'T' Division to police routes and approaches to scene. To direct pickets and transport to agreed parking places.

Confer with senior staff and ensure plan is agreed and fully understood.

Preferably 24 hours before start – brief all sector commanders, and show them scene – if possible all inspectors and sergeants also.

Keep briefing short and to the point, e.g. information – intention – method.

Emphasize need for all ranks to keep cool and not to be provoked.

Dress – standard dress must be emphasized in teleprinter messages and operation orders.[159]

On the day of the mass picket the police will try to establish a presence before the strikers arrive in strength so that advantage can be taken of the local geography. In particular, senior officers will be anxious to avoid the kind of situation that developed at Saltley where the police cordons were positioned at the bottom of a slope and so had to resist pressure from superior numbers by pushing uphill.[160] Once the police have taken up their positions arriving pickets will be directed to certain areas (e.g. the pavements) but denied access to others (e.g. the road in front of the factory gates). Cordons will be established to ensure that the pickets stay in the allocated areas but usually a few union officials will be allowed to stand in front of the police lines to exercise their right of peaceful persuasion. In such situations relations between the police and the pickets are generally quite good despite the pushing and shoving that tends to occur when a bus passes through the picket. Indeed, the police are briefed to establish rapport with the strikers in mass confrontation as well as during normal picketing.

this was included in the briefing at the Isle of Grain, 'Try to get along with the pickets and demonstrators who are there. Talk to them, have a joke with them, pass the time of day with them.' And in fact they did that . . . It even reached the stage, after the initial stoning and throwing of placards at the first bus that went through, whereby the officer in charge of a section of the line would say to the officers and the pickets, 'Right, here comes the next bus. Everybody get ready' and the policemen and pickets would put their shoulders against each other and he'd say, 'Right, heave!' and then the policemen and the pickets would heave against each other. And it was as good humoured and as good natured as that. (Superintendent)

As we have seen in normal picketing situations the establishment of rapport between police and pickets functions as a form of control in so far as the pickets become distracted from their main task. However, in the mass picketing situation rapport functions not so much to prevent picketing but to ease tensions and reduce the probability of violence. Foreign police forces have for several years consciously employed wit and humour in crowd control situations. For example, the West German police deliberately tried to lighten the atmosphere during a student protest against American involvement in Vietnam by booming from a loudspeaker attached to a water-cannon: 'Ladies and gentlemen, please move on or be prepared to get your bathrobes and towels ready; we are now going to have to stage some unusual acquatics.'[161] The crowd laughed, some people cheered and confrontation was avoided. In the USA psychological research on the possible use of humour as a police tactic in mass confrontations concluded that 'wit and humour is not a panacea for crowd control, but it is a new and possibly effective means of preventing or regulating disorder'.[162] There does not seem to have been any British research on the use of humour as a police tactic nor is there any evidence of the kind of conscious policy adopted by the West German police. Nevertheless, as we have noted, friendly behaviour is often encouraged at briefing sessons and individual officers sometimes consciously employ humour as a preventive tactic; an Inspector described how he 'defused' a 'nasty situation' by blowing his whistle and announcing that he had lost his biro; both police and pickets disengaged and spent several minutes looking for his pen on the ground.

Of course, when workers or lorries of coal attempt to enter the premises being picketed the strikers often attempt to push their way through the police cordons. Indeed, there have been occasions when pickets have managed to block the road in front of a colliery or factory entrance by breaking through the cordon or by occupying the ground before the police established control of the situation. At this stage in the confrontation the joking stops and more physical tactics are employed.

The first step, frequently advocated by officers, simply consists of trying to persuade the strikers to move off the road. This request may be underlined by a 'show of force' intended to convince the crowd of the futility of resistance. A Chief Superintendent explained how he cleared the road at a strike-bound factory by smartly marching up several Police Support Units (a PSU consists of 30 constables, three sergeants and an inspector who are younger, fitter and better trained than the average constable). The sudden arrival of so many extra police marching with military precision so overawed the pickets that they obediently moved out of the way.[163]

If the verbal warning and show of force fails to persuade the strikers to comply with police requests then a 'wedge' may be used to split the crowd and clear the road. The wedge is a formation of constables shaped like an arrow-head pointed at the crowd. It is an offensive tactic used to push its way into the strikers and split them into two groups; any number of men can be used, the bigger the wedge the more power it has. Once the pickets have been divided in this way cordons can be established to hold them back. There are basically four types of cordon: the open, the butcher's grip, the single belt and the double belt. The open cordon simply involves men standing close to but not touching each other and can be quickly transformed into the butcher's grip which is where the officers link arms at the elbow, clasping hands at chest height. The single belt involves each constable holding with his left hand the belt of the man in front, while the double belt is formed by each officer holding with both hands the belt of the second man on his left. The butcher's grip is the cordon which seems to be most often used in picketing situations.

The use of formations such as the wedge and the cordon have several advantages. First, they are effective in splitting or containing crowds. Second, they are relatively non-violent in that each officer has a specific job to do and is therefore controlled and occupied during offensive manoeuvres. Also both the wedge and the cordon depend upon officers maintaining linked arms so depriving them of the opportunity to lash out with fists or truncheon. Thirdly, these formations are not only relatively non-violent but can also readily be seen to be non-violent. It is difficult to convincingly portray a cordon of linked-armed police, possibly positioned with their backs to the pickets, as brutal agents of the repressive capitalist state. Finally, the rapid and disciplined adoption of an offensive formation such as the wedge constitutes in itself another show of force which may intimidate the crowd into retreating without resistance. As a Chief Inspector pointed out the mere sight of the wedge can cause a rapid 'loss of bottle'.

Several officers indicated that 'snatch squads' would be used to support the cordons and the wedge. Observers would be placed at vantage points to look, not only for those who are particularly aggressive, but also those who are known as 'rent-a-pickets'. The snatch squads would then be ordered to arrest these people and quickly extract them from the crowd: 'If you've got a good squad, say of three men, and one goes to one side and one goes to the other and one's behind him and takes him through the legs and grabs his balls, you've got him out before he knows it.'[164] One Commandant of a police training college said that he would have his snatch squad mingling with the pickets in plain clothes, but other officers disagreed with this approach. It was argued that plainclothes men would not have the same deterrent effect as a snatch squad of ten or so uniformed men positioned behind the pickets. Moreover, it was thought that the use of plainclothes men would be damaging in public relations terms: 'The media would make a meal of it.'[165] Finally, some officers considered it far too dangerous to use plainclothes men in this way since they would be exposed to 'grave risk of attack from angry pickets'.[166]

Tactics such as cordons, wedges and snatch squads are probably very effective as long as the police do not become grossly outnumbered (most officers advocated matching the pickets man for man) or the violence does not escalate beyond the usual pushing and shoving. If the situation deteriorates in either of these ways then 'we get tempted to try something a bit more military'.[167] A Chief Superintendent candidly noted that it 'all depends on the firmness of the government of the day' and that 'we can all feel the water'[168] and, presumably, under Mrs Thatcher the water is more conducive to floating the military option than under previous regimes. The actual tactics considered were riot shields, water-cannon (generally regarded as rather ineffective), rubber bullets, CS gas and deploying the military itself. Interestingly, one officer thought that the police would use rubber bullets and CS gas in a riot situation as a 'last ditch effort', but not in an industrial situation where 'the military would be given the problem'.[169] However, it should be emphasised that most officers strongly maintained that there would never be any need to resort to these more extreme measures as sufficient manpower using the wedge and if necessary riot shields should be able to cope with any industrial confrontation.

Although the police tactics outlined above seem to be relatively non-violent, especially compared with the baton-charges of earlier times, instances of brutality sometimes occur and it is to a consideration of these that we now turn.

Police brutality

Police violence during normal picketing is extremely rare. Indeed, only one of the 50 union officials interviewed could recall an example of aggressive police behaviour during small-scale local picketing:

our men stuck to the letter, slagged them, kept their hands off them but in one or two incidents, and I regret it myself, they started spitting on them. That's not my cup of tea and I took one or two of them up. I said, 'Look, that sort of thing hasn't got to happen, we've got to work with these fellows. These sort of things leave a nasty taste' etc. The day afterwards, the same thing happened. I went up to talk to their Branch Secretary, who was a personal friend of mine, in fact, and spelt out the same sort of thing, why we were there, what we were trying to achieve, it were in their interests etc. for the fast conclusion of the dispute and whilst I was talking to the Branch Secretary, and his members were behind him, this copper who was stood about just to keep law and order, there were one or two Superintendents, I don't know the rank, he just said something to the effect of 'Oh, bugger this carry on, come on through if you want to come through', and one of the lads, one of my Committee men who was stood at the side of me, he got hold of him and he just threw him to one side and he finished up on the deck. The lad reacted immediately, he got up and was going to go for the copper. Of course, I got hold of our lad to try to stop him doing so, but as he was going back towards the copper, the copper attacked him, and got hold of him and threw him down again. Then things got a bit out of hand. None of our men started any violence or anything like this, and the police got that man away and took him to the back of their cab [. . .]

I then went to see their governor and he were never seen again on the lines. They withdrew him, and he were never seen again on the lines. (NUM Branch Secretary)

However, in mass picketing situations police misconduct, although generally limited to back-heeling and elbowing, seems to have been far more widespread. Almost all the union officials interviewed said they had experienced this sort of behaviour during large-scale picketing. The following description of events outside the Grunwick factory is fairly typical in this respect:

The only time I could say I saw real physical violence was on the actual push back by the police when they kicked, they ripped my coat off me back. They didn't hold back then, they really pushed forward, they kicked out, back-heeled with them boots they have on, so that the point of the heel stuck into your leg, stamped on to your toes. (Grunwick picket)

Of course, formations such as the cordon and the wedge rely for success on the police maintaining linked arms and this tends to limit violence to pushing and back-heeling. On those rare occasions when police cordons broke under pressure punching as well as kicking seems to have taken place. This happened on at least one occasion during the Grunwick dispute:

the bus was due to come with the Grunwick workers, when all of a sudden everybody pushed forward, pushed forward, and then the riots started then [. . .] We were too strong for the first line of police so we pushed them forward easily and this is when they broke, the police broke then. And that's when they turned round and started hitting out and kicking at people. Oh, yes, fists, kicking, particularly kicking. If you thump somebody in face you've got all the evidence, but if you kick 'em on leg you can always say it was during the actual pushing forward that this happened. After a while they forced us back because replacements came out of the tunnel and forced us back, and the police who were there at first weren't so bad; they were quite friendly, when we were talking to them, but the second line of police were the Specials, and they really went to town then. (Grunwick picket)

Although, as we have seen, violence is generally limited to pushing and kicking some allegations of more serious police misconduct were made. For example, a NUM picket recalled an incident which occurred during the 1972 miners' strike outside Ipswich Docks:

I saw, there was a tanker coming out of big main gates, students were there and they were trying to hold this lorry back 'cos she were a blacked lorry coming out, and the students were gathering round and I saw one of the constables get hold of a young girl, she were no more than 17 years of age and drag her, her head hit floor, and they sent boot into her on floor. I complained at the time to the Chief Constable at Ipswich over it. We never heard no more about it but it were the day after when we had that meeting [i.e. with the police] things had been quietened off and I think that must have had something to do with it, because I took the constable's number at the time. (NUM picket)

Another NUM official witnessed this kind of police behaviour in Nottinghamshire:

I walked round the lorry, and as I walked round the lorry the police, there was this chap on his own, and they'd got him down on the floor and they really gave him some boot.

He walked away from the crowd and he was set on by the police. Now I don't know if he'd said something or what, but he wasn't a miner, he was a bloody butcher. He was actually nothing to do with us, he just happened to be in that street and most likely went to see what had happened, but they stamped on his hand. Would you believe it? Can't believe it, I can't. Things that they did. That was my first time I'd ever seen the police being forceful in a strike. (NUM Branch Secretary)

Similar accounts were provided of incidents during the picketing at Grunwick:

I can recall where pickets were on their way . . . towards the back of the bus, and I remember in particular one incident where they shouted, 'Roger, catch this chap' and there were at that time policemen running after a picket down the road; he were brought down in a rugby charge. Now, I don't know what had brought that scene about but certainly there were a concentration of a good number of policemen on this chap and once they'd brought him down then he stood a good deal of hammer because there were a number of policemen all around him and then he finished up being dragged up and down by his cardigan over his head. (NUM official)

Police brutality also seems to have occurred during the 1980 steel strike. One particularly vicious assault is alleged to have taken place on 7 February outside the Pressed Steel Fisher factory in Birmingham:

It were raining hard that night. One or two lorries had gone in and I think one of the lads, I don't know who it were, threw a brick. Well, then the SPG moved in, they got Kevin and dragged him into the gatehouse and beat him up – there were about eight of them, he didn't resist at all, he'd got no chance. We could just make out in the dark and rain through the windows bodies and shadows moving about. Well, when they'd finished with him they threw him out face down in a puddle. They became a bit worried then in case they'd fucking killed him and they took him to hospital; they were animals, animals. I saw the senior officer, him with the gold braid, an Inspector or whatever he was, and I was crying by this time, tears were streaming down my face and I said, 'Look you've won, you've bloody won, we don't want any more trouble. Feelings are running high, just tell me how many pickets you want and I'll try to get the others to go home.' He looked at me like I were shit and said, 'You fucking bastard. Fuck off before you get some too.' (ISTC official)

Several violent incidents were also reported during the mass picketing at Shearness:

There were a particular time when we had been marching round in front of Shearness. Police had thrown a cordon across road and we went to go through. One of them grabbed me. There were a large wall, I can't remember the names of the streets, a high wall, they got me up against that, about five of them, and kicked bloody hell out of me. It ended up me put in handcuffs but they kicked, just generally kicked. (ISTC official)

Another account was provided of similar aggressive police behaviour at Shearness:

A kid got his leg broke pushed against a fence. It hurt real bad, they'd shoved him against a wall. Another case where they got a kid and squashed his face against a wall. They took him up a side street where no one could see them. They dragged him by his legs face down so his face rubbed along the ground. I saw them pull someone else to the ground and kick him in the head and left him. (ISTC official)

Of course, brutal behaviour was not the sole prerogative of the police, as some union officials were prepared to admit. Indeed, one ISTC official was surprised how restrained the police were in response to his own violent behaviour:

I was arrested at Hadfields. I knocked this fucking copper down and the only thing they did to me were kept me handcuffed longer than rest. I were expecting getting bloody cracked when I got in cells at police station, but other than keeping me handcuffed longer than anybody else there were nobody came near me whatever. If I'd been out of area I reckon I'd have got bloody hammered. (ISTC official)

It seems, then, that a certain amount of kicking at shin level is fairly common in mass picketing situations and that both police and pickets engage in this sort of behaviour. However, in relatively rare instances the police, usually in secluded spots – up side streets, behind lorries, in gatehouses – have administered some brutal beatings. Perhaps the most serious police mis-behaviour has occurred away from the publicity of the picket line and in the relative privacy of the police station. For example, we have already noted that three of the strikers arrested during the Roberts–Arundel dispute were beaten up at Stockport police station (see p. 69).

A similar but less serious incident occurred, on at least one occasion, during the 1972 miners' strike:

I was at the back of the police who had all locked arms, and I said to two policemen, 'Would you let me through please, I want to go onto the road', so they let me through but as I went through I got a kick off one and a back elbow off the other as I went through. I turned round and said to the officer who had given me the elbow and I said, 'Now you know there's no need to do that' and as I said that a police Chief Inspector who stood by, they'd got a van taking cine film and everything by this time, and I said to him 'There was no need for you to do that', the Chief Inspector shouted, 'Arrest that man', and I were bloody buried with policemen. I could see blue sergeants and silver buttons and that's all I could see [. . .] Anyway they got me in the police mobile cell and off we went [. . .] And eventually we ended up at . . . police station and they filtered everybody through and took all the details, you know the personal details, name, address and all the rest of it, and I was the last to be dealt with [. . .] But anyway they got me in the cell, they took all my possessions off me and then eventually took me up to be finger-printed and photographed. Now I refused and they beat me up [. . .] I refused and the chap that was going to take my fingerprints, I said, 'What are you doing?' because he'd got hold of my hand. He said, 'We're taking your fingerprints.' I said, 'You're not taking my fingerprints unless you get a warrant from a magistrate.' So he said, 'You'd be better off if you give your fingerprints.' So I said, 'I'm not giving my fingerprints, so that's the end of that.' And with the hand he was holding he hurled me across the room, there's no other word for it, he hurled me across the room, and as I hit the wall on the other side of the room, he walked across the room and barged me into the wall. [. . .] He was abusive, he f'd and blinded at me and he said I would be locked up until the court sat, for a week. I wouldn't be allowed any visitors, and I would be better off – so I insisted that I wouldn't give my fingerprints. They got another policeman in and he was to take me down to the cell. When they took me down to the cell one of them gave me a kidney punch. He hit me in the back, just a straightforward punch, and I ended up in the cell. I seemed to be there for quite some time. (NUM Branch Secretary)

As one might expect most senior police officers were somewhat reluctant to admit that their men ever engaged in brutal behaviour towards pickets or prisoners. However, some officers recognised that there is a very real danger of this sort of thing happening during an industrial confrontation. One Chief Superintendent put it like this:

I would be foolish if I thought they were all angels. Policemen, you cannot do a policeman's job and remain an angel. If you do a policeman's job you are bound to know all the dirty tricks in the trade. All you can say really is that when a bloke's been throwing iron bars at the police or whatever he's liable to cop it when they get them. It's not good that that happens, but you've got to be realistic. You don't want me to sit here and say a lot of rubbish. (Chief Superintendent)

Senior officers who were aware of the likelihood of police overreaction stressed the various measures taken to prevent its occurrence. One Superintendent indicated that briefing sessions could be used for this purpose:

The frustration applies to bobbies as much as it does to the people, and the maintenance of morale, good spirits, is a problem . . . It's something you have to be consciously aware of, because a lot of the officers in disputes work a lot of long hours, away from their families, away from their homes. The steel strike lasted some four months. Officers were deployed on some 12 and 15 hours a day for four months. And they must become frustrated. So it is a problem that you've got to be aware of, that, aware of the possibility of them losing their temper, as much as anybody else, because they're frustrated. So the only way out of that is briefing [. . .] I think you would be briefing officers to the, you would be re-emphasizing what they already know, i.e. the thing's gone on for a long time, now. We appreciate that they are in a situation where frustrations may come but they must remember their role as officers of the law, serving the law, dealing with the law as it arises, and to guard against the dangers of becoming over-frustrated. You've got to identify that that is a possibility, and I think that is the only way you can tackle it. (Superintendent)

A Chief Superintendent, who was also the Commandant of a police training college, emphasised that the training given to both junior and senior officers was intended to reduce the possibility of overreaction:

Ideally the police should react with the amount of physical force that is necessary to achieve the object that they're seeking to achieve. That is a typical lawyer's answer. The truth, of course, is this. Is that when you put an 18½-year-old behind a shield and you throw pieces of rock at him and iron bars at him, that can make him very angry and is likely to make him very angry. Now when he gets out and he has to be physical when you get into the situation where you're going to punch somebody you don't half do it, you really do it, and therefore the danger of overreacting in a public order situation when young police officers are involved, and they have to be young because they have to be fit enough to do it, the danger of the police violence escalating, or the police physical force escalating beyond that which is necessary is a very real danger. But, because it's a very real danger we spend considerable time here in trying to train people to understand that and therefore to be careful of doing just that . . .

Of course, the fact that officers are trained at police colleges to avoid overreaction in public order situations does not necessarily mean that they will put their training into practice in real confrontations. Indeed, one Superintendent suggested that senior officers turn a blind eye to kicking and elbowing by constables:

I'm sure it goes on, tempers get frayed or you have a mischievous policeman who wants a bit of action. So far as the senior officer knowing anything about it, I don't think they bother all that much because, it sounds awful, but if you've got a dog job to do, if you've got a dog, you've got to give it a lump of sugar now and again . . . It's a bit like Generals turning a blind eye to rape and pillaging in war time.

Summary

From the end of the Second World War until the 1970s there was, aside from the Roberts–Arundel strike in 1967, hardly any disorder associated with industrial disputes. This comparatively peaceful period is often contrasted with the following years of industrial and political violence, but as we have seen, the strikes of the 1970s were remarkable for their general lack of violence. It is true that strikers engaged in more illegal behaviour – obstructing the police and the highway, damaging lorries and even intimidating workers – than they had in the previous twenty-five years, but this was relatively non-violent crime. Moreover, in a longer historical perspective the mass pushing and shoving, which upsets many commentators, can be seen as a solution to the problem of making picketing effective without resorting to violence. One can be excused for thinking that many of the objections against alleged violent picketing are really objections against effective strike action itself.

The historical trend towards the centralisation of intelligence collection and contingency planning that we noted in the last chapter continued during the post-war period. Nevertheless, there have been new developments in the strategy and tactics of social control. At the strategic level we have seen the emergence of the police as the sole agency responsible for maintaining public order; the army and volunteer organisations are no longer considered appropriate in an industrial context. In order to fulfil this public order role the police have developed and refined a centrally co-ordinated mutual aid system comprised of PSUs that enables them to respond with sufficient manpower to any threat of industrial disorder. At the tactical level there has been a closure between the action of strikers and the reaction of police. Instead of basically non-violent strikers being confronted by police baton-charges, both sides tend to engage in limited action that typically takes the form of pushing and shoving.

This relatively orderly pattern of confrontation has been superseded, notably during the miners' strike of 1984–5, by a more violent style of industrial conflict. However, before we turn our attention to these developments, in Chapter 7, it is worth pausing to consider some of the factors which have brought about the transition from stoning and shooting at Featherstone to pushing and shoving at Saltley.

6

Victory without violence

What sort of factors lie behind the changes in the nature of industrial disorder which we have revealed in the preceding chapters? There seem to be at least three contributory historical developments: (1) Constitutionalisation, (2) The growth of the media, and (3) The democratisation of civil liberties.

1. Constitutionalisation

Strikers and government

The close association of the trade union movement with a political party committed to democratic reform rather than revolutionary change has had a restraining effect on the behaviour of strikers. As we shall see, union officials and strike leaders have been anxious to avoid violence during industrial disputes on the probably correct assumption that such action would have a detrimental effect on the Labour Party's political fortunes.

However, at the time of the Featherstone shootings in 1893 the miners' unions do not seem to have been sufficiently well organised at local level to adequately control the behaviour of their members (see Chapter 2). Moreover, the idea of separate working-class representation in Parliament was still very new; Keir Hardie's Independent Labour Party had only just been formed and the political implications of industrial disorder had not yet become apparent. In these circumstances, given the coal owners' policy of employing blackleg labour and the severe hardship suffered by strikers, it is hardly surprising that the violent behaviour we have characterised as 'stoning' occurred.

By the time of the South Wales coal strike in 1910 most union officials had become aware of the political need to avoid violence and consequently urged their followers to engage only in peaceful picketing.[1] Even C. B. Stanton, the miners' agent, who 'made his first violent marks in Labour politics by firing a revolver in a revolutionary demonstration'[2] repeatedly advocated non-violence.[3] Moreover, on several occasions union officials and strike committee members actually tried to restrain physically their men during violent clashes:

I was at the lower end of Tonypandy tonight at 7 o'clock . . . when a request came for the assistance of the Strike Committee and myself to quell the disturbance at the Glamorgan Collieries, and we at once proceeded to the scene, and I am glad to say that we eventually induced thousands of men to return quietly to their homes. In scores of incidences the men, if they returned home by the usual road, would have to pass the police, and we induced them, rather than to risk another conflict, to return home by circulous routes.

Thousands of men followed us . . . and at every point of vantage we stopped and held short meetings. When addressing the men we urged them, if they had any regard for us, as their leaders, and for their own cause and for the honour of labour, to leave the matter in the hands of their responsible leaders, and to refrain from all acts of violence.

I particularly emphasized the fact that in my opinion the attack on the power station in smashing the windows, and the looting of shops was calculated to do us infinite harm as a body of workmen; that it would alienate public sympathy, and retard settlement.[4]

Although such attempts by union officials to prevent violence were by no means entirely successful they do seem to have been sufficient to ensure that violent picketing rather than stoning occurred (see Chapter 3).

Political considerations in 1910 also constrained the behaviour of the authorities. We have already noted that Churchill's policy was to use troops only if the local police and the Metropolitan reinforcements were unable to control the situation. There seems little doubt that this course of action was to some degree determined by the composition of Parliament; the Liberals, in order to maintain a majority over the Conservatives, frequently had to rely on the support of Labour and Irish Nationalist Members of Parliament. Clearly, a more repressive policy could have seriously jeopardised the future of the Liberal Government. However, in addition to these immediate political considerations there were also good historical reasons for avoiding bloodshed.

In the past the use of lethal force against defenceless working people had been counterproductive in several ways. Opposition from a broad section of political opinion could be expected and this often proved extremely embarrassing for the Government. This occurred, as E. P. Thompson reveals in his book *The Making of the English Working Class*, after the Peterloo Massacre in 1819:

For a time, ultra-Radicals and moderates buried their differences in a protest movement with which many Whigs were willing to associate . . .

If Peterloo was intended to curb the right of public meeting it had exactly the opposite consequences. Indignation provoked Radical organization where it had never before existed, and open-air demonstrations were held in regions hitherto under the spell of the 'loyalists'.[5]

A similar reaction followed the Featherstone shootings in 1893; vigorous speeches condemning the action of the troops were made in Parliament and an effigy of the Home Secretary surmounted with a Death's head and cross bones was carried through Trafalgar Square.[6] Even thirteen years after the shootings, Asquith, who as we have seen played only a very minor role in the events at Featherstone, was still occasionally greeted by the chant:

> For he's the Featherstone murderer,
> For he's the Featherstone murderer,
> For he's the Featherstone murderer,
>   And so say all of us.[7]

But the use of bloody repression was equally as damaging to the *status quo* at a more reflective and philosophical level. If the Government was merely concerned with implementing the collective will of the people then why was it necessary to suppress violently those same people? In short, the rhetoric of the liberal democratic state was to some extent undermined by the actuality of physical coercion. A bare outline of this kind of argument can be discerned in an extract from a pamphlet published after the Featherstone shootings:

A cry of indignation arose from every lover of progress. The bloody spectre of military repression had again reared its head in our land. Visions of Peterloo swept before men's imaginations ... Progressive-minded men learned with amazement that under the 'most democratic Government of our times' the capitalist was permitted to goad the workers to the point of desperation, and that when the latter broke forth into manifestations of revolt, they were to be shot down like dogs.[8]

Churchill was well aware of this kind of reaction to past repression and was no doubt anxious to avoid its recurrence in relation to Tonypandy. It seems then that a conjunction of immediate and long-term political considerations caused him to send Metropolitan police to the strike area in an attempt to avoid bloodshed and consequent adverse public reaction.

However, by this time a well-organised Labour movement was ready to gain political advantage by publicising and exaggerating any seemingly coercive action of the state. It is not, therefore, surprising that in socialist mythology Churchill became personified as the heartless agent of capitalism who sent troops to shoot the miners at Tonypandy.[9] Some forty years after the event, during the general election campaign of 1950, Churchill was still trying to clear his name in this respect. Speaking in Cardiff on 8 February he addressed himself to the 'cruel lie' spread by 'socialists and communists' that he had 'used troops to shoot down the Welsh miners'.[10] But Tonypandy proved itself to be still something of a political hot potato. Within twenty-four hours a Labour Minister, Ness Edwards, accused Churchill of having a 'convenient memory' and quoted various 1910 newspaper reports which he said proved that military forces had been used against the miners (Churchill had rather underplayed the role of the military in his outline of 'the true story of

Tonypandy').[11] The national press took up the issue and once again the name of Tonypandy made headlines. Churchill accused Edwards of: 'a desire to spread an untruthful impression among the South Wales miners'.[12] Edwards replied that: 'The masquerade of truth which is being indulged in by Mr Churchill about his action in sending the troops against the Welsh miners is deplorable in a statesman of his eminence.'[13] At this point in the debate the President of the NUM, Sir William Lawther, publicly stated that Churchill had been just as much the enemy of the miners in 1910 as he was in 1950.[14] The political flak continued to fly for some time and it seems that the intrusion of Tonypandy into the election campaign did Churchill some real harm.[15]

These political limitations on the use of physical force continued and indeed intensified during the inter-war years. It is no coincidence that the emergence of the Labour Party as a major political power occurred more or less at the same time as the decline of serious industrial disorder. In particular the Trades Union Congress (TUC) made strenuous efforts to avoid violence during the General Strike of 1926. For example, the following extract taken from the TUC Strike Order clearly reveals the importance placed on maintaining orderly behaviour:

they the Trades Councils and union officers shall be charged with the responsibility of organizing the Trade Unionists in dispute in the most effective manner for the preservation of peace and order . . .
A strong warning must be issued to all localities that any person found inciting the workers to attack property or inciting the workers to riot must be dealt with immediately. It should be pointed out that the opponents will in all probability employ persons to act as spies and others to use violent language in order to incite the workers to disorder.[16]

Repeated messages to the strikers urging orderly behaviour were made throughout the stoppage via newspapers, posters and pamphlets.[17] In some places stewards were appointed to keep order at meetings and during picketing while in other areas strikers were urged to stay at home and 'look after the wife and kiddies'.[18] The General Council of the TUC directed that in all districts where large numbers of workers were idle, sports and other entertainments should be arranged to keep people busy.[19] The famous football match between police and strikers at Plymouth was, it seems, not so much an illustration of police tact and diplomacy as an example of the TUC's order-maintaining arrangements.[20] In any case, one can hardly accuse the Plymouth police of tact on this occasion as scuffles broke out after the match when a striker's house was searched.[21]

As we have already seen (in Chapter 4) the various measures taken by the TUC to prevent disorder were generally very effective. Of course, these steps were taken not only to maintain the Labour Party's democratic image but also to deny the authorities any excuse for engaging in systematic repression. It may be that the TUC leadership realised that the political constraints on the Government had been seriously weakened by the atmosphere of panic which functioned to legitimise and encourage repression (see pp. 61–6). In these circumstances the prevention of violence became one of the TUC's major objectives for both political and humanitarian reasons.

The failure of the General Strike discredited the idea of direct action capable of achieving revolutionary change and henceforth the Labour movement concentrated on parliamentary politics in order to improve the lot of working people. This rejection of the revolutionary road to change has of course increased yet further the importance of maintaining public opinion during industrial disputes. The problem facing trade unionists today is not so much how to picket effectively a colliery or factory but how to do so without alienating a broad section of public opinion. As we have seen the optimum solution to this problem seems to be to restrict violence to mere pushing and shoving. All the 50 union officials interviewed thought that the Labour Party could be damaged by any greater use of violence during an industrial dispute. Moreover, the respondents had strong links with the Labour Party; they were all paid-up members, two were councillors, one was the election agent for the sitting MP and another was the brother of an MP. Obviously this close identification with the Labour Party would make these people highly sensitive to the political implications of industrial disorder.

Indeed, union officials pointed out that public opinion was important for a variety of reasons. One official stressed that peaceful behaviour could win public approval which would in turn strengthen the union's bargaining position: 'If you can set that negotiating position up and convince as many people that what you're doing is reasonably right, then general public can play a very great part in what you're doing' (NUM official). A Branch Secretary emphasised that the wives and families of strikers were an important section of the public that could be alienated by violence on the picket line:

if you keep violence down to a minimum on the line, the picket line, as I did as a steward, you didn't give the newspapers any chance to say anything provocative about the strikers and what actually happens is that if they do get something provocative and something bad to write about the strike it has an effect on the families when they get home. The wives and people like that will get on to the strikers to come away from that picket line or to resolve it or to get back into work. Whereas if you give them no reason to say anything – by behaving non-violently – and you can get the paper to highlight the trouble, what's happening inside the factory or the reasons why you're actually out on strike you stand more of a chance at winning the points of view [. . .] The families are the ones that suffer when people are out on strike, like the wives. They stop you all sorts of security, if you're a striker you get no social security, just the wife and kids. You don't get your strike pay from the union until after the dispute is over, so you've nothing coming in bar that, so you've a lot of pressure from your family and it's a strong woman who can withstand that pressure when the money's running down. And if they see something in the papers like 'The violence on the line',

'These people are out for nothing but violence', 'Anarchy in the middle of the picket', and stuff like that it tends to weaken the position of the strike, from the family point of view. And the wife plays a hell of a lot, a big part in whether a strike is successful or whether it isn't. (Grunwick picket)

An ISTC official thought that an adverse public reaction would affect the enthusiasm of the pickets themselves:

Public opinion is very, very, very important indeed. Very important. It's my belief that the person who's assisting you in the picketing duty, he will gladly and freely assist in every way he can while he believes he's doing the right thing. But if public opinion is so pressurizing him into believing he's doing the wrong thing then you'll lose his support, so I think it's very very important to get public opinion behind you. (ISTC official)

One NUM Branch Secretary was sharply reminded that public opinion could be alienated by scenes of disorderly picketing some four years after the last miners' strike:

First instance when they put it [i.e. mass picketing] on television it's always pickets or anybody who's demonstrating who's at fault. It's always their fault, in my eyes. It's never the police, because them who's never had nowt to do with picketing or demonstrating the first thing they say is, 'Look at that fucking lot'. You go down south on holiday and you've only got to mention you're a miner and that were it. A woman brayed me, that were three years since, with her brolly in Newquay 'cos I'd switched her electric off and fought with police. I said, 'You silly old twat, my electric were off too.' She hit me on top of my head with her fucking brolly. I said 'I'll throw you in that harbour in a minute, you silly old twat.' (NUM Branch Secretary)

Public opinion, it seems, has become a vital concern of union officials for party political and various other reasons. All the respondents said that they had taken various steps to reduce the probability of violence exceeding passive obstruction during picketing. For example, there was widespread agreement about the desirability of keeping outsiders off the picket line:

we send the nut cases away. We don't have them there. You always get stewards on a picket line and a steward will attend to them. As soon as you get involvement from ultra-left, absolute ultra-left, people like the Socialist Workers Party, International Socialists, coming selling their newspapers and things like that, the best thing you can do is to get them away as soon as you can because they have a temper and anarchist attitude and will deliberately stir up trouble between the police and pickets. (Grunwick picket)

As well as excluding outsiders from picket lines union officials also tried to prevent disorder by keeping their men fully occupied:

Most of the time during our dispute, apart from the picketing, I'd get them nearly all involved. I'd allocated them all jobs, and I think this takes a lot of heat out of things. I'd got them chopping fish up and distributing groceries and going to see the women and children, to see about problems with kiddies' shoes and hardship cases. We were very well organized and I think a lot of people learnt a lot from what we did during that dispute. (NUM Branch Secretary)

In addition the strikers would be constantly reminded at briefing sessions of the need to behave in an orderly fashion. As one NUM Branch Secretary put it:

I would have been briefing these lads every day, and I would have also, like the coach of the football team who tells them to play hard but play fair [. . .] In that sense I would be a coach. But I would also be saying to people that they must keep out of trouble and if anybody raises a fist to strike you, well you must defend yourselves, etc. But because of the position that I'm in I'm bound to say that I would be telling these men that they've got to be disciplined and not to break the law. (NUM Branch Secretary)

Those strikers who were thought to be aggressive or short-tempered would often not be allowed onto the picket lines and numerous instances were cited of angry men being sent home.[22] If, despite these various preventive measures, disorder nevertheless occurred, then union officials would intervene to restore order:

I had two or three occasions when one of the lads got a bit aereated at Cadeby Bridge and I said, 'Cut it out. Look, we don't want no bloody trouble. Let's have it right. If anybody comes and anybody starts acting awkward, all well and good. But don't say nowt to police, don't make no cross talk to 'em that might be damaging to our picket line. Just have a few words to them in conversation if you like, but don't cause any trouble.' [. . .]

We had one incident where one of our lads went a bit berserk and he made a grab for a policeman and six of our big lads got hold of him and pulled him back. I went to police side and said, 'Now look, leave it alone. He's got a bit upset.' They said, 'If he comes again, we'll bloody have him and that's it' and he got a bit nasty did Sergeant. I went back to our lad and gave him a right good ticking off and sent him home. (NUM Branch Secretary)

It seems, then, that union officials are anxious to avoid violence and have devised several methods of controlling their members during picketing situations. But, of course, the political constraints on industrial disorder are more evident in some circumstances than in others. For example, the miners' strike of 1974 took place during a general election campaign and this caused the NUM to discourage actively both violence and mass picketing. What *The Times* described as a 'strict code of behaviour' was drawn up by the NUM and circulated to the Area Secretaries who in turn instructed the local branch secretaries accordingly.[23] The code restricted the numbers on any particular picket line to six and laid down that no picketing at all was to take place without the express approval of the National Strike Committee. Each area was requested to establish close liaison with the local Chief Constable and make the official NUM picket identification badge known to him.[24] Finally, under the heading 'discipline' officials were urged to 'impress on pickets that they must behave in a disciplined and peaceful manner even if they are provoked'.[25]

It is clear that NUM leaders at national and local level went to great lengths to restrain their members and in the event there were no serious incidents of violence. After the strike Owen Briscoe, the NUM Yorkshire Area Secretary, noted how effective political considerations had been in producing this orderly behaviour:

Our biggest problem has been frustration rather than a lack of discipline. Miners are not fools. They almost all vote Labour and they were aware of the effect trouble at the picket line would have had on the election.[26]

Although, as we have seen, political constraints generally operate to restrict violence to mere pushing and shoving there are occasions, such as an impending election, when even this form of confrontation is not acceptable. In these circumstances picketing is limited to a sort of symbolic confrontation where a small number of pickets face one or two policemen. The law is observed and no physical contact between the two sides takes place, thus reducing the probability of offending public opinion.

So far we have noted that trade unionists have become increasingly politicised in the sense that they wish to win the support of public opinion and that this places tight limits on the degree of physical coercion that can be used on picket lines. We have also seen that governments operating within a democratic system need to maintain general public approval and that this similarly limits the social control options available to them. However, the police too are subject to various political pressures that influence their response to industrial disorder and it is to a consideration of these pressures that we now turn.

The police

At the time of the Featherstone shootings the police and indeed military response to industrial disorder appears to have been controlled by the local magistrates who were often also the employers of the men in dispute. It is no exaggeration to say that the police acted as an employer's private army during the late nineteenth and early twentieth centuries.[27] However, by the time of the South Wales coal strike in 1910 this collusion between property owners and the forces of law and order was proving something of an embarrassment to the Liberal Government who directly intervened to prevent military force being deployed under magisterial control. Now, it was the Home Office rather than the local employers and magistrates who controlled police operations and, as we have seen, engendered a more impartial style of law enforcement. Of course, in 1910 central control was only imposed on a very temporary basis in response to a particular incident. It was not until the inter-war period that local police forces began to look to the Home Office for guidance and advice rather than succumb to the pressures of local magistrates and employers. Nevertheless, it was recognised that something ought to be done to free the police from local control in order to restore their legitimacy as an unbiased order-maintaining force. Captain B. W. Childs, Macready's intelligence officer and later head of Special Branch, proposed that working-class magistrates should be appointed to balance the influence of the employers.[28] It was decided that, although sound in principle, such a policy could not be implemented while the 1910 disturbances continued. However, the widespread industrial unrest of 1911 together with the perceived sense of crisis that accompanied it triggered a reversion to a more repressive style of order maintenance and local police forces continued to act as strikebreaking organisations.

It was not until after the First World War that the structure of the police system was altered, weakening local influences and strengthening central ones. These changes were the direct result of the recommendations of the Desborough Committee which had been set up after the police strike of 1919 to consider conditions of service, rates of pay and methods of recruitment.

The Police Act of 1919 gave effect to the Desborough Committee's central recommendations and thus immediately commenced a process of centralisation; Chief Constables were encouraged 'to look beyond their local boundaries to a concerted lead from Whitehall'.[29]

Of course, centralisation was not achieved overnight. Predictably local interests fiercely resisted the diminution of their influence over the police and the small borough forces were not abolished until 1946, while watch committees retained powers of appointment, promotion and discipline until 1964. However, the important point is that from 1919 a police service began to emerge that was conscious of itself as an independent organisation with aims and objectives that did not necessarily coincide with those of the local property-owning classes. Moreover, this new service was susceptible to central rather than local political pressures and regarded the Home Office not the local justice as its natural leader.

So during the inter-war years a Chief Constable might well have found himself subject to pressure from local interests, from central government and from the police organisation itself, but the local influence was rapidly weakening while central and organisational pressures were intensifying. Indeed, T. A. Critchley, the police historian, has noted that:

By 1939 . . . the Home Office had built up a position of quite remarkable influence in police affairs, when it is remembered how detached the department had been before the First World War, and how the absence of central leadership and lack of concern had reflected on the well-being of the men. Latterly, the prolific 'advice' and 'guidance' contained in Home Office circulars on all manner of subjects became a euphemism for 'direction'; and chief constables, resentful of any attempt at interference from outside, would look to an informal exchange with the Home Office to settle almost any problem.[30]

Central control of policing increased both during and after the Second World War. In particular the number of forces was cut in 1946, in the late

1960s and yet again in 1974. Today there are forty-three police forces in England and Wales compared with 117 in 1962 and 239 in 1857. The sheer size of the new police areas has militated against local control and has increased the power of both the Chief Constables and the Home Office.

It is interesting to note that the centralisation process began during the inter-war period at about the same time as Labour Party councillors were beginning to form the majority party on some councils.[31] However, it would be an extremely crude conspiracy theory which suggested that central control increased so that repressive policing could be maintained despite the emergence of Labour-dominated local authorities. On the contrary, as we have seen, governments have been well aware that any sanctioning of repressive police action against strikers could seriously jeopardise their chances of re-election. Draconian measures in an industrial context became no longer politically feasible. Indeed, increased central political influence has probably led to a reduction of aggressive control measures. This is certainly the view of many junior and intermediate ranks in the police. For example, an Inspector commented:

These senior officers they're all into this low profile, softly, softly, community relations approach, and let these strikers get away with just about every offence short of murder. I think we've been too softly, softly for too long and that's a view shared by many ordinary policemen. We're the ones who at the end of the day get the kicks, bottles and bricks coming at us. We ought to just once move in hard – that's all it would take and we'd have no more problems. These senior officers, well, they're all too scared to do that. They're worried about questions being asked in Parliament, about their chances of promotion, about being criticized, about whether they'd have to explain to Scarman why they did this, that or the other, about whether the Home Secretary would call for a report, etc., etc. (Inspector)

Further evidence of this view is provided by a survey of police attitudes to trade unionism carried out by Robert Reiner. He found that rank and file policemen felt that they were often restrained from fully enforcing the law during industrial disputes by senior officers.[32] One constable, with a somewhat confused sense of history, alleged that senior officers were frightened of looking 'like right-wing Nazis charging in to break up the Peterloo massacre'.[33]

It seems probable then that the centralisation process has functioned to constrain the police reaction to industrial disorder and has motivated the development of relatively non-violent tactics such as the cordon and the wedge. As we have seen, this kind of tactical development has enabled the police to enforce the law in strike situations without exceeding political limitations which rule out the use of more violent methods.

Of course, constitutionally the police are supposed to be a neutral law enforcement agency independent of political influence. However, there seems little doubt that the Government does influence the policing of industrial disputes both in terms of the overall approach and in terms of particular operational decisions. One Superintendent drew attention to this disjunction between the rhetoric of political independence and the actuality of Home Office influence:

The moment anyone alleges a policeman is politically influenced he goes bananas, whereas you and I know at the end of the day even the police force, especially the Metropolitan police, has some degree of political overtone, bearing in mind we're Home Office controlled. If anything happens, the Home Secretary wants to know. And he's there, isn't he? But operationally he doesn't get involved. But, of course, he does make known their views and I suppose who pays the piper plays the tune at times. (Superintendent)

Similarly, a Chief Superintendent said:

The miners here are capable of putting 50,000 men on the street. If they all come, it becomes an impossible situation, so by that time I shall probably have moved into the situation of national negotiation. It would be over my head, it would be Chief Constable, the Home Secretary, the whole big issue. And I have little doubt that the Chief Constable would be perhaps getting advice from government. (Chief Superintendent)

Although political pressure from central government seems to have generally functioned to restrain the police response to industrial disorder there have been particular instances when its application has been intended to promote more vigorous policing. According to a Chief Constable pressure of this kind was exerted during the picketing of the Saltley coke depot in 1972:

The miners' strike of '72 was of paramount importance to the Heath Government; their whole incomes policy and credibility depended on standing firm against the miners. And Saltley was the symbolic apex of the strike; after that they were lost, they never really recovered from it, although of course they didn't actually call an election until the '74 stoppage. Derrick Capper [the Chief Constable of Birmingham] must have been under tremendous political pressure to keep that Saltley depot working. I know he must have been subjected to intense pressure not to give way on that one. (Chief Constable)

But, as we saw in our account of the 1972 miners' strike, the gates at Saltley were closed despite the alleged pressure to keep the depot working.

It seems, then, that the Birmingham police were somewhat reluctant to use more violence than mere pushing and shoving even when they could be reasonably certain of government support for tougher measures. This was because the local force itself was subject to certain political pressures in addition to those emanating from central government. After all, thousands of local engineering workers joined the picket line as did many representatives of the local community and it was this, according to one Chief Superintendent, that ruled out more aggressive tactics:

the Chief Constable of the day, Mr Capper, who is now dead, he realized that he couldn't win and it was a battle lost in a war, if that's the right term to use, as it was at that time. Because the unions were really well organized, weren't they? There were magistrates on the picket lines. There were magistrates organizing the movement of vehicles. There were members of the local council there, it was a political dispute [. . .]

Capper didn't use more violent tactics such as baton charges, CS gas or rubber bullets . . . This is why we have the type of police service we have, and if we are going to use the other methods, then we change the pattern of the police service and we're going over to riot squads, aren't we? and semi-military organizations where we say, 'We are going to preserve the peace at all costs, and you are going to do as you're told.' Mr Capper there took the other view and I don't think, given the sort of community involvement he'd got there, he could have done any other. (Chief Superintendent)

This concern for the local community was not unique to Saltley. According to James Brownlow, the Chief Constable of South Yorkshire, a low profile was adopted during the steel strike for precisely the same reason:

It is not sufficient for a Chief Constable to purely and simply have regard to the law in such situations, he must look at the overall problem and in doing so endeavour to appreciate the feelings of all those involved in the dispute. In the case of the steel strike, my personal knowledge of the industry and of its workforce led me to the conclusion that in maintaining the Queen's peace every attempt should be made to retain the goodwill of everyone and that force should be used only as a last resort. Bearing in mind the fact that almost every family in Sheffield is connected in one way or another with the steel industry, my task during the early part of this year [i.e. 1980] was clear – the South Yorkshire Police had to maintain order but at the same time be fully conscious of the overwhelming importance of performing its task with tact and diplomacy. To have done otherwise in such a sensitive area would have been totally counter-productive both in the short and long terms.[34]

Indeed, there was unanimous agreement among senior officers not only about the desirability of not alienating the local community but also about the need to maintain public approval for their actions. A Chief Superintendent pointed out that industrial disputes 'draw the police into the political arena' in a supremely visible manner and therefore require 'complete impartiality'.[35] Similarly, a Superintendent with special responsibility for public order training said:

In our society if we arrest a man for stealing everybody else says, 'serve him right', but where you get into an area where you are arresting a man in relation to his work then there are emotions involved here that are not as clear cut to the average guy as there are with the ten commandments for instance. We know that so we have a lot more, if not sympathy because that doesn't come into it, we have a lot more understanding of the fact that we've got to give him enough rope before we hang him. (Superintendent)

It certainly seems, then, that the need to maintain public support functions to restrict the physical options that are available to the police. A Superintendent shrewdly commented:

We have to be seen to be pushed into whatever action we take. It's like the riots, really. Last summer we just stood there behind our shields and were seen night after night to be passively taking the bricks and the bombs. It's only after you've been seen by the public to lose at one tactical level that you can escalate to the next level. It's a bit like ascending a tactical stair-case; you have to be seen to be pushed up each step. You lose at one level so that you can justify going on to the next level in order to win. (Superintendent)

The police, of course, 'lost' at Saltley and it was this defeat which justified the reorganisation of the mutual aid system, the establishment of the National Recording Centre and tactical developments such as the wedge. To a lesser extent, the police were also seen to lose during the summer riots of 1981 and this led to the development of 'riot squads' armed with short shields and truncheons, specially trained to charge and disperse hostile crowds. As we shall see, in the next chapter, these strategic and tactical innovations enabled the police to 'win' the 1984–5 miners' dispute, albeit at some considerable cost both to their image and to their relationship with mining communities.

The growth of the media

They [i.e. strikers] can be rough and tough as many a copper's found out before now. But they soon learned the same lesson we did at the demos in the early days when the TV cameras were so keen to pan on to the odd drawn truncheon or frogmarched militant student.[36]

The above comments of a senior police officer indicate that the presence of television cameras has a restraining effect on the behaviour of pickets and police. This is hardly surprising given both the desire of police and unions to win public approval and the capability of television to transmit scenes of industrial disorder into virtually every home in the country.

Our own investigation revealed that union officials were certainly well aware of the need to avoid violence in situations that might be filmed. For example, one NUM official commented:

I think newsreel on TV generally just show bad points and it does create a bad image with the public, because they don't show any good things, they'll show the bad things. I mean, there are some good points go off on a picket line, a lot of good things happen, and there is times when you're very successful on a picket line, where you've convinced a bloke, and he accepts what you've said and he'll say, 'I'm in total support and wish you luck', and you don't generally get that sort of thing on media, you just get odd flare up. But because media will show odd flare up we have to impress on our blokes, 'Keep calm, don't retaliate, no violence.' (NUM Branch Secretary)

Of course, the presence of the media might actually provoke disorderly behaviour. James Brownlow noted that this seemed to have happened during the steel strike:

One interesting point which did emerge was that during the early morning filming of the demonstrators [i.e. the mass picketing at Hadfields], it was necessary for the TV crews to use spotlights. As soon as the spotlights were switched on the demonstrators pushed and jostled, but when they were switched off they promptly resumed their passive posture. Remarkably, the relationship between the demonstrators and the police officers did not seem to be affected by these changes of mood.[37]

However, it should be remembered that even when strikers play to the cameras their behaviour is usually limited to verbal abuse and the familiar pushing and shoving. Indeed, two NUM Branch Secretaries said that they would organise a display of this kind in order to demonstrate the strength of feeling on the picket line. Nevertheless, they stressed the need to avoid serious violence so as not to alienate public opinion:

I'd get the television people down on the picket line. I'd 'phone them up and say 'Come along.' And we'd make it so we had enough pickets on there to make a show. Because nine times out of ten if you've got a long strike you're left with a skeleton picket that can do no harm to anybody. It's a fire, three or four pickets and a tent. Well nobody's going to be interested in filming that. I'd get enough people there to give an impressive display. I'd get them to shout and push a bit. I think it's important to look active and perhaps angry, it helps convince people of the justice of your case ... I don't think shouting and pushing does union any harm, it's when fists start flying and coppers get hurt, that's when image gets a bit tarnished. (Grunwick picket)

It seems reasonable to conclude, then, that the televising of picketing generally functions to reduce violence, although in a minority of cases it may actually encourage a certain amount of limited aggression.

There is considerable evidence to suggest that the increased social visibility of industrial confrontation has also had a restraining effect on police tactics and behaviour. For example, a Chief Constable thought that the growth of the mass media coincided with and accounted for the decline of the baton-charge as a public order tactic:

What you must remember is that during the first half of the twentieth century public order policing was in fact very private. It was public in the sense that it was carried out on the highway or wherever, but it was private in the sense that only those present, probably a few hundred at most, saw what transpired. Alright, there were newspaper reports, but to read about a baton charge does not have the same impact as seeing it. Also, I don't think the papers used to publish photographs to the same extent as they do now. That's right isn't it? The development of the media must have had a tremendous effect on tactical thinking. You can imagine the significance, suddenly literally millions of people are able to see for themselves what happens. I'm convinced that's why baton charges are no longer used. You can imagine the public outcry if people saw on television the police baton-charging pickets. (Chief Constable)

Further support for the view that the media acts as a restraining influence on the police was provided by a Superintendent:

I think that one of the advantages pre the media was that if a matter occurred, the Cornish tin miners' strike [in 1913] or whatever, then it could be put down, if you want to use that expression, a lot easier. One of the big problems of dealing firmly with anything is the television, if we're talking about a short-cut solution. So we are very much aware of the media which controls to some extent police action. So that action, when it's seen on the film, has got to be seen to be reasonable. If we act unreasonably, then yes, we could alienate the public, not in the issue but in the way that we deal with them. That weakens our ability to control at a muscular level which is one of our functions, a situation that has to be taken into account [. . .] We've got to protect our image and would prefer to baton charge without the television if it was necessary, because it's not pretty. The necessity of it is another matter. (Superintendent)

Similarly, a Superintendent commented:

as a policeman I am conscious that there are sections of the media who are there watching the police to see if any policemen lose control of themselves in those situations [i.e. industrial disputes] and if they do find a policeman who does something he shouldn't, then that becomes the headline, rather than the violence in the other direction. [. . .] Just one or two officers who lose control, that makes the news and everybody's tarred with the same brush. (Superintendent)

This common feeling of being 'under the microscope'[38] has functioned to reduce violence in several ways. Firstly, senior officers, aware of the harm that can be done to the police image, have tightened control over their men. As one Superintendent put it:

The fact that television and press reporters are going to be there with their cameras sharpens up our control and discipline. It sharpens up the Commander's awareness of his need to supervise and to ensure that there is no open violence, open aggressiveness, on the part of the police, and I think that at the end of the day our primary consideration of course, is not necessarily to uphold the letter of the law, but to ensure that everyone behaves in a reasonable way. (Superintendent)

Secondly, as an Inspector in charge of public order training at a police college revealed, constables are trained not to react violently in situations where they might be filmed or photographed:

The worst situation is where the police officer loses control of himself and uses more action than is required, and that's where we get the bad publicity and that's where we have to train the officers concerned that no matter what the provocation and no matter how emotional the situation, they really have just got to use the minimum amount of force required. (Inspector)

Finally, it seems that junior policemen are reluctant to adopt aggressive tactics if the media are present. Indeed, a Chief Inspector pointed out that there was, in at least one force, an unofficial policy of not using truncheons for this reason:

They wouldn't draw their staffs because there's been such a concerted effort by the media to photograph that sort of thing . . . I'm told, in the Met., there's a reluctance now to draw staffs. Which I think is sad, but that's the way the PCs on the ground see it. So they're looking to their own defence, if you like. Whilst you might think, I might think and they might think that they've got very good grounds for drawing their staffs, what's subconscious at the back of their minds is 'What if the press is on this, I'm in trouble.' (Chief Inspector)

There is little doubt, then, that the increased visibility of public order policing has functioned to reduce violence. However, the media can also be used to increase public support and sympathy for the police and several senior officers were well aware of this. The Commandant of a police training college clearly revealed how conscious the police are of the need to gain public sympathy and how they go about achieving this:

Both sides, if you want to use that expression, are trying to provoke the other side by all sorts of things into being the ones that look bad on television and the whole issue of the strike and everything else gets lost. That's the Monty Python bit about it. [. . .] The police could do that by appearing to be over reasonable, and the propaganda machine of the union and the propaganda machine of the police is waiting for an opportunity to magnify whatever situation arises. If a striker were to get knocked down and killed by a vehicle, that is very sad for the guy, but it is good for the propaganda machine. If a police officer gets struck down by a milk bottle, that's bad for him, but it's good for the police and that's not a question of making it happen but being an opportunist . . . Also the Commander can educate his men into the fact that the television is there and it is better to take a battering and get sympathy than win and lose it, but having done that, not to lose the day. You see, we have a number of objectives. One is not to lose the day, the other is to come out of it with a reasonable image and this is harder.

There is also some evidence to suggest that the police have actually stage-managed incidents to win public sympathy. For example, the Metropolitan Police at one time trained an especially comely horse, the 'Brigitte Bardot' of police horses, to fall down feigning death in order to win support from the animal-loving British public.[39] Similarly, allegations have been made that during the Grunwick dispute an elderly policeman with white hair would, when the television cameras were on him, writhe about on the ground clutching his stomach as if injured.[40] This kind of careful and calculated concern with appearances reveals both how important the police consider public opinion and how the presence of the media can affect their behaviour.

The democratisation of civil liberties

since the 1930s, civil liberties have become more widely available and have been more widely used. It is the continuation of a fluctuating process that has been going on for hundreds of years. The Whig ideologists of the nineteenth century were very good at tracing the development of English freedom from Saxon times while simultaneously oppressing their factory workers. Some of our liberties are indeed ancient, but only in the twentieth century have they been taken up on any scale by ordinary people.[41]

This popular colonisation of old aristocratic rights and freedoms was reflected in and reinforced by the foundation of pressure groups such as the Haldane Society of Socialist Lawyers (1930) and the National Council for Civil Liberties (1934). In more recent times the continuation of the process has been indicated by the introduction of statutory legal aid, the multiplication of Citizens' Advice Bureaux and the establishment of 'neighbourhood' or 'community' law centres.[42] Clearly, a detailed evaluation of the effect of all these developments on police behaviour is beyond the scope of the present work. Nevertheless, we can point to civil libertarian involvement in trade disputes and the police reaction to that involvement as evidence of the tightening constraints on police methods.

Organisations like the National Council for Civil Liberties have monitored, since the 1930s, police action in relation to industrial disputes. For example, in 1937 during the Harworth Colliery strike, Ronald Kidd, the Secretary of the NCCL, visited Harworth Colliery and other places in Nottinghamshire in order to investigate complaints about police behaviour. In March the NCCL published a pamphlet which recorded the results of Kidd's investigations. It concluded that:

Whatever the cause, there can be no reasonable doubt, I think, that there have been serious irregularities in the conduct of the police during the dispute and this, coupled with the attitude and composition of the local Bench and with the methods of serving summonses and making charges, has led to a feeling throughout the district that the general administration of law and order in the County is being used in a manner which must do infinite harm to a belief in the traditions of public administration and justice.[43]

Eventually the NCCL, supported by internationally famous authors such as H. G. Wells, E. M. Forster and G. D. H. Cole, even forced the Government to reduce the prison sentences imposed on some of the strikers.[44]

The techniques used by the NCCL at Harworth – observation by respected individuals, the publication of pamphlets and the application of parliamentary pressure – have been repeated during many police operations. For instance, during the Grunwick dispute observers reported back to the NCCL incidents involving aggressive police behaviour. One observer, a probation officer, wrote:

I was deeply disturbed by the tactics of the police last Monday. The usual neutrality shown by the police on such occasions was absent and I saw and heard a police Inspector shouting in response to a speech by the Chairman of the Brent Trades Council that he 'didn't care if the buggers were paid nothing'. I also saw people who were peacefully picketing being snatched by the police and arrested. To my mind they were not guilty of obstruction and if they were, were certainly not asked to move along by the police.

After the bus had gone into the gates and as the crowd was moving away towards Dollis Hill tube station the police drove everyone on the pavements up the road in a totally unnecessary manner. I saw an elderly woman being jostled by policemen, and eventually reduced to tears. During this manoeuvre the police brutally arrested people that were passing innocuous comments to them.[45]

Similar reports were made by other observers and their allegations were taken up by MPs or passed on directly to the Home Secretary.[46] In addition legal representation and advice was provided at local police stations for many of those arrested on the picket line. According to one picket the presence of community lawyers had a restraining effect on the police:

When we got to the station, by the time we reached the station there were literally hundreds of people milling around. We were just taken, finger-printed, they were going to photograph, but I objected to photographs, and then we finished up in a cell for two or three hours that day.

In fact there were legal people there from law centres who were advising us and I understand that the charges were being made meant that to some degree some people couldn't afford any of the fingerprinting. I thought they'd get really nasty with the ones that refused but they just seemed to accept it. On the whole they treated us all right – I think it might have been different if the law centre people weren't there. (Grunwick picket)

To what extent the activities of organisations such as law centres and the NCCL have affected police conduct is difficult to assess, but the comments of police officers themselves suggest that the impact has been considerable:

if you think in terms of fifty to sixty years ago perhaps the policeman gave as good as he got and things were quits. The recipient didn't go to the National Council for Civil Liberties, to the Citizens' Advice Bureau, to the local Legal Aid Centre, to the station to complain. Well, now they do all those things so the police officer doesn't hazard himself professionally. One could take the view that he is much more professional now in that respect in that he doesn't administer summary justice, he places the prisoner before the law, for the course of law to be run. Whether that is good for the prisoner or not is a different matter [. . .] But why we do not police on that basis now, is because so many people have access to invoke punitive measures on the policeman, so he's no longer prepared to hazard his job. [. . .] I think it's a greater availability of the law to the population as a whole, and it's also an awareness by the population of the availability of the law, and the avenues it offers to them to seek redress for whatever wrong. (Chief Inspector)

It seems, then, that there has been something of a shift from traditional to rational, from informal to formal policing during the last fifty years or so. This shift has been influenced by the civil rights organisations which have themselves emerged as a consequence of the democratisation of traditional liberties. Although all aspects of police work have become more formal it is suggested that the restraining influence of the civil libertarians is particularly effective in relation to public order policing which is highly visible and can be easily monitored.

Summary

By the late 1970s industrial confrontation had become a sophisticated political game in which two sides, police and pickets, battled for public opinion. Of course, strikers still tried to obstruct 'blacklegs' or materials and the police still tried to enforce the law, but both sides attempted to achieve their conflicting objectives without losing public approval. This meant that violence beyond mere pushing and shoving was generally regarded as counterproductive in strike situations.

However, in the mid 1980s this historical trend towards non-violence appears to have been reversed; once again stone-throwing pickets have been charged by baton-wielding police. It is to an examination of this new and more violent pattern of confrontation that we now turn.

7

Industrial confrontation after the riots

> once the mind has achieved another diameter of thought it doesn't return to its original size. We've got all this stuff and it may well be that you can put a helmet on, pick up a truncheon and shield, pull your visor down and achieve more with one man than you did before with three. It's very tempting.
>
> (Chief Superintendent)

As we have seen, the police responded to their 'defeat' at the Saltley coke depot in 1972 by revitalising the mutual aid system, establishing a National Recording Centre and introducing techniques, such as the wedge, into public order training. These innovations enabled later disputes – Neap House Wharf, Grunwick and the steel strike – to be successfully policed in a relatively non-violent manner. However, following the widespread rioting of 1981 there was once again a perceived need to review public order tactics and training. In many instances constables had been reduced to standing passively behind their long shields, like sitting ducks at a shooting gallery, while missiles and even petrol bombs rained down upon them. Formations, such as the wedge, that had worked so well during the industrial disputes of the seventies, were obviously of little value in these much more disorderly riot conditions. Yet the use of more drastic crowd control techniques, such as CS gas and rubber bullets, were considered either ineffective or counter-productive in terms of public relations.

The solution was the development of riot squads, armed with short portable shields and truncheons, whose function was to charge the crowd at speed thus preventing a static stone-throwing situation from developing. Unfortunately, the sheer time and effort put into this reorganisation of public order training, with its emphasis on riot shields, has led to formations such as the wedge becoming somewhat redundant.

Since 1981 public order training has become, in effect, riot control training. This has meant that a sort of tactical gap has opened in the police response to the relatively restricted violence of industrial conflict. Moreover, associated with the emphasis on riot control is a new 'hardline' attitude. After all, if one is gearing up for a riot subtle tactics such as the use of wit and

humour or the need for liaison and co-operation are, naturally enough, not
at the forefront of the mind. This tougher attitude, together with the new
riot tactics, has played a significant part in escalating industrial confrontation beyond the pushing and shoving of the seventies to a new, more
violent, level.

Industrial confrontation after the riots: chronology

The National Graphical Association dispute

A first glimpse of the application of riot tactics in an industrial context was
provided, in the autumn of 1983, during a closed shop dispute between the
National Graphical Association (NGA) and the Messenger Group of
newspapers. The most significant picketing since the 1980 steel strike,
involving on one occasion some 4,000 pickets, took place outside Mr Eddie
Shah's print works.

Initially, the picketing took the, by now, familiar form of pushing and
shoving. The police, who on occasions more than equalled the number of
pickets, were easily able to ensure that delivery vans could leave the print
works at will. For example on 23 November police cordons held back some
600 pickets; one policeman was injured when a breeze-block wall fell over
and only two arrests were made.[1] The pickets, as in former disputes, were
prepared to use more violence against property than they were against people
and the tyres of some delivery vans were slashed, but the situation hardly
amounted to the 'wild anarchy and chaos' alleged by Mr Shah.[2] In subsequent days the number of pickets increased but again the impressive police
presence, including PSUs from other areas, ensured the delivery vans free
passage. Mr Shah confidently claimed that the pickets would need 'three
armoured tanks, a couple of helicopters with machine guns and about 600
men from 2 Para' to stop the newspapers leaving.[3]

On 30 November some 4,000 people, the largest mass picket since Grunwick, collected outside the Warrington print works. The police, as usual,
used cordons to push the crowd back to make way for delivery vans. According to press reports the pickets remained cheerful during the initial pushing
and shoving, but the mood changed when the police called up reinforcements who seized union banners and confiscated the pickets' public address
system.[4] At this point some stones and bottles were thrown, a senior officer
warned of possible baton-charges and a squad in full riot gear appeared.[5]
Missiles continued to be thrown, a policeman yelled 'Come on, let's go and
get these bastards' and the riot squad drove into the crowd, splitting it into
two.[6] Stoning intensified and barricades were set ablaze. At the end of the
day 43 people were injured, including 25 police, and 73 arrested.[7]

However, the constraints on industrial violence that we noted in the last chapter seemed to be far more effective at curbing picketing than the Government's employment legislation, which the unions had so far ignored, for following media coverage of the disorder described above the NGA immediately suspended mass picketing at Warrington.[8] The whole affair is of interest because it reveals the readiness of the police to employ tactics such as the baton-charge, a technique which at the time had not been used in an industrial context since before the war, that had been perfected for very different riot conditions. A similar willingness to revert to a more violent style of confrontation was also evident in the subsequent miners' strike.

The miners' strike

On Tuesday 6 March 1984 Ian McGregor, the Chairman of the National Coal Board, confirmed the existence of a plan which provided for around 20 pits (with a loss of 120,000 jobs) to be closed down over the next twelve months.[9] Understandably, especially since the same number of pits had been lost during the existing year, Arthur Scargill, the President of the NUM, described this as the 'savage butchery' of the industry.[10] The response of Yorkshire's 56,000 miners was less rhetorical; they decided to turn the union's four-month overtime ban into an all-out strike from the following Monday. Miners' leaders in Scotland, South Wales, Kent and Durham quickly followed suit and what became known in the press as the 'rolling coal strike' was underway. However, it soon became clear that in some areas the rank and file were not unanimously in favour of the stoppage; even in traditionally militant South Wales there was a majority against strike action.[11] In such a fragmented situation persuasion, peaceful or otherwise, was obviously going to be of crucial importance in ensuring the success of the strike.

Almost immediately picketing began in earnest; on 12 March groups of strikers gathered at Harworth, Cresswell and Bevercotes in Nottinghamshire, while at Scotland's Bilston Glen Colliery 300 miners bellowed abuse and obscenities from behind police cordons.[12] The first disorder occurred on 14 March when some members of a 200-strong force of pickets were involved in scuffles with police at Nottinghamshire's Ollerton Colliery; ten miners were arrested and three policemen were slightly injured.[13] In South Wales angry miners, who had rejected the strike call by 2 to 1, claimed the coalfield had been brought to a standstill by 'mob rule'.[14] On the following day the first death of the strike occurred at Ollerton Colliery when Yorkshire picket David Jones collapsed and died after running several hundred yards to his car. Later, police and pickets joined in a two-minute silence for the dead man. Further clashes between police and pickets were reported from the Nottinghamshire coalfield and a total of 23 arrests were made.[15]

By Monday 19 March some 8,000 police had been mobilised; David Hall, the Chief Constable of Humberside and controller of the National Recording Centre, spoke of the 'most mobile and sophisticated police reserve yet assembled in Britain'.[16] As if to verify his comments, that same day police roadblocks were placed around the Nottingham headquarters of the NUM as 270 delegates voted to return to work. Spotter planes and police helicopters flew overhead and tracker dogs patrolled nearby fields to ensure that delegates could meet in an atmosphere free from intimidation.[17] The police were clearly reacting, possibly overreacting, to the strike in a highly organised manner. Outside many Nottinghamshire pits police outnumbered pickets by as many as 3 to 1 and at Harworth some 3,000 police were deployed to control 30 entirely peaceful pickets.[18] At Thoresby Colliery a cordon of 200 police kept 50 strikers from even talking to the working miners. An Inspector, appropriately using 1984 'double think', said they are 'demonstrators not pickets' therefore the police were entitled to stop them approaching the working miners.[19] In Derbyshire the County Council's Policy Committee described the police operation as 'intimidatory and totally unnecessary';[20] a view shared by even some of the working miners at Newstead Colliery who walked out in protest at the level of policing.[21] According to a working miner at Ollerton Colliery the police rather than the pickets seemed to be doing the obstructing: 'Some mornings we haven't been able to get into the pit canteen . . . bloody place is packed out with coppers tucking into bacon butties.'[22]

The first two weeks of the strike were relatively orderly; by 23 March only 96 arrests had been made and most of these were for nothing more serious than obstruction.[23] Indeed, many of these arrests had taken place not on the picket lines but at police roadblocks as a policy of 'immobilizing the militant miners in their home villages' was put into action.[24] But despite this general lack of violence, police chief David Hall warned that the police might be issued with riot shields; a statement which indicates the same willingness to ascend the 'tactical staircase' as was evident during the earlier NGA dispute.[25]

On 23 March at Hem Heath Colliery car windscreens were smashed and plastic bags full of urine were thrown at working miners, action which led to a protest sit-in by four non-strikers at 3,000 feet underground.[26] Four days later minor disorder occurred outside the NCB's Doncaster headquarters where eight police were injured in the 'heaving and pushing'.[27] Early April saw police reinforcements drafted into the Lancashire area as fears mounted of a clash between pickets and pitmen who had voted to return to work. An article in *The Times* noted 'The very pervasiveness of the police presence is beginning to displace picketing as the locus of the argument. And that shift plays into the hands of the left'[28] – an opinion difficult to contradict, particularly in view of the relatively orderly nature of the dispute so far.

In South Wales, at the Port Talbot Steelworks, minor clashes between police and pickets occurred on 3 April and again two days later.[29] On 8 April, Gerald Kaufman, the Shadow Home Secretary, presented the Chief Constable of Nottinghamshire, Charles McLaughton, with a dossier of complaints about police behaviour; 'I had names, dates and policemen's numbers.'[30] The Chief Constable, apparently, 'in some matters showed considerable concern'.[31] Meanwhile, the Home Secretary, Leon Brittan, had dismissed allegations that police had tapped the telephones of the NUM and had disguised themselves as pickets.[32] A denial that is difficult to reconcile with previous police practice (see pp. 96–100) and a subsequent admission by David Owen, Chief Constable of North Wales, that he had deployed officers in plain clothes during the strike.[33]

Disorder occurred at the Cresswell and Babbington collieries on 9 April when a total of 78 arrests were made and six policemen and one miner were slightly injured.[34] Three days later moderate miners' leaders were manhandled after an executive meeting of the NUM, cans and fruit were thrown, 52 arrests were made and a bottle-cap with four screws sticking out was thrown at police lines but fell short.[35] Sporadic incidents of a less serious kind continued to be reported throughout April; at Sutton Manor Colliery on Merseyside the tyres of two vans and a roadsweeper were slashed, a working miner was punched in the face at Hem Heath Colliery and there were scuffles at Wivenhoe near Colchester as pickets tried to stop imported coal leaving the quayside.[36]

By May the frustration caused by seemingly ineffective strike action and the massive police presence in the coalfields spilt over into more serious violence. Stones were thrown when some 6,000 'moderates' staged a 'right to work' demonstration, outside the NUM's Nottinghamshire headquarters, and were met by a counter-demonstration of 1,500 strikers.[37] At Harworth Colliery, 10,000 pickets walked over fields to evade police roadblocks; there were scuffles and some stones were thrown.[38] There were also clashes at Ravenscraig, where the police had been placed on 'red alert', at Wivenhoe, and at the Golbourned Colliery, Lancashire, where 1,000 pickets gathered.[39] On 3 May 2,000 strikers managed to circumnavigate police roadblocks at Cotgrove and threw various missiles at working miners; there were 18 arrests, but no reported injuries.[40]

The most violent picketing so far took place at Ravenscraig on 6 and 7 May when about 1,000 pickets clashed with an equal number of police. Stones, bottles and bricks were thrown, one constable's collar-bone was broken, several pickets were led away bleeding and mounted police made repeated charges. One picket said, 'You know the expression: "riding rough shod over someone" – well that's what is happening here – literally'.[41] Further disorder occurred at Hunterston on 8 May when mounted police were again deployed; missiles were thrown, two police and five pickets were injured. Less serious incidents also took place at Cresswell Colliery, Wivenhoe and Ramsgate in Kent where more than 200 miners gathered to prevent the unloading of oil from a tanker. During a miners' rally in Mansfield glasses and bottles were thrown, 12 police were injured and 60 arrests made.[42]

Towards the middle of May widespread intimidation of working miners at places other than the picket lines began to be regularly reported for the first time.[43] Detectives in Nottinghamshire were said to be investigating 'scores' of these incidents, while Warwickshire police issued a list of 100 such cases.[44] On 18 May the Home Secretary announced that special police teams of detectives had been formed to 'combat intimidation' and that they would be supported by extra uniformed men 'patrolling on foot throughout the day and increasing levels of activity during the high risk periods'.[45] It seems that the massive police operation designed to ensure working miners a safe passage through the picket lines had also displaced violence and intimidation away from the colliery gates and back into the community.

At the end of May there was a dramatic escalation of violence at the Orgreave coking plant near Rotherham. Arthur Scargill called for a mass blockade and many miners, unaware of the significant changes that had taken place in police tactics since 1972, optimistically talked of 'doing a Saltley'.[46] On 29 May, 1,500 pickets clashed with 1,700 police from 13 different forces; smoke bombs, firecrackers, fence-posts, stones and bricks were thrown.[47] For the first time since the 1940s mounted police baton-charged strikers as did foot squads in full riot gear – 64 people were injured and 84 were arrested.[48] On the following day the number of pickets and the level of disorder increased; again the riot squads using shields and truncheons went into action and again they faced a barrage of missiles. Wire was stretched across the road to trip horses, a portakabin was set ablaze and police announced the existence of 'a riot situation'.[49] There were 16 injuries, 35 people, including Arthur Scargill, were arrested and *The Times* declared 'a crisis of law and order'.[50] Following a day's lull trouble again flared up on 1 June when cordons of police, 30 men deep, held back some 4,000 pickets. Missiles were thrown and riot tactics, including baton-charges, were again used. There were 19 arrests and 20 injuries including a picket with a fractured skull who was given the kiss of life by a police sergeant. However, following widespread condemnation of violent picketing by miners' leaders, trade unionists and the leader of the Labour Party the mass picketing at Orgreave continued for a while on a much more orderly basis. For example on 6 June, Tony Clement, the Assistant Chief Constable in charge of the police operation, noted that 'apart from pushing' and one incident involving the throwing of paint stripper 'there had been very little violence', despite the presence of 3,000 pickets.[51]

Several incidents occurred throughout early June; 110 miners were arrested during a protest march in London, 200 angry miners stoned a police station at Maltby near Rotherham and the second fatality took place when a picket was killed in an accident with a lorry.[52] But the focus of attention shifted back to the Orgreave coke depot on 18 June when a mass picket by 10,000 led to the most violent scenes of the dispute so far. Stones and bottles were thrown at the police line which at one point gave way under pressure, mounted men made repeated baton-charges as did the helmeted riot squads. Three vehicles were set on fire, sharpened stakes were set in the ground to deter 'cavalry charges' and policemen clapped and cheered as injured pickets were led away.[53] Seventy-nine people were injured and 93 were arrested. Tony Clement, the police Commander, said that it was 'a miracle' no one had been killed.[54]

Less serious incidents continued to be reported from various parts of the country; there were scuffles at the Bilston Glen Colliery in Scotland, while stones were thrown at the NCB's Doncaster offices, but at Orgreave police and pickets shared cold drinks.[55] July was relatively peaceful. Of course, there were clashes, notably at Port Talbot, Bilston Glen, Cresswell and the Bentinck Colliery near Mansfield, but nothing approaching the violence at Orgreave seems to have occurred.[56] In August there was something of a reversion from obstruction to destruction; this started in the Derbyshire and Nottinghamshire coalfield when 30 lorries used to transport coal through the picket lines were sabotaged in one week.[57] Similar events continued; on 6 August a representative of the 'South Notts hit squad' rang BBC Radio Nottingham to claim responsibility for vandalising a coal transport depot at South Normanton causing £4,000 worth of damage.[58] Two days later 1,000 stone-throwing pickets launched a night attack on Silverstone and Harworth collieries; cars and pit windows were smashed and a police spokesman said he was convinced the strikers had 'given up picketing in favour of vandalism'.[59] Within a week another coach depot was attacked at Pleasley Vale and five buses used to ferry working miners through the picket lines were burnt out.[60] A few days later, on 15 August, three coaches used to take men into Hem Heath Colliery were set on fire during the night and were totally destroyed.[61]

A return to more conventional confrontation occurred on 16 August at the Gasgoigne Wood Colliery when two strikers, the first in militant Yorkshire, decided to return to work. At dawn a burning barricade blocked the colliery approach road and riot squads with helmets and short shields moved into position. However, despite the presence of thousands of pickets, the largest gathering since Orgreave, nothing more violent than pushing and shoving was reported.[62] The next day a more serious confrontation took place; bricks, clods of earth and bottles were thrown at the police, some of whom lost their temper and broke from the cordon to deliver a spontaneous baton-charge.[63] Riot squads were brought up but the disorder was over in minutes; nine policemen and four pickets were injured.[64]

By late August the long hot summer was nearing its end but without any corresponding reduction of temperature in the coalfields. In Yorkshire, at Kiveton Colliery, a police horse was stoned to the ground and three policemen were cut by broken glass when their coach was attacked by angry miners, while in South Wales strikers occupying crane cabins at Port Talbot threw a variety of missiles at police 120 feet below.[65]

During the first week of September it was announced that so far 676 policemen and an unknown number of pickets had been injured while some 6,427 people had been arrested mainly for public order offences such as obstruction and breach of the peace.[66] These totals increased as further disorder occurred throughout the following months. On 18 September, Kiveton Colliery was again the focus of attention when missiles including bags of urine and used contraceptives were thrown at mounted police who responded with the, by now familiar, baton-charge.[67] In South Wales more lethal projectiles such as lumps of concrete and large stones were launched from motorway bridges at convoys of lorries transporting coal from Port Talbot to the Llanwern Steelworks, action, according to the local police, which amounted to attempted murder.[68] An ambush of a different kind took place at Silverwood Colliery on 28 September when hundreds of pickets attacked a convoy of police dog transporters; eight policemen were injured and two vans were overturned.[69] In subsequent weeks several other incidents were reported which indicate that, at least in some areas, the police themselves had become the target for attack. At Longannet in Scotland, PC Daniel Hutchinson was injured when a brick was thrown through the window of his panda car while on 16 October WPC Janet Smith was knocked to the ground and kicked following an attack on the Grimethorpe police station.[70]

A return to mass confrontation occurred, this time at Brodsworth Colliery, on 19 October, when mounted and foot police in full riot gear made several baton-charges before dispersing a crowd of stone-throwing miners. Within a week a similar incident occurred at Denby Grange Colliery, near Wakefield, this time both fireworks and steel ball-bearings were thrown at the police; 44 officers were injured.[71] On 8 November there was another direct attack on the police when a crowd attacked Stainforth police station, breaking every window in the building and overturning several cars.[72] The following day saw serious disorder at Cortonwood, South Yorkshire, when 4,000 pickets clashed with 1,000 police; bricks, bottles and ball-bearings were thrown and a workman's cabin was set ablaze and rolled towards the police lines.[73] However, what was described by the police as 'the worst violence yet' occurred in the Yorkshire coalfield on 12 November when shops were broken into, barricades set on fire and petrol bombs (all of which failed to ignite) thrown in an attempt to dissuade strikers from returning to work in response to the Coal Board's special 'Christmas bonus' offer.[74]

By mid November, then, the pattern of confrontation had become clear;

symbolic, small-scale picketing involving no disorder at all, occasional mass confrontations, some of which clearly involving considerable violence, intimidation of working miners, the destruction of property and sporadic direct attacks on the police themselves.

Industrial confrontation after the riots: analysis

There seems no doubt that the long-drawn-out miners' strike which began in March 1984 was more violent than any other post-war industrial dispute. Consider, for example, the following newspaper report of the disorder which occurred on 18 June at the Orgreave coking plant:

> A second charge is made. One mounted police officer is struck, and slumps in his saddle. Policemen are yelling for ambulance crews.
> A police officer in charge of a group of men with short shields and truncheons tells them to take prisoners. The men, dressed in riot gear, run forward and attack the pickets with truncheons . . .
> A picket, blood pouring from a head wound, is held semi-conscious by a policeman and helped towards an ambulance. Police nearby clap and cheer.[75]

The killing of David Wilkie, on 30 November, a taxi driver who was transporting non-strikers to work in South Wales, was also indicative of the extent to which the level of violence had escalated. It is interesting to note that until this incident there was no record of strikers having killed anyone during the last hundred years.

It is important, however, to place drastic events like those described above in perspective. Most picketing during the dispute consisted of a small two- or three-man presence that was completely orderly and required no policing at all. It was only when mass pickets were called that disorder occurred and even then violence in excess of aggressive pushing and shoving was by no means inevitable, as a Chief Inspector recalled:

> We would say to them, 'Bus is coming in five minutes – get ready lads', and the pickets would sort themselves out and get ready for the push and we would get ready and have a good push. Nothing more violent than that ever happened, even when we had literally thousands there. Of course they would shout and swear at the buses going through the line, 'You fucking scabs!', that sort of thing, but one of our superintendents, he's a bit religious, he said to them 'Can't you shout something else? Why do you have to swear? It's not very nice.' And the next time the buses went through they all shouted out, 'You bounders.' (Chief Inspector)

Indeed, by March 1985, some twelve months after the start of the strike, serious disorder seems to have taken place on no more than 15 occasions.[76] Nevertheless, it is clear that these incidents do indicate a new and more violent pattern of confrontation.

Several factors have accounted for the shift away from the successively less violent trajectory revealed in earlier chapters. As we have already noted, police tactics, since 1981, have themselves tended to escalate industrial confrontation. For example, the deployment of riot shields, which happened on several occasions before any missiles were thrown, may actually encourage stoning.[77] As a Chief Superintendent, with special responsibility for public order, commented:

It's a funny thing, but the uniform is sort of sacred; there's extreme reluctance on the part of the public to touch it. Even on picket lines you can see the reluctance of the demonstrators to make contact – for them it must be like jumping off the high board for the first time. Now when you place a chunk of plastic between you and them that reluctance goes. I sometimes think riot shields almost invite people to throw things at you. It's putting the idea in their minds. It was interesting but during the riots the kids who were throwing bricks and stones at us, and some of them were literally kids, were throwing at the shields, not at the men. If they'd really wanted to hit us they could have thrown the bricks up in the air so they dropped over the front line of shields like Harold or whatever did at the battle of Hastings. (Chief Superintendent)

Moreover, the tactical gap, created by the neglect of the wedge and the emphasis on riot shields in public order training, has meant that pickets feel that they no longer have any chance of succeeding by mere pushing. The great beauty of a tactic like the wedge was that it allowed the police to win on what was perceived to be equal terms without destroying the strikers' hopes of future victory. A NUM official who had picketing experience during the 1972 coal strike, the Grunwick dispute and the 1984 miners' stoppage contrasted the wedge with later riot tactics:

It's one of those sights, if anybody's never seen it you don't understand how effective it is. They start grunting and groaning and pumping their legs in unison. They get all the hard coppers at the front, kitted out with guards and cricket boxes, and all the sheep in the middle, like. They just march straight into you and push you out the way. Well, we learnt from them and started doing the same to them to break through their cordons, we nearly did it on several occasions, but fair do's, they were a bit better at it than us. Maybe if strike had lasted a bit longer and we'd had more practice or if we'd got a few more lads, we could have beat them.

Today, you've no chance. There's a lot more of them and if you look like you're going to break through hard guys are called in, them with shields and bloody truncheons. Well, your unarmed picket can't compete with that sort of thing. I don't condone it but I can understand why some of lads start throwing things. (NUM official)

Some of the tactics developed after Saltley, such as the turning back of miners *en route* to the picket lines and the increased police presence, co-ordinated by the National Recording Centre at Scotland Yard, have also frustrated strikers. In particular, the PSUs have not always gone out of their way to lower the tension in the coalfields:

In my view the PSUs have caused a lot of the trouble – it's very difficult to get them to be friendly. Because they're only in an area for maybe a couple of weeks they've got no vested interest in building up relationships with the community. If anyone attempts to talk to them they just tell 'em to piss off – it's because they're young, under 40, physically fit, riot trained and some, I'm sorry to say, go looking for trouble. (Chief Inspector)

However, it seems that when PSUs are sent to areas where there is already a notoriously bad relationship between police and public they are accepted by the community as a welcome change; 'something quite different from what they've been used to'.[78]

Perhaps, as one Inspector alleged, it depended on where the PSU was from; 'those from mining areas showed an understanding and sympathy that was completely lacking with PSUs from other areas, especially the Met.'[79] According to the pickets the position was not so complex; all the trouble was caused by the 'hard bastards' drafted in to break the strike.[80]

Although it is not certain to what extent the attitude of the PSUs contributed to the increased disorder it is clear that their effectiveness displaced violence from the picket line. In short, conventional picketing has now become a set battle that the strikers cannot win; faced with certain defeat at the pit gates hit and run tactics have become the only feasible alternative. Intimidation of working miners, the destruction of Coal Board property and attacks on police stations are evidence of a frustrated backlash itself engendered by the success of tactics designed, ironically, to ensure that the police retain control without resorting to more violent methods. In addition, there is no doubt that the police were pressurised by central government into adopting a 'hard line' approach. We have already noted that senior officers 'feel the water' (see p. 109) and its temperature was clearly signalled within days of the stoppage. On 16 March, the Attorney-General, Sir Michael Havers, urged the police to act 'vigorously and without fear or favour'.[81] Within a week the message was reinforced by the Home Secretary who said that 'the police have a right to take what action is necessary'.[82] Such public statements, together with private communications, clearly left police chiefs in no doubt as to what was expected of them. As Peter Joslin, Chief Constable of Warwickshire, said, 'We are no push over, enough is enough.'[83]

There is some evidence to suggest that, just as in the past (see Chapter 3), such political pressure from central government is related, at least to some extent, with acts of police brutality on the picket lines. In marked contrast with the responses of union officials questioned about the disputes of the 1970s all the NUM members interviewed about their experiences in the 1984 strike could relate examples of unjustified police violence. The following incident is, in many ways, typical:

It were a bit rough, like; a minority were chucking things at police then riot squads with truncheons charged at us. Well, it were bloody chaos; people running in all directions. I saw coppers – they got this chap on ground and kicked hell out of him. Later on, I was walking back home with two mates when police van pulls up and out gets four or five coppers and they just laid into us. I got cut lips and big bruises –

others were worse. Eric's nose got broke – we didn't resist at all. All of us were in our fifties. It's destroyed what little faith I had left in police I can tell you. (NUM Branch Secretary)

As well as reports of indiscriminate violence[84] during picketing and of attacks on individual or small groups of strikers it also seems that on one or two occasions the police have raided clubs and meeting places. For example, a miners' club at Rossington was broken into by police who allegedly began 'kicking our members. One policeman tried to restrain one or two of the policemen but they still carried on. I was hit at back of head and a number of our men were laid on floor.'[85] This kind of unnecessarily aggressive policing can only have contributed to the escalation of violence already engendered by the new riot tactics and mutual aid system.

Of course, other factors in addition to police tactics have played a part in bringing about an increased level of violence. Obviously the miners were far from united from the outset of the strike. Ray Chadburn, the Nottinghamshire NUM Area President, sadly noted, 'We have brother against brother, father against son, man against wife . . . throughout a great deal of the British coalfield.'[86] Not surprisingly, many of the more disorderly scenes occurred when pickets tried to prevent working miners from entering collieries; tempers are easily lost when former workmates 'do the dirty' on you.[87] In addition, the sheer length of the stoppage, with miners' families forced to survive on reduced and sometimes delayed social security benefits must have increased frustration and possibly contributed to violence on the picket line. It may also be that the new militant majority on the NUM Executive are not so committed to reform via the Labour Party in Parliament as their moderate predecessors, and this in turn could have loosened the constraints on industrial violence noted in the previous chapter. Arthur Scargill, in particular, resolutely refused to condemn picket-line violence; 'the only action I would condemn is the decision to go back to work'.[88] Indeed, in view of the kind of factors considered above, it is perhaps surprising that the miners' strike was not even more disorderly.

Conclusion and implications

Our investigation into the policing of industrial disputes has revealed several distinct forms of disorder. In the 1890s strikers often attempted to destroy the property of their employers and responded to intervention by the forces of law and order with spirited defiance that took the form of stoning. Destruction of property gave way to the violent obstruction of non-strikers in the years immediately preceding the First World War, while the inter-war period was notable for the decline of industrial disorder. Since the 1940s violence has tended to be, until comparatively recently, restricted to the pushing and shoving which was dominant during disputes such as the 1972 miners' strike and Grunwick. In the 1980s industrial disorder seems to have reverted to a style similar to that which prevailed at Featherstone with strikers sabotaging property and stoning police.

We have also seen that just as there are several historically distinct forms of disorder so too are there corresponding control tactics. Shooting by the army later gave way to batoning by police, for example at Tonypandy, which in turn was replaced by the cordons and wedges used in more modern times to contain and control pickets in a relatively non-violent manner. Following the summer disturbances of 1981 public order tactics have once again become more violent with riot squads armed with short shields and truncheons charging and batoning strikers.

Six patterns of confrontation have, then, occurred during the period of our study (see Fig. 1), each of which has tended to be less violent than its predecessor; that is, until the 1980s when a reversion to an earlier and more violent pattern has taken place. Although these patterns of confrontation indicate how industrial conflict has changed they do not explain why these changes have occurred. As we have seen three historical developments, the constitutionalisation of strikers and police, the growth of the mass media and the democratisation of civil liberties, have played an important part in bringing about the transition from one pattern to another. Moreover, we found that the development of public order tactics in the early 1980s, together with increased political support for more vigorous policing, have accounted, at least in part, for the tactical reversion to batoning noted earlier in the text. Similarly, the return to destruction and stoning by striking miners in 1984 can be explained by reference to factors such as the new police tactics, increasing frustration and isolation from the restraining influence of the Labour movement.

As for the future, there is every reason to suppose that the violence of the miners' strike will not generally be repeated in subsequent disputes. It seems that several unique features – the lack of wholehearted support from other unions, the marked absence of internal unity, the militant leadership, the sheer length of the stoppage – prevented the constraints on violence which had proved so effective in the past from being fully operative. However, there is clear evidence of the continued presence of these restraining influences. Throughout the stoppage Labour leaders repeatedly deplored picket line violence. Neil Kinnock, in particular, made what one left-wing magazine called 'convulsive condemnations' whenever he spoke on the subject of the strike.[1] In addition, written instructions to 'play it cool' were issued to pickets on several occasions.[2] Moreover, on picket lines, even at the scenes of the more disorderly confrontations, strikers seemed well aware of the importance of non-violence. For example, a picket at the Orgreave coking plant said 'we don't want any bricks thrown, all we want is a good push'; another commented 'we don't want anyone hurt, we don't want even the police hurt'.[3] Even some pickets who admitted throwing missiles said they were opposed to violence but had momentarily lost their temper because of 'brutal policing' and the frustration of watching 'thousands of waggons pass through the line'.[4] It seems, then, that the return to 'stoning' may be a temporary phenomenon; a throwback in the evolution of successively less violent styles of industrial disorder. On the other hand, one must remain cautious for these constraints on violence have, to some extent, been offset by modern police tactics which tend to generate a vicious spiral of violence and destruction. The links in this fatal nexus, which may lead ultimately to a widening gulf between police and public, are illustrated in Fig. 2.

Although we have drawn attention to the application of riot control tactics to industrial situations it is worth noting that public order policing is still subject to various constraints. For example, one of our police respondents revealed that more repressive tactics could be used against black rioters than would be considered in an industrial situation:

I don't want the police to use rubber bullets or CS gas at all. Gas is very unreliable; it can blow back on you. With baton rounds you can say with certainty that for every so many thousand fired, someone's going to be killed. The police need the support of the public in order to operate efficiently, public opinion wouldn't support the use of baton rounds or CS gas against strikers . . . they'd support CS gas and all the other things against rioters, but not against strikers. (Superintendent)

Whether the police are tolerant or repressive in a given situation depends, then, not on personal or institutionalised prejudice but on the perceived

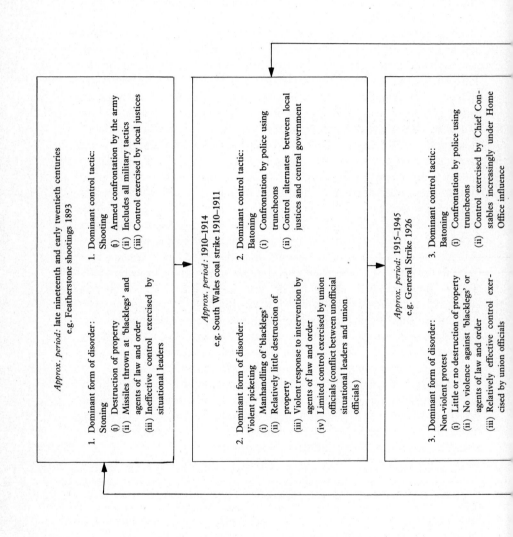

Approx. period: late nineteenth and early twentieth centuries
e.g. Featherstone shootings 1893

1. Dominant form of disorder:
   Stoning
   (i) Destruction of property
   (ii) Missiles thrown at 'blacklegs' and agents of law and order
   (iii) Ineffective control exercised by situational leaders

1. Dominant control tactic:
   Shooting
   (i) Armed confrontation by the army
   (ii) Includes all military tactics
   (iii) Control exercised by local justices

Approx. period: 1910–1914
e.g. South Wales coal strike 1910–1911

2. Dominant form of disorder:
   Violent picketing
   (i) Manhandling of 'blacklegs'
   (ii) Relatively little destruction of property
   (iii) Violent response to intervention by agents of law and order
   (iv) Limited control exercised by union officials (conflict between unofficial situational leaders and union officials)

2. Dominant control tactic:
   Batoning
   (i) Confrontation by police using truncheons
   (ii) Control alternates between local justices and central government

Approx. period: 1915–1945
e.g. General Strike 1926

3. Dominant form of disorder:
   Non-violent protest
   (i) Little or no destruction of property
   (ii) No violence against 'blacklegs' or agents of law and order
   (iii) Relatively effective control exercised by union officials

3. Dominant control tactic:
   Batoning
   (i) Confrontation by police using truncheons
   (ii) Control exercised by Chief Constables increasingly under Home Office influence

148

Approx. period: 1946–1980
e.g. miners' strike 1972

4. Dominant form of disorder: Pushing and shoving

(i) Relatively non-violent obstruction of 'blacklegs', materials and police and police. Effective control exercised by union officials

4. Dominant control tactic: Pushing and shoving

(i) Unarmed relatively non-violent confrontation by police, includes the use of wedges and cordons

(ii) Control exercised by Chief Constables under Home Office influence

Approx. period: 1946–1980
e.g. miners' strike 1974

5. Dominant form of disorder: symbolic confrontation

(i) Limited number of pickets

(ii) No physical contact with 'blacklegs' or police

(iii) Very effective control exercised by union officials and stewards

5. Dominant control tactic: Symbolic confrontation

(i) Limited number of police

(ii) No physical contact with pickets

(iii) Control exercised by Chief Constables under Home Office influence

Approx. period: 1980s
e.g. miners' strike, 1984–5

6. Dominant form of disorder: Stoning

(i) Destruction of property
(ii) Missiles thrown at 'blacklegs' and agents of law and order
(iii) Periodic loss of control by union officials

6. Dominant control tactic: Batoning

(i) Confrontation by police using truncheons and riot shields
(ii) Control exercised by Chief Constables under Home Office influence

Figure 1. The changing nature of industrial confrontation

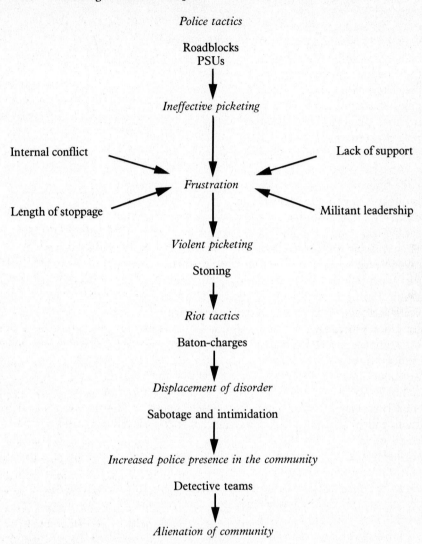

Figure 2. The escalation of disorder during the 1984–5 miners' strike

political consequences of repression and these, it would appear, are greater in the industrial context than in relation to Britain's black population.[5]

Moreover, the same kind of factors which in the past contributed to the development of non-violent police tactics were also present during the miners' strike. The National Council for Civil Liberties launched an enquiry, supported by some police authorities, into the policing of the dispute and despatched 50 observers to the picket lines.[6] Media coverage sometimes homed in on aggressive behaviour; on one occasion a policeman was seen, on ITN's 'News at Ten', to strike a seemingly passive picket several hefty blows with his truncheon.[7] In addition, several Labour MPs, including the Shadow Home Secretary, and many local authorities criticised the police response to the strike.[8] However, there is less reason in the case of the police to suppose that these constraining factors will force a return to pushing and shoving. The Thatcher administration's support for 'hard line' policing seems likely to ensure that the tactical gap in police training is not closed; baton-wielding riot squads, it seems, are here to stay.

What has disappeared, without much notice ever being paid to its existence, is the informal control exercised by the community over the police. Today it is difficult to imagine a Chief Constable allowing a coke depot to be closed down by mass picketing for fear of alienating his local population. The mutual aid system, which relies on police from other areas, riot tactics and the unmistakable 'get tough' messages from central government have combined to far outweigh any influence on the police that the local community can bring to bear. This, of course, means that some kind of formal democratic control is desperately required if the police, as they often claim, are really to police with consent. As we have seen, directions and guidance from the Home Office often amount to *de facto* control, but this, given the absence of significant party political disagreement over any aspect of policing, is only democratic in a very narrow sense. Similarly, cosmetic community policing and token liaison committees will not suffice. The drift from a police service to a police force will only be checked by the acquisition of real power by community representatives. Such a development could lead to a modification of those police tactics which have themselves contributed to increasing levels of disorder.

Surely, the time is ripe for the police to recognise in their training a distinction between industrial and other forms of disorder. After all, different forms of public disorder conform to different patterns and are subject to different constraints. Our study has shown that the constitutionalisation of the working class, through political enfranchisement and the development of a strong trade union and Labour Party has, on the whole, restricted industrial violence. Yet, there has been no comparable political mobilisation by the people of Britain's deprived inner cities and therefore fewer constraints on disorder. There is a very real danger that the unreflective application of tactical solutions devised for one context may contribute to escalating disorder in the other.

We end with the essentially simple question: What do we want the police for? To help enforce elected governments' industrial policy or to serve, as best they can, the various needs of local people? Which more closely resembles the ideal of democratic policing and which the Orwellian police state?

Notes

1. Introduction

1 *The Guardian*, 19 June 1984.
2 See, for example, Carol Ackroyd, Karen Margolis and Tim Shallice, *The Technology of Political Control*, 2nd edn (Pluto Press, 1980).
3 Interview with Chief Superintendent, 2 September 1981.
4 Interview with Superintendent, 5 August 1981.
5 Interview with Assistant Chief Constable, 18 September 1981.

2. Stoning and shooting

1 Report of the Committee appointed to inquire into the circumstances connected with the disturbance at Featherstone on 7 September 1893. Parliamentary Paper, C 7234 (1893), p. 6.
2 *Ibid.*, p. 1.
3 *The Times*, 1 August 1893.
4 *The Times*, 2 August 1893.
5 Parliamentary Paper, C 7234, p. 112.
6 *Ibid.*
7 *Ibid.*
8 J. J. Terrett, *The Rt. Hon. H. H. Asquith, M.P. and the Featherstone Massacre* (Twentieth Century Press, n.d.), p. 5.
9 Parliamentary Paper, C 7234, p. 2.
10 *Ibid.*
11 *Ibid.*, p. 7.
12 *Ibid.*, Minutes of Evidence, p. 103.
13 Parliamentary Paper, C 7234, p. 3.
14 *Ibid.*, p. 4.
15 *Ibid.*
16 *Ibid.*, Minutes of Evidence, p. 9.
17 Parliamentary Paper, C 7234, p. 8.
18 *Ibid.*, p. 6.
19 *Ibid.*
20 *Ibid.*, pp. 8–9.
21 *The Times*, 9 September 1893.
22 Parliamentary Paper, C 7234, p. 6.
23 See, for example, *ibid.*, Appendix III; *The Times*, 28 August 1893, 26 October

1893; J. E. Williams, *The Derbyshire Miners* (Allen & Unwin, 1962), p. 333; *Derbyshire Times*, 2 and 9 September 1893.
24 G. Rudé, *The Crowd in History, 1730–1848* (Wiley, 1964), p. 34.
25 Parliamentary Paper, C 7234, p. 1.
26 *Ibid.*
27 See, for example, *Police Review*, 30 October 1893; *The Times*, 1 August; 21 August; 17 October; 19 October; 20 October; 31 October 1893.
28 See, for example, *The Times*, 5 September 1893; Parliamentary Paper, C 7234, Appendix III.
29 *Derbyshire Times*, 9 September 1893.
30 *The Times*, 21 August 1893.
31 Parliamentary Paper, C 7234, Minutes of Evidence.
32 T. A. Critchley, *The Conquest of Violence* (Schocken Books, 1972), pp. 66–8.
33 Rudé, *The Crowd in History*, p. 35.
34 Major O. Teichman, *The Yeomanry as an aid to the Civil Power, 1795–1867* (Army Historical Research, 1940), vol. 19, p. 80.
35 L. Radzinowicz, *A History of English Criminal Law* (Stevens, 1968), vol. 4, p. 235; see also Teichman, p. 142.
36 *Ibid.*, p. 202.
37 Lieut-Gen. Sir W. Napier, *The Life and Opinions of General Sir Charles J. Napier* (1857), vol. 2, p. 63.
38 Reports from Assistant Hand-Loom Weavers Commissioner Part II (43–1), PP (1840), vol. 23, p. 53. See also Radzinowicz, *English Criminal Law*, vol. 4, pp. 236–8.
39 *Ibid.*, pp. 279–81.
40 Home Office Papers, HO 45/9377/41103/11 dated 21 March 1875.
41 Select Committee on the Employment of Military in Cases of Disturbance, PP (1908), pp. 4 and 5.
42 *Ibid.*, p. 4.
43 *Ibid.*, p. 4.
44 Parliamentary Paper, C 7234, Minutes of Evidence, p. 4.
45 *Ibid.*, p. 29.
46 *Ibid.*, p. 36.
47 *Ibid.*, p. 25.
48 *Ibid.*, p. 29.
49 *The Times*, 14 September 1893.
50 Parliamentary Paper, C 7234, p. 8.
51 *Ibid.*, p. 9.
52 *Ibid.*, p. 85.
53 For an account of the Oliver affair see Critchley, *Conquest of Violence*, pp. 110–11.
54 See T. Bunyan, *The Political Police in Britain* (Quartet, 1977), p. 63.
55 T. C. Mather, *Public Order in the Age of the Chartists* (Manchester University Press, 1959), p. 183.
56 *Ibid.*, p. 165.
57 Parliamentary Paper, C 7234, p. 10.
58 *Ibid.*, p. 4.
59 *Ibid.*, p. 5.
60 *The Times*, 11 September 1893.
61 Parliamentary Paper, C 7234, Minutes of Evidence, p. 10.

62 *The Times*, 13 September 1893 and 16 October 1893.
63 R. Quinault, 'The Warwickshire County Magistracy and Public Order, 1830–1870', in J. Stevenson and R. Quinault (eds.), *Popular Protest and Public Order* (Allen & Unwin, 1974), pp. 182–3.
64 Parliamentary Paper, C 7234, Minutes of Evidence, p. 7.

3. The pivotal period

1 O. Morgan, 'The Merthyr of Keir Hardie', in G. Williams (ed.), *Merthyr Politics: The Making of a Working Class Tradition* (University of Wales Press, 1966), p. 74.
2 R. P. Arnot, *The Miners; Years of Struggle* (Allen & Unwin, 1953), p. 59.
3 Colliery Strike Disturbances in South Wales, November 1910, Parliamentary Paper, Cd 5568 (1911), p. 4.
4 *Ibid.*, p. 10.
5 *South Wales Daily News*, 8 November 1910.
6 Parliamentary Paper, Cd 5568, p. 31.
7 *The Times*, 8 November 1910.
8 D. Evans, *Labour Strife in the South Wales Coalfield, 1910–1911* (Educational Publishing Co. Ltd, 1911), p. 108; B. Holton, *British Syndicalism 1900–1914* (Pluto Press, 1976), p. 81.
9 Transcript of an interview with ex-PC W. Knipe, 1973, Oral History Collection, South Wales Miners' Library, Swansea; *Western Mail*, 8, 9 November 1910; *Rhondda Leader*, 5, 12 November 1910; *South Wales Daily News*, 9 November 1910.
10 Holton, *British Syndicalism*, p. 81; Evans, *Labour Strife in the South Wales Coalfield*, pp. 40–9.
11 D. Smith, 'Tonypandy 1910: Definitions of Community', *Past and Present*, No. 87 (May 1980), p. 170.
12 Parliamentary Paper, Cd 5568, p. 49.
13 *South Wales Weekly Post*, 12 November 1910.
14 Smith, 'Tonypandy 1910', pp. 166–7.
15 *South Wales Weekly Post*, 12 November 1910; see also *Western Mail*, 9 November 1910; *Rhondda Leader*, 12 November 1910.
16 W. Childs, *Episodes and Reflections* (Cassell, 1930), p. 82.
17 Transcript of an interview with Bryn Lewis, 1973, Oral History Collection, South Wales Miners' Library, Swansea.
18 *South Wales Daily News*, 9 November 1910; *Western Mail*, 9 November 1910.
19 *Sunday Times*, 13 November 1910.
20 *Rhondda Leader*, 12 November 1910.
21 Smith, 'Tonypandy 1910', p. 168.
22 *South Wales Daily News*, 9 November 1910; *Rhondda Leader*, 12 November 1910; *Western Mail*, 9 November 1910; see also Smith, 'Tonypandy 1910', *ibid.*
23 *The Times*, 28 June 1911; *The Times*, 26 June 1911.
24 *The Times*, 30 June 1911.
25 *The Times*, 7 July 1911.
26 General Sir Nevil Macready, *Annals of an Active Life* (Hutchinson, 1924), vol. I, p. 160.
27 Quoted in G. Askwith, *Industrial Problems and Disputes* (Murray, 1920), p. 149.

28 The German gunboat *Panther* put in at the port of Agadir in Morocco. Britain feared, probably correctly, that this was the first step in a German plan to establish a naval base in Morocco which would threaten Gibraltar and the sea route through the Mediterranean to India. The Germans eventually withdrew, following strong warnings from Britain, and recognised French predominance in Morocco in return for cession of half of the French Congo to Germany.

29 The Employment of Military During Railway Strike 1911, Parliamentary Paper, 1911 (323) XLVII, p. 693, pp. 3–9.

30 R. P. Arnot, *The Miners: Years of Struggle* (Allen and Unwin, 1953), p. 101.

31 *Ibid.*, p. 102.

32 *The Times*, 2 March 1912.

33 Quoted in R. P. Arnot, *South Wales Miners 1898–1914* (Allen & Unwin, 1967), p. 294.

34 Table constructed from reports published in *The Times* during March 1912.

35 D. Williams, *Keeping the Peace* (Hutchinson, 1967), p. 184.

36 K. O. Fox, 'The Tonypandy Riots', *Army Quarterly*, vol. 104 (October 1973), p. 73.

37 Parliamentary Paper, Cd 5568, p. 48.

38 Macready, *Annals of an Active Life*, vol. I, p. 137.

39 *Ibid.*, p. 152.

40 Parliamentary Paper, Cd 5568, p. 16; R. A. Leeson, *Strike: A Life History 1887–1971* (Allen & Unwin, 1973), p. 148.

41 *South Wales Daily News*, 10 November 1910.

42 Macready, *Annals of an Active Life*, vol. I, p. 139.

43 *Ibid.*, p. 137.

44 *Ibid.*, p. 155.

45 Parliamentary Paper, Cd 5568, p. 48; see also p. 26.

46 Diary of Captain Lindsay, Glamorgan R.O. 1889–1941 (the 1910 diary is missing), See also Smith, 'Tonypandy 1910', pp. 173–4.

47 Macready, *Annals of an Active Life*, vol. I, p. 140; see also p. 132.

48 *Ibid.*, p. 135.

49 R. S. Churchill, *Winston S. Churchill* (Heinemann, 1967), vol. II, Companion, Part 2, 1907–1911, p. 1116.

50 *The Times*, 23 August 1911.

51 L. Masterman, *C. F. G. Masterman* (Nicholson and Watson, 1939), pp. 206–7.

52 Churchill, *Winston S. Churchill*, vol. II, Companion, Part 2, 1907–1911, p. 1274.

53 G. Askwith, *Industrial Problems and Disputes* (Murray, 1920), p. 150.

54 Churchill, *Winston S. Churchill*, vol. II, Companion, Part 2, 1907–1911, pp. 1263–4.

55 *The Times*, 8 August 1911.

56 Parliamentary Paper, Cd 5568.

57 *Ibid.*, p. 31.

58 *Ibid.*, p. 49.

59 *Ibid.*, p. 21.

60 Childs, *Episodes and Reflections*, p. 85.

61 Parliamentary Paper, Cd 5568, p. 25.

62 Evans, *Labour Strife in the South Wales Coalfield*, p. 104.

63 Childs, *Episodes and Reflections*, p. 79.

64 Parliamentary Paper, Cd 5568, pp. 16 and 21.

65 Macready, *Annals of an Active Life*, vol. I, p. 140.

66 *Ibid.*, pp. 142 and 135; see also Childs, *Episodes and Reflections*, p. 84.
67 Macready, *Annals of an Active Life*, vol. I, p. 153.
68 Parliamentary Paper, Cd 5568, p. 18.
69 *Ibid.*, p. 18; see also p. 30.
70 Macready, *Annals of an Active Life*, vol. I, p. 154.
71 *Ibid.*, p. 147.
72 Arnot, *South Wales Miners*, pp. 202–4.
73 *Ibid.*
74 *The Times*, 9 November 1910.
75 *The Times*, 16 December 1910.
76 *Hansard*, vol. XX (20 HC 1910), 24 November 1910, p. 413.
77 *Ibid.*
78 *South Wales Daily News*, 23, 28, 29, 30 November 1910; *Wales Weekly Post*, 3 December 1910; *Police Review*, 2 December 1910; *Daily Mail*, 8 November 1910.
79 *Hansard*, vol. XX (20 HC 1910), 24 November 1910, Adjournment Debate.
80 Parliamentary Paper, Cd 5568, p. 52.
81 *Ibid.*
82 *Ibid.*, p. 53.
83 Table constructed from information provided in Parliamentary Paper, Cd 5568.
84 Fox, 'The Tonypandy Riots', p. 75.
85 Childs, *Episodes and Reflections*, p. 87.
86 *Police Review*, 16 December 1910.
87 Parliamentary Paper, Cd 5568, p. 7.
88 *Ibid.*, p. 8.
89 *Ibid.*, p. 33.
90 Askwith, *Industrial Problems and Disputes*, p. 164.
91 Masterman, *C. F. G. Masterman*, p. 205.
92 *Ibid.*, p. 208.
93 *The Times*, 12 August 1911.
94 Masterman, *C. F. G. Masterman*, p. 207.
95 *The Times*, 17 August 1911.
96 *The Times*, 11 August 1911.
97 Churchill, *Winston S. Churchill*, vol. II, Companion, Part 2, 1907–1911, p. 1291.
98 *The Times*, 30 August 1911.
99 *Ibid.*
100 K. Hardie, 'Killing No Murder', 1911, cited in R. and E. Frow, and M. Katanka, *Strikes: A Documentary History* (Charles Knight, 1971), p. 145.
101 *The Times*, 30 August 1911.

4. The decline of violent labour protest

1 M. Foot, *Aneurin Bevan* (Paladin, 1975), vol. 1, pp. 72–3.
2 B. Thomson, Sir, *Queer People* (Hodder and Stoughton, 1922), pp. 272–3.
3 T. Jones (edited by K. Middlemas), *Whitehall Diary* (O.U.P., 1969), vol. 1, p. 66.
4 *The Times*, 31 August 1918; see also *The Times*, 2 September 1918.
5 *Daily Mail*, 22 July 1919.
6 *Daily Mail*, 24 July 1919, see also *Daily Mail*, 26 July 1919.

7 *The Times*, 4 August 1919; see also G. W. Reynolds and A. Judge, *The Night the Police Went on Strike* (Weidenfeld and Nicolson, 1968).
8 R. H. Desmarais, 'The British Government's Strike-breaking Organization and Black Friday', *Journal of Contemporary History*, 6, No. 2 (1971) p. 121.
9 *Daily Mail*, 20, 22 October 1920.
10 R. P. Arnot, *The Miners: Years of Struggle* (Allen and Unwin, 1953), p. 296.
11 *Daily Mail*, 16 May 1921.
12 *Daily Mail*, 14 April 1921.
13 *Durham Chronicle*, 15 April 1921; *Derbyshire Times*, 9 April 1921.
14 *Daily Mail*, 7 June 1921.
15 *Police Review*, 17 June 1921.
16 *Ibid.*
17 R. H. Desmarais, 'Strikebreaking and the Labour Government of 1921', *Journal of Contemporary History* (1973), p. 165.
18 R. W. Lyman, *The First Labour Government* (Chapman and Hall, 1957), p. 219.
19 *The Times*, 20 February 1924.
20 By 1925 the Triple Alliance had become defunct and the TUC now represented the trade union movement in negotiations with government.
21 *Daily Mail*, 6 May 1926.
22 Cited in C. Farman, *The General Strike May 1926* (Rupert Hart-Davis, 1972), p. 185.
23 *Daily Mail*, 10 May 1926.
24 Cited in Farman, *General Strike*, p. 192.
25 *Ibid.*
26 *Daily Mail*, 6 May 1926.
27 *Derbyshire Times*, 24 July 1926; see also *British Gazette*, 12 May 1926; J. E. Williams, *The Derbyshire Miners* (Allen & Unwin, 1962), p. 702.
28 *Police Review*, 28 May 1926; *Daily Mail*, 11 May 1926.
29 *Police Review*, 21 May 1926.
30 For accounts of public disorder during this period see W. Hannington, *Unemployed Struggles* (E. P. Publishing Ltd, 1973); W. Hannington, *Never on Our Knees* (Lawrence and Wishart, 1967); S. Bowes, *The Police and Civil Liberties* (Lawrence and Wishart, 1966).
31 Bowes, *Police and Civil Liberties*, p. 28 and p. 32.
32 *The Times*, 26 April 1937.
33 Desmarais, 'The British Government's Strikebreaking Organization and Black Friday', p. 114.
34 General Sir Nevil Macready, *Annals of an Active Life* (Hutchinson, 1924), vol. II, pp. 418–19.
35 *Review of the Work of the Strike Committee*, PRO, CAB, pp. 58–9.
36 Desmarais, 'Strikebreaking and Black Friday', p. 114.
37 T. Bunyan, *The Political Police in Britain* (Quartet, 1977), p. 258. See also *State Research Bulletin*, vol. 2, No. 8 (October–November 1978), pp. 14–15.
38 Desmarais, 'Strikebreaking and Black Friday', p. 120.
39 *Ibid.*, pp. 120–1.
40 *Ibid.*, p. 125; *Daily Mail*, 12 April 1921.
41 L. S. Amery, *My Political Life* (Hutchinson, 1935–53), vol. 2, p. 217.
42 HO 45399004/1.
43 Home Affairs Committee, Conclusion No. 101, included in CAB 27/82.
44 Desmarais, 'Strikebreaking and Black Friday', p. 126.

45 Desmarais, 'Strikebreaking and the Labour Government of 1921', pp. 168–9.
46 *Ibid.*, p. 167.
47 *Ibid..*
48 T. Bunyan, *The Political Police in Britain* (Quartet, 1977), p. 262.
49 Table constructed from information provided in T. A. Critchley, *A History of Police in England and Wales* (Constable, 1978), p. 200; T. Cliff, *The Crisis* (Pluto Press, 1975), p. 97; Farman, *General Strike*, p. 194.
50 Cited in Farman, *General Strike*, pp. 41–2.
51 *Ibid.*, pp. 188–9.
52 Farman, *General Strike*, p. 194.
53 Bunyan, *Political Police*, p. 264; see also *State Research Bulletin*, vol. 2, No. 8 (October–November 1978), p. 15.
54 Thomson, *Queer People*, p. 274.
55 Sir B. Thomson, *The Scene Changes* (Collins, 1939), p. 314.
56 *Ibid.*, p. 297.
57 Thomson, *Queer People*, p. 274.
58 Thomson, *The Scene Changes*, p. 338.
59 Macready, *Annals of an Active Life*, vol. II, p. 417.
60 Critchley, *A History of Police*, p. 188.
61 *Police Review*, 1 April 1920.
62 T. Barnes, 'Special Branch and the First Labour Government', *The Historical Journal*, 22, No. 4 (1979), p. 943.
63 *Ibid.*, p. 945.
64 Sir Wyndham Childs, *Episodes and Reflections* (Cassell, 1930), p. 209.
65 Barnes, 'Special Branch and the First Labour Government', p. 945.
66 J. Symons, *The General Strike* (Cresset, 1957), pp. 112–13.
67 *The Times*, 15 January 1980; see also T. A. Critchley, *The Conquest of Violence* (Schocken Books, 1970), p. 192; Farman, *General Strike*, pp. 201–2.
68 *Daily Mail*, 6 May 1926.
69 Farman, *General Strike*, p. 201.
70 Hannington, *Unemployed Struggles*, pp. 146–53; see also Farman, *General Strike*.
71 Farman, *General Strike*.
72 *Ibid.*, pp. 201–2.
73 See, for example, R. Hayburn, 'The Police and the Hunger Marches', *International Review of Labour History*, 17, No. 3 (1972), pp. 625–44 and Hannington, *Unemployed Struggles*, Chapter VIII.
74 Bunyan, *Political Police*, pp. 155–6.
75 Thomson, *Queer People*, p. 273.
76 Desmarais, 'Strikebreaking and Black Friday', p. 116.
77 Jones, *Whitehall Diary*, vol. I, p. 97.
78 *Ibid.*, p. 99.
79 *Ibid.*
80 *Ibid.*, pp. 99–101.
81 Desmarais, 'Strikebreaking and Black Friday', p. 122.
82 *Ibid.*
83 C.P. 1706, 29 July 1920, CAB 24/110.
84 *Police Chronicle*, 1 October 1920.
85 *Hansard*, 6 August 1925.
86 Childs, *Episodes and Reflections*, pp. 213–14.
87 *British Gazette*, 6 May 1926.

88 *Daily Mail*, 8 May 1926; Jones, *Whitehall Diary*, vol. I, p. 97.
89 *Daily Mail*, 10 May 1926.
90 *Police Chronicle*, 20 May 1921.
91 *British Gazette*, 8 May 1926.
92 Symons, *The General Strike*, p. 159.
93 *Daily Mail*, 7 May 1926.
94 Critchley, *A History of Police*, p. 200; see also D. Thomson, *England in the Twentieth Century* (Penguin, 1965), pp. 115–16.
95 *Glasgow Herald*, 1 February 1919.
96 *Glasgow Herald*, 19 April 1919.
97 Farman, *General Strike*, p. 196.
98 R. A. Leeson, *Strike: A Live History 1887–1971* (Allen & Unwin, 1973).
99 Bowes, *Police and Civil Liberties*, p. 27.
100 Farman, *General Strike*, p. 196.
101 *Ibid.*
102 *Ibid.*, pp. 195–6.
103 Leeson, *Strike*, p. 91.
104 *Police Review*, 28 May 1926, Report of Commissioner of Police of the Metropolis for the Year 1926, Cmd 2882, p. 7.
105 Farman, *General Strike*, p. 199.
106 E. Burns, *The General Strike: Trades Councils in Action* (Labour Research Department, 1926), p. 73.
107 *Derbyshire Times*, 4 September 1926.
108 Burns, *The General Strike*, p. 105.
109 Cliff, *The Crisis*, p. 107; CPGB 8th Party Congress, Report, p. 13; G. A. Phillips, *The General Strike: The Politics of Industrial Conflict* (Weidenfeld and Nicolson, 1976), p. 204; Burns, *The General Strike*, p. 69.

5. Pushing and shoving

1 A. W. Gouldner, *Patterns of Industrial Bureaucracy* (Routledge and Kegan Paul, 1955); see also A. W. Gouldner, *Wildcat Strike* (Routledge and Kegan Paul, 1955).
2 J. Arnison, *The Million Pound Strike* (Lawrence and Wishart, 1970), pp. 16–17.
3 *Manchester Evening News*, 6 December 1966.
4 *The Times*, 7 December 1967.
5 *The Times*, 7 December 1967; 23 February 1967.
6 *The Times*, 23 February 1967.
7 *Ibid.*
8 *The Times*, 23 September 1967.
9 Arnison, *Million Pound Strike*, p. 74.
10 *The Times*, 23 February, 2 September, 18 November, 23 November 1967.
11 *Ibid.*, p. 75.
12 B. Whitaker, *The Police in Society* (Eyre Methuen, 1979), pp. 254–5.
13 T. Hall, *King Coal* (Penguin, 1981), p. 167.
14 *Ibid.*, p. 170.
15 T. F. Lindsay and M. Harrington, *The Conservative Party 1918–1979* (Macmillan, 1979), p. 271.
16 A. Scargill, 'The New Unionism', *New Left Review* (July–August 1975).
17 *The Times*, 13 January 1972, 14 January 1972 and *The Guardian*, 18 January 1972.

18 *The Times*, 11 January 1972.
19 *The Times*, 18 January 1972.
20 J. E. Trice, 'Methods of and Attitudes to Picketing', *Criminal Law Review* (May 1975), p. 273.
21 *The Times*, 19 January 1972.
22 *The Times*, 20 January 1972.
23 *Daily Mail*, 20 January 1972.
24 Hall, *King Coal*, p. 183; see also *The Times*, 22 January 1972.
25 *The Sun*, 28 January 1972; see also *The Times*, 22 January 1972.
26 Trice, 'Picketing', p. 273.
27 *The Guardian*, 1 February 1972.
28 Hall, *King Coal*, p. 188.
29 *Ibid.*
30 *The Miner*, April 1972.
31 A. J. McLeod, 'Police and the Pickets', unpublished paper, Department of Law, Manchester Polytechnic, 1978, p. 51.
32 Quoted in R. Clutterbuck, *Britain in Agony* (Penguin, 1980), p. 66.
33 Hall, *King Coal*, p. 189.
34 McLeod, 'Police and the Pickets', p. 52.
35 *Ibid.*
36 Scargill, 'New Unionism', p. 15.
37 *The Miner*, April 1972.
38 Clutterbuck, *Britain in Agony*, p. 67; Hall, *King Coal*, p. 190; Scargill, 'New Unionism', pp. 15–16; *Birmingham Post*, 8 February 1972.
39 Clutterbuck, *Britain in Agony*, p. 69.
40 *Ibid.*, p. 68.
41 *Ibid.*, p. 69.
42 Scargill, 'New Unionism', p. 18.
43 *Ibid.*, p. 19.
44 Trice, 'Picketing', p. 275.
45 Table constructed from information in Clutterbuck, *Britain in Agony*, pp. 65–76; Hall, *King Coal*, pp. 189–91; McLeod, 'Police and the Pickets', pp. 50–8.
46 *The Guardian*, 15, 16 and 18 February 1972.
47 *The Miner*, June 1972.
48 *Birmingham Post*, 15 February 1972.
49 S. Cranidge, 'Report on the Police Operation at the Trent and Humber Ports in the Scunthorpe Division of the Lincolnshire Constabulary between 20 July and 21 August 1972', Lincolnshire Constabulary 1972, p. 2 (unpublished confidential report).
50 *Ibid.*, p. 6.
51 *Ibid.*
52 *Ibid.*, pp. 8–9.
53 *Ibid.*, p. 11.
54 McLeod, 'Police and the Pickets', p. 63.
55 *Ibid.*
56 Cranidge, 'Police Operation at the Trent and Humber Ports', pp. 9–13.
57 *Ibid.*, pp. 14–17.
58 *Ibid.*, pp. 18–19.
59 *Ibid.*, p. 20.
60 *The Guardian*, 15 August 1972.
61 Table constructed from information in Cranidge, 'Police Operation at the Trent and Humber Ports' and McLeod, 'Police and the Pickets'.

62 See, for example, J. Rogaly, *Grunwick* (Penguin, 1977); J. Dromey and G. Taylor, *Grunwick: The Workers' Story* (Lawrence and Wishart, 1978); Lord Justice Scarman, 'Report of Inquiry into Dispute between Grunwick Processing Laboratories and Members of APEX', Cmnd 6922 (HMSO, 1977); G. Ward, *Fort Grunwick* (Temple Smith, 1977); Clutterbuck, *Britain in Agony*, pp. 202–23; McLeod, 'Police and the Pickets', pp. 70–86.

63 Scarman, 'Report of Inquiry'; *The Times*, 23 July 1977; *Sunday Telegraph*, 26 June 1977.

64 Rogaly, *Grunwick*, p. 125.

65 *Ibid.*

66 Clutterbuck, *Britain in Agony*, p. 69.

67 *Socialist Worker*, 11 June 1977.

68 *Socialist Worker*, 23 May 1977; 11 June 1977.

69 *The Times*, 14 June 1977.

70 *Ibid.*

71 *Ibid.*

72 *The Observer*, 26 June 1977; *The Times*, 14 June 1977.

73 *New Society*, 30 June 1977, p. 655.

74 *The Times*, 25 June 1977.

75 *New Society*, 30 June 1977, p. 655.

76 *Ibid.*, p. 656.

77 *The Times*, 25 June 1977.

78 Rogaly, *Grunwick*, p. 87.

79 *The Times*, 22 June 1977; see also Clutterbuck, *Britain in Agony*, p. 213.

80 *The Times*, 23 June 1977.

81 *The Times*, 28 June 1977. Scargill was not the only one from the Barnsley contingent to be arrested; Maurice Jones the editor of the *Yorkshire Miner* was charged with insulting behaviour. Later when released on bail, Jones fled to East Germany and sought political asylum rather than face the charges arising from his arrest. On his return (Scargill flew over and brought him back) Jones alleged that Special Branch officers had threatened to harm his children. *The Times*, 25 July 1977; *The Guardian*, 16 July 1977; *Daily Telegraph*, 18 July 1977.

82 *The Times*, 24 June 1977; ITN News at Ten, 24 June 1977.

83 Rogaly, *Grunwick*, p. 108.

84 *The Times*, 24 June 1977.

85 *Socialist Worker*, 2, 9 and 16 July 1977.

86 *Militant*, 1 July 1977.

87 *The Times*, 12 July 1977.

88 Clutterbuck, *Britain in Agony*, p. 215.

89 *The Times*, 12 July 1977.

90 *Daily Telegraph*, 23 July 1977.

91 *The Times*, 9 August 1977; see also McLeod, 'Police and the Pickets', p. 81; Clutterbuck, *Britain in Agony*, p. 216.

92 *The Times*, 8 November 1977.

93 *The Times*, 8 January 1980.

94 Report by the Chief Constable of South Yorkshire submitted to the Police Committee on 2 June 1980, Appendix C., p. 1, unpublished.

95 *The Guardian*, 12 January 1980; *The Times*, 12 January 1980.

96 *The Times*, 17 January 1980.

97 *The Guardian*, 30 January 1980; see also *The Times*, 30 January 1980.

98 *The Times*, 30 January 1980.

99 *The Times*, 31 January 1980.

100 *The Times*, 1 February 1980.
101 *The Guardian*, 8 February 1980; *The Times*, 8 February 1980.
102 *The Times*, 12 February 1980.
103 *The Times*, 13 February 1980.
104 Report by the Chief Constable of South Yorkshire submitted to the Police Committee on 2 June 1980, Appendix C, p. 5; *The Times*, 14 February 1980.
105 *Ibid.*, p. 6; *The Times*, 15 February 1980.
106 *Ibid.*
107 *The Guardian*, 21 February 1980; see also *The Times* 21 February 1980.
108 *The Guardian*, 21 February 1980; *The Times*, 21 February 1980.
109 *The Times*, 25 February 1980; Report by the Chief Constable of South Yorkshire submitted to the Police Committee on 2 June 1980, Appendix C, p. 6.
110 Table constructed from information in the Report by the Chief Constable of South Yorkshire, *ibid.*; *The Times*, 9 January 1980; *The Times*, 13 and 15 February 1980 and Employment Committee, Minutes of Evidence, 27 February 1980, 462–ii, pp. 35–6.
111 *The Times*, 13 March 1980; Report by the Chief Constable of South Yorkshire submitted to the Police Committee on 2 June 1980, Appendix C, p. 7 and Appendix D.
112 *The Guardian*, 7 March 1980; see also *The Times*, 7 March 1980.
113 *The Times*, 2 April 1980.
114 Interview with NUM official, 23 September 1981.
115 See *The Sun*, 15 February 1980; *Daily Mail*, 15 February 1980.
116 Interview with NUM Branch Secretary, 15 October 1981.
117 Interview with NUM Branch Secretary, 23 September 1981.
118 *Ibid.*
119 *The Times*, 21 January 1980.
120 T. Bunyan, *The Political Police in Britain* (Quartet, 1978), pp. 265–9.
121 *Sunday Times*, 7 February 1971.
122 *Daily Express*, 12 January 1973; *Daily Telegraph Magazine*, 15 July 1973.
123 *Sunday Times*, 22 February 1976.
124 *The Times*, 13 November 1973.
125 See Clutterbuck, *Britain in Agony*, p. 215.
126 Bunyan, *Political Police*, p. 293.
127 *Ibid.*
128 *The Economist*, 27 May 1978; *The Times*, 18 April 1978; *State Research Bulletin*, vol. 3, No. 14 (October–November 1979), p. 19.
129 *The Guardian*, 22 February 1979; *The Guardian*, 17 March 1979; *State Research Bulletin*, vol. 3, No. 14 (October–November 1979), pp. 19–21.
130 Interview with Superintendent, 13 July 1981.
131 Interview with Superintendent, 5 August 1981.
132 Interview with ISTC official, 8 November 1981.
133 Interview with Superintendent, 20 January 1981.
134 Interview with ISTC officials, 8 November 1981.
135 *The Times*, 31 January 1968.
136 *Socialist Worker*, 25 June 1977.
137 Dromey and Taylor, *Grunwick*, p. 135.
138 Interview with Superintendent, 20 January 1981.
139 *New Statesman*, 1 February 1980.
140 *Ibid.*
141 *Daily Telegraph*, 4 September 1984.
142 Interview with Chief Superintendent, 11 November 1981.

143 Interview with Superintendent, 20 January 1981.
144 Interview with Superintendent, 16 April 1982.
145 Interview with NUM Branch Secretary, 2 October 1981.
146 *The Times*, 4 February 1980.
147 *The Guardian*, 7 December 1981.
148 Interview with Superintendent, 13 July 1981.
149 *Ibid.*
150 T. A. Critchley, *A History of Police in England and Wales* (Constable, 1967), pp. 179–81.
151 *State Research Bulletin*, vol. 3, No. 19 (Aug–Sept 1980), pp. 153–8.
152 S. Cranidge, 'Supplementary Report on the Police Operation at the Trent and Humber Ports in the Scunthorpe Division of the Lincolnshire Constabulary between 20 July and 21 August 1972', unpublished, Lincolnshire Police, 1972, p. 1.
153 Report by the Chief Constable of South Yorkshire submitted to the Police Committee on 2 June 1980, Appendix F, p. 2.
154 Interview with Chief Superintendent, 29 July 1981.
155 *Ibid.*
156 Paper presented at Bramshill Police Staff College 'carousel' course, 'Public Order – The Industrial Perspective', 15 February 1981–26 February 1981, p. 1.
157 *Ibid.*
158 Interview with Superintendent, 30 September 1981.
159 Paper presented at Bramshill Police Staff College 'carousel' course, 'Public Order – The Industrial Perspective', 15 February 1981–26 February 1981, pp. 1–2.
160 Interview with Assistant Chief Constable, 18 September 1981.
161 *New York Times*, 6 November 1967.
162 J. F. Coates, 'Wit and Humour: A Neglected Air in Crowd and Mob Control', *Crime and Delinquency*, 18, Part 2 (April 1972), pp. 190–1.
163 Interview with Chief Superintendent, 29 July 1981.
164 Interview with Chief Superintendent, 20 January 1982.
165 Interview with Superintendent, 16 April 1981.
166 *Ibid.*
167 Interview with Chief Superintendent, 20 January 1982.
168 *Ibid.*
169 *Ibid.*

6. Victory without violence

1 See, for example, *South Wales Daily News*, 24 November 1910.
2 O. K. Morgan, 'The Merthyr of Keir Hardie', in G. Williams, *Merthyr Politics: The Making of a Working-Class Tradition* (University of Wales Press, 1966), p. 65.
3 *South Wales Daily News*, 24 November 1910.
4 *South Wales Daily News*, 9 November 1910.
5 E. P. Thompson, *The Making of the English Working Class* (Penguin, 1968), pp. 756–7.
6 J. J. Territt, *The Right Hon. H. H. Asquith MP and the Featherstone Massacre* (Twentieth Century Press, n.d.), p. 17.
7 *Ibid.*, p. 3.
8 *Ibid.*, p. 6.
9 See R. S. Churchill, *Winston S. Churchill*, vol. II, *Younger Statesman 1901–1914* (Heinemann, 1967), p. 373; J. H. McEwen, 'Tonypandy: Churchill's

Albatross', *Queens Quarterly*, LXXVIII, No. 1 (Spring 1971), pp. 83–94.
10 *The Times*, 9 February 1950.
11 *The Times*, 9 and 10 February 1950.
12 *The Times*, 13 February 1950.
13 *Ibid.*
14 *Ibid.*
15 H. G. Nicholas, *The British General Election of 1950*, 2nd edn (Cass, 1968), p. 94.
16 R. P. Arnot, *The General Strike, May 1926: Its Origin and History* (Kelley, 1967), p. 162.
17 See, for example, *Daily Herald*, 4 May 1926 and *British Worker*, 5 May 1926.
18 E. Burns, *The General Strike May 1926: Trades Councils in Action* (Labour Research Department, 1926), p. 31; T. A. Critchley, *The Conquest of Violence* (Schocken Books, 1972), p. 190.
19 Critchley, *Conquest of Violence*, p. 189.
20 Burns, *General Strike*, pp. 27–8.
21 R. Reiner, 'Political Conflict and the British Police Tradition', *Contemporary Review*, 236 (April 1980), p. 195.
22 Interview with NUM Branch Secretary, 25 September 1981; interview with ISTC official, 13 November 1981.
23 *The Times*, 8 February 1974.
24 *Ibid.*
25 *Ibid.*
26 *The Times*, 6 March 1974.
27 K. O. Fox, 'The Tonypandy Riots', *Army Quarterly*, 104 (October 1973), p. 75.
28 *Ibid.*
29 T. A. Critchley, *A History of Police in England and Wales* (Constable, rev. edn, 1978), p. 198.
30 *Ibid.*, p. 219.
31 T. Bunyan, *The Political Police in Britain* (Quartet, 1976), p. 72.
32 R. Reiner, 'Police and Pickets', *New Society*, 7 July 1977, p. 14.
33 *Ibid.*
34 J. Brownlow, 'The South Yorkshire Steel Strike', *Police: The Magazine of the Police Federation*, June 1980, p. 20.
35 Interview with Chief Superintendent, 11 November 1981.
36 *Police Review*, 25 February 1972.
37 Brownlow, 'The South Yorkshire Steel Strike', p. 22.
38 Interview with Chief Inspector, 12 March 1982.
39 Reiner, 'Political Conflict and the British Police Tradition', p. 191.
40 J. Dromey and G. Taylor, *Grunwick: The Workers' Story* (Lawrence and Wishart, 1978), pp. 135–6.
41 B. Cox, *Civil Liberties in Britain* (Penguin, 1976), p. 13.
42 See A. Byles and P. Morris, *Unmet Need* (Routledge and Kegan Paul, 1977), Chapter 1, 'The Legal Advice and Assistance Act 1972, Legal Aid Act 1974'.
43 R. Kidd, *The Harworth Colliery Strike* (NCCL, 1973), p. 11.
44 R. P. Arnot, *The Miners in Crisis and War* (Allen and Unwin, 1961), p. 215.
45 Letter to the NCCL, 11 November 1977.
46 Letter to the NCCL, 7 November 1977; letters to the Home Secretary, 15 and 16 June 1977.

7. Industrial confrontation after the riots

1 *The Times*, 24 November 1983.
2 *Ibid.*
3 *The Times*, 30 November 1983.
4 *The Times*, 1 December 1983.
5 *Ibid.*
6 *Ibid.*
7 *Ibid.*
8 *The Times*, 2 December 1983.
9 *The Times*, 7 March 1984.
10 *Ibid.*
11 *The Times*, 10 March 1984.
12 *The Times*, 13 March 1984.
13 *The Times*, 15 March 1984.
14 *Ibid.*
15 *The Times*, 16 March 1984.
16 *The Times*, 19 March 1984.
17 *Ibid.*
18 *The Times*, 20 March 1984.
19 *The Times*, 21 March 1984.
20 *The Times*, 22 March 1984.
21 *The Times*, 24 March 1984.
22 *The Times*, 13 April 1984.
23 *The Times*, 23 March 1984.
24 *The Times*, 2 April 1984.
25 *The Times*, 19 March 1984.
26 *The Times*, 28 March 1984.
27 *Ibid.*
28 *The Times*, 2 April 1984.
29 *The Times*, 6 April 1984.
30 *The Times*, 9 April 1984.
31 *Ibid.*
32 *The Times*, 7 April 1984.
33 *The Times*, 14 April 1984.
34 *The Times*, 10 April 1984.
35 *The Times*, 13 April 1984.
36 *The Times*, 14 and 19 April 1984.
37 *The Times*, 2 May 1984.
38 *The Times*, 3 May 1984.
39 *The Times*, 4 May 1984.
40 *Ibid.*
41 *The Times*, 7 and 8 May 1984.
42 *The Times*, 15 May 1984.
43 *The Times*, 18 and 19 May 1984.
44 *The Times*, 19 May 1984.
45 *The Times*, 18 May 1984.
46 *The Times*, 29 May 1984.
47 *The Times*, 30 May 1984.
48 *Ibid.*
49 *The Times*, 31 May 1984.
50 *Ibid.*

51 *The Times*, 7 June 1984.
52 *The Times*, 8, 16 and 18 June 1984.
53 *The Times*, 19 June 1984.
54 *Ibid.*
55 BBC TV News, 19 June 1984.
56 *The Times*, 25, 27 and 28 July 1984.
57 *The Times*, 7 August 1984.
58 *The Times*, 6 August 1984.
59 *The Times*, 8 August 1984.
60 BBC TV News, 12 August 1984.
61 *The Times*, 17 August 1984.
62 *Ibid.*
63 *The Times*, 18 August 1984.
64 *Ibid.*
65 *The Times*, 1 September 1984.
66 *The Times*, 14 September 1984.
67 *The Times*, 19 September 1984.
68 *The Times*, 26 September 1984.
69 *The Times*, 29 September 1984.
70 *The Times*, 9 and 17 October 1984.
71 *The Times*, 20 and 26 October 1984.
72 *The Times*, 9 November 1984.
73 *The Times*, 10 November 1984.
74 *The Times*, 13 November 1984.
75 *The Times*, 19 June 1984.
76 This figure is based on an analysis of reports contained in *The Times* for the relevant period.
77 Interview with Chief Inspector, 5 November 1984.
78 Interview with Inspector, 6 November 1984.
79 Interview with Inspector, 3 November 1984.
80 Interview with NUM picket, 10 November 1984.
81 *The Times*, 17 March 1984.
82 *The Times*, 24 March 1984.
83 *The Times*, 19 March 1984.
84 See also *The Times*.
85 BBC TV News, 12 November 1984.
86 *The Times*, 6 April 1984.
87 Interview with NUM official, 14 November 1984.
88 BBC TV News, 12 November 1984.

8. Conclusion and implications

1 *Socialist Worker*, 9 October 1984.
2 Interview with NUM official, 14 November 1984.
3 ITN News at Ten, 1 June 1984.
4 Interview with NUM official, 14 November 1984.
5 See, for example, *Police Out of Brixton*, Revolutionary Communist Pamphlets No. 10 (April 1981), pp. 10–14.

6 *Daily Telegraph*, 14 August 1984.
7 ITN News at Ten, 18 June 1984.
8 See, for example, *The Times*, 21 September and 18 October 1984.

Index

accountability of police, *see under* police

Ackton Hall Colliery, 8, 13, 14, 19, 29

Advisory, Conciliation and Arbitration Service (ACAS), 84

Amalgamated Union of Engineering Workers (AUEW), 68, 69, 75

Amery, L. S., 55

Anderson, Sir John, 56

army, *see under* military

arrests, 49, 53, 59, 60, 65–6, 69, 70, 71, 73, 75, 76, 77, 78, 81, 82, 83, 85, 87, 88, 89, 90, 91, 99, 103, 104, 135, 136, 137, 138, 139, 140, 141

Asquith, H. H., 32, 35, 44, 118

Association of Professional, Executive and Computer Staff (APEX), 72, 84, 85, 88, 99

Barker, Captain, 6, 10, 11, 12, 18

baton-charges, *see under* police

Bhudia, Devshi, 83

Black Friday, 50, 55, 62, 63

black people and police, *see under* police

Bolshevism, 64

Boyce, Samuel, 25, 40

Brent Trades Council, 84, 132

Brownlow, James, 98, 102, 127, 128

brutality, *see under* police

bugging, *see* telephone tapping

Campbell, Duncan, 100

Capper, Sir Derrick, 76, 126, 127

Carrington, Lord, 96

centralisation of police, *see under* police

chartism, 16, 20

Childs, Captain Sir Wyndham, 30, 38, 39, 60, 63, 124

Churchill, Sir Winston, 25, 26, 27, 28, 29, 36, 37, 40, 42–4, 49, 62, 117, 118

citizen guard, 54

Civil Constabulary Reserve, 57, 58

Civil Contingencies Committee (CCC), 95

civil defence, 58, 95, 101

Civil Liberties, 116, 131–3, 146

Colliery Officials and Staff Association (COSA), 72

Communist Party, 60, 74, 85

community policing, 151

contingency planning, 53–8, 95–6, 114

Corden, Inspector, 11

cordons, *see under* police tactics

County and Borough Police Act 1856, 15–16

Criminal Investigation Department (CID), *see under* police

Critchley, T. A., 59, 124

crowd control, *see under* police, tactics

Davidson, J. C. C. 56

deaths occurring during industrial disputes, 19, 40–1, 45–7, 73, 136, 140, 142

democratisation of civil liberties, 131–3, 147

Desai, Jayaben, 83, 84

Desborough Committee, 17, 124

destruction of property by strikers, 12, 23, 25, 27, 29, 33, 46, 50, 51, 69,

70, 89, 90, 135, 137, 139, 140–3, 146, 147
dock strikes, *see under* strikes
Dodsley, Walt, 64
Dromey, Jack, 84
Duggin, James Arthur, 19

Emergency Powers Act 1920, 54, 55
Emergency, States of, *see under* States of Emergency

Featherstone, 6–24, 33, 34, 47, 52, 53, 70, 115, 116, 118, 123, 146, 148
First World War, 5, 47, 48, 53, 124, 146
flying pickets, 13, 71, 89

Geddes, Eric, 53, 62
General Staff, 61, 62
General Strike, 51–2, 56, 58, 60, 61, 63–6, 70, 101, 118, 120, 148
Gibbs, James, 19
Gill, Deputy Chief Constable, 7, 8, 10–12, 22
Gormley, Joe, 71
Grantham, Ray, 84, 87, 88, 99
Gristey, Len, 84
Grunwick industrial dispute, 5, 83–8, 91, 99, 100, 110, 111, 131, 132, 134, 135, 143, 146

Hadfields Steel Works, 89–91, 112, 128
Haldane, R. B., 27, 32
Hankey, Sir Maurice, 61
Hardie, Keir, 41, 42, 43, 46, 116
Hartley, Bernard, J.P., 6, 12, 18
Harworth Colliery Strike, 52, 53, 132, 137
Heath, Edward, 77, 95
Henry, Sir Edward, 27
Holliday, Mr, 9, 10, 11, 12, 14, 18
Home Office, 16, 17, 20, 26–9, 35, 36, 38, 39, 43, 44, 45, 53, 56, 59–60, 95, 123, 124, 125, 126, 151
Home Secretary, 16, 23, 26, 33, 34, 35, 36, 38, 40, 44, 53, 56, 57, 73, 77, 85, 100, 118, 125, 126, 132, 138, 139, 144
Horridge, Justice, 34
humour as a police tactic, 107, 135

Independent Labour Party, 13, 116
industrial disputes, *see* strikes
Industrial Unrest Committee (IUC), 53
informers, *see under* police
intelligence collection, 19–22, 38–9, 58–61, 79, 96–100, 104, 138
intimidation, 11, 14, 17, 24, 49, 67, 78, 85, 90, 91, 114, 137, 139, 142, 143
Iron and Steel Trades Confederation (ISTC), 3, 88, 89, 90, 92, 93, 94, 100, 103, 111, 112, 121

Jellicoe, Lord, 95
Jones, Reverend D., 41, 44
justices of the peace, *see under* magistrates

Labour Government, 51, 56, 95, 96
labour movement, 52, 53, 77, 118, 120, 147
Labour Party, 74, 116, 117, 120, 125, 139, 145, 151
Lalley, Jack, 74
Law, Bonar, A., 62
Liberal Party, 26, 47, 117
Lindsay, Captain, 26, 27, 18, 35, 36, 44
Llewellyn, Mr, 36, 40
Lloyd George, D., 32, 44, 49, 53, 62

MacDonald, Ramsey, 44
Macready, General Sir Nevil, 27, 28, 32, 35, 36, 38, 39, 40, 54, 59, 124
magistrates, 8, 9, 10, 12, 16, 18, 20, 21, 23, 35, 40, 45, 52, 123, 124
Mann, Tom, 34
marching gangs, 12–13, 21, 23, 28
Mark, Sir Robert, 95
Masterman, Charles, 44
Matthews, Fred, 73, 74
Maudling, Reginald, 73, 77
media, 1, 108, 116, 128–31, 136, 146, 150–1
methodology, 2–4
Metropolitan Police, *see under* police
Metropolitan Police Act 1829, 15
MI5, 59, 60, 96
military
    aid to civil power, 14–19, 95
    and industrial disputes, 8, 9, 10, 12,

military (*cont.*)
  17–19, 24, 27–8, 32–8, 49, 51, 55,
  67, 96, 101, 109, 117, 118, 146
  and intelligence collection, 21, 38–9,
  59, 60
militia, 14
miners' strikes, *see under* strikes
ministries, 58, 59
Moylan, J. F., 28, 29, 38, 39
mutual aid, *see under* police

Napier, General Sir Charles, 16, 20,
  96
National Coal Board (NCB), 70, 71,
  72. 77, 136, 137, 140, 141, 144
National Council for Civil Liberties
  (NCCL), 131, 132, 133, 150
National Graphical Association industrial dispute, 135–6, 137
National Recording Centre (NRC), *see
  under* police
National Security Committee (NSC),
  95
National Union of Mineworkers
  (NUM), 3, 70, 71, 72, 73, 74, 76,
  77, 90, 91, 92, 93, 94, 95, 97, 100,
  103, 109, 110, 111, 113, 119, 120,
  121, 122, 128, 129, 136, 137, 138,
  143, 144, 145
Neap House Wharf, 78–83, 89, 98,
  101, 134

obstruction, 25, 29, 33, 39, 46, 47, 67,
  78, 84, 85, 89, 91, 92, 103, 133,
  140, 141
Organisation for the Maintenance of
  Supplies (OMS), 56–7
Orgreave coking plant, 139, 140, 142,
  147

Pentonville Five, 78
Peterloo, 15, 117, 118, 125
picketing, 25, 26, 29, 40, 48, 50, 52,
  67, 69, 70, 71, 73, 74, 75, 76, 77,
  78, 82, 83, 84, 85, 87, 88, 89, 90,
  91–4, 102, 103, 116, 119, 121,
  129, 135, 136, 139
police
  accountability, 151
  baton-charges, 7, 22, 24, 26, 40–1,
    43, 45, 48, 51, 52, 64, 65, 66, 109,
    114, 127, 129, 130, 135, 136, 139,
    140, 141, 146
  and black people, 147, 150
  brutality, 40–3, 64–6, 69–70, 85, 89–
    90, 109–14, 144–5
  centralisation of, 48, 123–5
  cordons, 29, 79, 80, 81, 85, 86, 90,
    91, 106, 107, 108, 110, 111, 125,
    135, 136, 137, 139, 146
  CID, 39, 48, 59
  discipline, 130
  informers, 21, 60, 97
  injuries, 68, 69, 70, 75, 77, 81, 82,
    83, 88, 90, 91, 135, 136, 138, 139,
    140, 141
  intelligence collection, 19–22, 79,
    96–100, 104, 138
  manpower, 17, 24, 110
  metropolitan, 12, 16, 17, 20, 25, 26,
    28, 32, 35, 36, 37, 38, 42, 43, 44,
    54, 117, 118, 126, 131, 144
  mutual aid, 16, 17, 101, 114, 128,
    134, 145, 151
  National Recording Centre, 2, 95,
    128, 134, 137, 143
  plainclothes, 20, 21, 59, 98, 108, 138
  riot equipment, 109, 127, 128
  Scotland Yard, 20, 39, 60, 61, 95,
    143
  snatch squads, 86, 108
  Specials, 25, 54, 55, 57, 65, 66, 101
  Special Branch, 59, 60, 96, 97, 98,
    100, 124
  strikes, 49, 59
  support units, 2, 79, 80, 81, 82, 101,
    107, 114, 135, 143, 144, 150
  surveillance, 21, 60, 61, 96
  tactics, 22, 23, 39–40, 43, 85, 86,
    102–9, 134–5, 143, 144, 145, 146,
    147, 150, 151
  training, 134, 143
  wedge, 107, 108, 110, 125, 128, 134,
    143, 146
Popay, William, 20
Prime Minister, 60

rail strikes, *see under* strikes
Red Friday, 51, 56
Reiner, Robert, 125
riots, 14, 28, 29, 33, 50, 52–3, 76, 110,

127, 128, 134, 135, 136, 139, 140, 143

Riot Act, 12, 19, 24, 45, 46, 69

riot shields, 109, 134, 137, 139, 140, 143

Roberts–Arundel industrial dispute, 67–70, 114

Rogaly, Joe, 87

Rudé, George, 13

Russell, Captain, 7, 8, 9, 10, 17

Russian Revolution, 61

Saltley coke depot, 73, 74, 75, 76, 77, 78, 79, 83, 84, 87, 95, 101, 106, 115, 126, 127, 128, 134, 139, 143

Scargill, Arthur, 74, 75, 76, 87, 88, 136, 139, 145

Scarman, Lord Justice, 84, 87, 125

Scotland Yard, *see under* police

Second World War, 52, 66, 70, 101, 114, 124

Shah, Eddie, 135

Special Branch, *see under* police

special constables, *see under* police

Socialist Workers Party (SWP), 85, 87, 88, 121

States of Emergency, 55, 56, 57, 67, 71, 77, 95

strikes
  by building workers, 51
  by dockers, 31, 67, 78–83, 95
  by engineering workers, 67–70
  by miners, 1, 2, 6–31, 33–34, 47, 50, 67, 70–8, 122, 136–145
  by police, 49, 59, 124
  by print workers, 135–6
  by railwaymen, 32, 33, 37, 44, 49, 50
  by seamen, 31
  by steelworkers, 88–91
  see also: deaths occurring during industrial disputes, Featherstone, General Strike, Grunwick industrial dispute, Harworth Colliery Strike, National Graphical Associ-ation industrial dispute, Roberts–Arundel industrial dispute, Tonypandy

Strike Committee, 53, 54

Stuart, Major, 45, 46

Supply and Transport Committee (STC), 54, 55, 56, 57, 61, 62

telephone tapping, 61, 99–100, 138, *see also* police, intelligence collection

Thatcher, Margaret, 96, 109, 151

Thomas, D. A., 35, 40

Thompson, E. P., 117

Thomson, Sir Basil, 48, 58, 59, 60, 61, 62, 63

Tocher, John, 69

Tonypandy, 5, 27–31, 38, 40, 41, 42, 44, 47, 50, 52, 70, 117, 118, 119, 146

Trade Disputes Act 1906, 26, 32

Trades Union Congress, 51, 52, 60, 61, 62, 65, 119, 120

Transport and General Workers Union (TGWU), 51, 68, 74, 76

Triple Alliance, 49, 50, 53, 55, 62

troops, *see* military

Troup, Sir Edward, 27

unemployment, 52

vehicles, stopping of by pickets, 73–7, 79, 80, 89, 90, 92, 93, 94, 140

volunteers, 54, 55, 56, 57, 101, 102, 114

Volunteer Service Committee (VSC), 55

wedge, *see under* police

Wedgwood, Josiah, 56

Weir, Stuart, 85, 86

Wilson, Harold, 95

Wilson, PC Trevor, 87

Wise, Audrey, 87

Yeomanry, 15